Social Workers and Labor Unions

Recent Titles in
Contributions in Labor Studies

Social Workers and Labor Unions

HOWARD JACOB KARGER

Contributions in Labor Studies, Number 26

GREENWOOD PRESS

New York
Westport, Connecticut
London

Library of Congress Cataloging-in-Publication Data

Karger, Howard Jacob, 1948–
    Social workers and labor unions / Howard Jacob Karger.
      p. cm. — (Contributions in labor studies, ISSN 0886–8239 ;
no. 26)
    Bibliography: p.
    Includes index.
    ISBN 0–313–25867–8 (lib. bdg. : alk. paper)
    1. Trade-unions—Social workers—United States. I. Title.
II. Series.
HV43.2.U6K37   1988
331.88'1136132'0—dc19   88–3127

British Library Cataloguing in Publication Data is available.

Library of Congress Catalog Card Number: 88–3127
ISBN: 0–313–25867–8
ISSN: 0886–8239

First published in 1988

Greenwood Press, Inc.
88 Post Road West, Westport, Connecticut 06881

Printed in the United States of America

The paper used in this book complies with the
Permanent Paper Standard issued by the National
Information Standards Organization (Z39.48–1984).

10 9 8 7 6 5 4 3 2 1

To the memory of my grandfather,
Abraham Schwartz, a gentle Rumanian carpenter
who taught me about both love and unions.

"The most militant workers with whom I have to contend with are the social service workers. They are the greatest militants in the world. They are going out on strike every Monday and Thursday, and you know why? Because nobody takes them seriously."

—Victor Gotbaum, Former Executive Director, District Council 37, American Federation of State and County Municipal Employees, AFL-CIO. The quote is from a paper presented at a symposium held at the University of Kansas in November 1976.

Contents

Preface

There are over 125,000 unionized social workers in the United States. In light of those numbers, a surprising dearth of literature exists on social workers and labor unions. The reasons for this paucity of scholarship involve a complex series of questions.

Perhaps, as some writers suggest, large numbers of social workers have a bias against unionism. Clearly, a significant number of academics and practitioners perceive unionism as antiprofessional. Because unions emphasize employee rights, other social workers believe that unionism runs counter to the best interests of clients, many of whom are highly vulnerable. Still others conclude that the profession of social work is built upon the foundation of altruism, and the self-serving nature of unions is believed to be in direct opposition to values of self-sacrifice. Another group of social workers flee from unionism because of the bad press it has received in the past few decades, especially regarding corruption and gangsterism. Other social workers believe that American unionism is in its death throes, and, therefore, why bother to write about a movement that is no longer viable? Finally, some academics and practitioners believe that unions are inextricably linked to public welfare, an area that provides little interest for certain sectors of the social work community. For whatever reasons, little more than a handful of literature has been written on social workers and labor unions since the 1940s.

Although the relationship between social work and organized labor goes back to the turn of the century, it has only been in the last fifty years or so that professional social workers have had the option to join a protective labor organization. Therefore, in many ways the relationship between organized labor and unionized social workers is in its infancy.

This book is intended to cover a broad spectrum of social work and organized labor. The first chapter, "A History of Early Social Work and Labor Unions, 1900–1947," supplies a glimpse into the complex circumstances that marked the often uneasy relationship between professional social workers and labor unions. This chapter is divided into two sections: part one examines the period from the late 1880s to the early 1920s, when social workers helped workers, notably female, to organize; part two explores the years between 1930 and 1947, a period in which social workers organized themselves.

"The Common Goals of Labor and Social Work" explores the complementary goals of labor and social work by examining its historical context, the similar struggles waged by the National Association of Social Workers (NASW) and public service unions, and by assessing significant areas of agreement between professional social work associations and public sector unions.

The third chapter explores social work licensure, a fundamentally divisive issue separating professional social work organizations and public sector unions. More specifically, the chapter provides a description of legal regulation and examines the position of NASW and the unions on licensure.

"Reclassification: NASW and the Unions" examines reclassification, a second area of disagreement between public service unions and professional social work organizations. More specifically, the chapter probes the issue of reclassification; examines the positions of NASW, American Federation of State and County Municipal Employees (AFSCME), and the hypothetical public; and attempts to understand the policy implications of reclassification. The Michigan reclassification plan is used as a case study.

"The Compatibility of Labor and Social Work" addresses the negative and positive views of unionism held by social workers, the reasons for antiunionism, and the positions of NASW on collective bargaining.

"Labor Relations Laws and Social Workers" focuses on labor laws and the profession of social work. This chapter considers federal labor laws affecting social workers, reviews various Executive Orders and the Civil Service Reform Act of 1978, and provides an overview of state and local labor relations laws.

Milton Tambor's "The Social Service Union in the Workplace," examines overall social service workplace issues including collective bargaining, union organizing, the reaction of management to unionization, negotiation of the labor contract, and the administration of the labor agreement.

David Stoesz's "Privatization: Prospects for Unionizing Social Work-ers," examines the implication of privatization for union organizing. "Computer Technology and the Human Services," which I coauthored with Larry Kreuger, examines the psychological, sociological, and power relationships that characterize the computerized social service workplace.

"De-Skilling Social Workers: The Industrial Model of Production and the Delivery of Social Services" probes the effects of the industrial model of production on the delivery of social services. The author suggests a set of criteria that can be used in the development of alternative measures of worker and agency productivity.

Frederic G. Reamer's "Social Workers and Unions: Ethical Dilemmas," examines the values and ethical choices that must be made by unionized social workers. The author discusses the implications of ethical choices, especially on social workers' "divided loyalties" to clients, employers, and the general public. The chapter concludes with a discussion of the rel-evance of ethical theory to the variety of value choices social workers face in the world of work.

"Social Workers and Public-Sector Labor Relations: A Case Study of the Missouri Department of Social Services and the Communications Workers of America" inquires into key labor relations principles that impact upon the unionization of public sector social workers. The re-lationship between the Missouri Department of Social Services (Mo. DoSS) and the Communications Workers of America (CWA), Public Employees Division, is used as a case study to illustrate the conflict that often permeates public-sector labor relations.

Leslie B. Alexander's "Professionalization and Unionism: Compatible After All?," examines the common view that unionization and profes-sionalization are inherently antagonistic. The author attempts to resolve this question by examining the conditions under which these two pro-cesses are incompatible or complementary.

A special appreciation is extended to Leslie Alexander, Tom Beer, Larry Kreuger, Frederic Reamer, David Stoesz, and Milton Tambor, for believing in this project since its inception.

Many people helped bring this book to completion. Early support came from Connie Bryant, Vice-President, Public Employee Division, Com-munications Workers of America (CWA). Vic Crawley and Rick Bass, both of CWA, provided me with the opportunity to work with unionized members of the Missouri Department of Social Services. Other debts are owed to the research staff of the American Federation of State and County Municipal Employees (AFSCME), the NASW research and leg-islative staff, and the social science librarians at the University of Mis-souri-Columbia.

A very special thanks is extended to Roland Meinert, Director, School of Social Work, University of Missouri-Columbia for providing me with the "protected time" necessary to complete this book.

An apology is offered to Saul and Aaron for having to put up with my moods and frustrations, and for my having missed some of the best family times. My deepest appreciation, however, goes to Connie, my critic, partner, and friend.

I

THE HISTORICAL BACKGROUND OF SOCIAL WORK AND UNIONISM

1

A History of Early Social Work and Labor Unions, 1900–1947

HOWARD JACOB KARGER

The purpose of this chapter is to provide a glimpse into the complex circumstances that marked the historical relationship between professional social workers and organized labor. The chapter is divided into two sections: part one examines the period from the late 1880s to the early 1920s, when social workers helped workers—notably female—to organize; part two explores the years between 1930 and 1947, a period in which social workers organized themselves.

The relationship between social work and organized labor was born in several of the larger settlement houses that dotted America's urban landscape.[1] Witnessing the impact of industrialization, settlement house leaders knew firsthand the misery produced by an unfettered market economy. For example, employers in the 1910 New York garment industry demanded that their female employees work an average of fifty-six hours weekly, often requiring them to do home work in their after hours. Wages for learners in this industry (about 25 percent of the work force) were from three to four dollars a week. For average operators (about 60 percent of the work force) salaries ranged from seven to twelve dollars weekly, sometimes going higher.

Women working in department stores in Baltimore averaged around fifty-six hours a week, with some working as much as sixty-five hours. During the Christmas rush the average work week was seventy hours. Eighty-one percent of women working in these stores earned less than $6.70 per week, an amount that had been calculated as necessary for a single woman to be self-supporting.[2]

Wages in most industries were not standardized and thus were based solely on the whims of the employer. Both men and women worked for what they could get. According to settlement workers, women and children were the most exploited, with most industrial women being between the ages of 15 and 25.

The female work force mushroomed between 1870 and 1910. By 1910, 10 percent of all workers were women, and the labor force participation of married women reached 25 percent of the total female work force, an increase of almost 50 percent since 1890.[3] Despite the large number of women workers, only 25 percent of the states in the late 1890s had adopted maximum hour laws for women, and in only three of those states were the laws effective. The legal work limit was ten hours per day in regulated states.[4]

In response to the egregious working conditions of women, social work reformers attempted to increase public awareness and influence policy through social survey reports and direct action. For example, Mary van Kleeck found that despite the sixty hour a week law passed in some states, women were working as long as seventy hours weekly. In an attempt to expose the deplorable conditions of women workers, van Kleeck wrote a series of books for the Russell Sage Foundation on the heavily female bookbinding, millinery, and artificial-flower trades.

Moved by these injustices, many of the larger settlement houses supported organized labor. For example, labor unions met regularly in Boston's Denison and South End Houses, in New York's Henry Street Settlement, and in Chicago's Hull House, Chicago Commons, and the University of Chicago Settlements.

Among the best known of the settlement leaders was Jane Addams, founder of Chicago's Hull House. According to Mary Anderson, a former head of the Federal Women's Bureau, "it was around Miss McDowell [Head Resident, University of Chicago Settlement House] and Miss Addams, in the early days, that the whole movement for the organization of women and the improvement of their working conditions centered."[5]

Addams maintained "that a settlement that is drawn into the labor issues of its city can seem remote to its purpose only to those who fail to realize that so far as the present industrial system thwarts our ethical demands, not only for social righteousness but for social order, a settlement is committed to an effort to understand and, as far as possible, to alleviate it."[6] As an expression of her philosophy, Addams became involved in several strikes throughout the early 1900s, including the Chicago stockyards strike of 1904, strikes involving the building trades, a waitress strike in a downtown restaurant, and her most important strike involvement—the 1910 garment workers strike against Hart, Schaffner, and Marx.[7]

Prompted by Ellen Gates Starr, the cofounder of Hull House, Addams entered the 1910 garment workers strike to organize a relief fund for striking workers. Despite her good intentions, Addams quickly found herself in an awkward position—all three partners, Hart, Schaffner, and Marx, were generous contributors to Hull House. By 1910 Addams had become a labor arbitrator of sorts as well as a channel of communication between the two sides.[8]

Support for labor unions also came from other settlement quarters. Robert Woods, Head Resident of Boston's South End House, wrote that "the greatest improvement in all the conditions of labor that has been wrought during these recent years, is without all possible question, the result of working class organization."[9] Ellen Gates Starr believed that "if one must starve, there are compensations in starving in a fight for freedom that are not found in starving for employer's profits."[10]

The outrage felt by social workers at the plight of working women was translated into their support of labor unions and the right of men and women to collectively bargain. This concern spawned two separate yet related organizations: the National Women's Trade Union League (WTUL) and the National Consumers League (NCL).

SOCIAL WORK REFORMERS AND THE WOMEN'S TRADE UNION LEAGUE

An example of the position taken by social work reformers in the movement to organize women is illustrated by their role in the WTUL. Founded at the 1903 American Federation of Labor (AFL) convention, the WTUL was not an official union, but a quasi-educational organization which operated as the industrial wing of the mainstream women's movement. Although membership was open to anyone who promised to assist women in organizing into trade unions, a policy ensured that the majority of the board would be women workers. In effect, the WTUL was a hybrid organization that included both leisure-class activists and trade union members.

The initial founders of the WTUL were Mary Kenney O'Sullivan, a veteran of the Illinois campaign for the legislative protection of women workers, and William English Walling, a settlement resident and the socialist grandson of a Kentucky millionaire. Excited by a similar organization he had seen in England, Walling returned to the United States and immediately contacted O'Sullivan. After a brief deliberation, they decided to found the WTUL at the 1903 AFL convention, even though only four women delegates were allowed admittance.

Despite lackluster support by the AFL leadership—a problem that would persistently plague the organization—by the end of the convention the new organization had officers, a constitution, and a program consisting of five demands: (1) the organization of all workers into trade unions, (2) equal pay for equal work, (3) an eight hour day for all workers,

(4) a minimum wage scale, and (5) women suffrage.[11] Local leagues were set up almost immediately in Chicago, New York, and Boston.

Mary Kenney O'Sullivan was in many ways a prime example of a working-class reformer and trade unionist. As a young bookbinder in Chicago, Kenney joined the Ladies Federal Labor Union in 1888, a catch-all union chartered by the AFL. In 1889 Kenney met Jane Addams and moved to Hull House, which she used as a base to organize the book-binders, shirtwaist workers, and other female-dominated trades. During her residency at Hull House, Kenney helped support the passage of the Illinois Factory Act, an important piece of legislation which provided protection for women and child workers.

In 1892, Samuel Gompers offered Kenney a job as the AFL organizer for women, a position she occupied for six months until the AFL terminated her because of a lack of funds. After returning to Chicago, Kenney took a job as a factory inspector under Florence Kelley, and shortly afterward married John O'Sullivan, a trade union activist. Kenney moved to Boston, continued her trade union activities, and later became a central figure in the WTUL.

Throughout its early history the WTUL was strongly influenced by settlement leaders and their followers. For example, the first national officers consisted of Mary Kenney O'Sullivan, Jane Addams, Mary McDowell (head of University of Chicago Settlement), Lillian Wald (head of New York's Henry Street Settlement), and Lenora O'Reilly.[12] The board of the New York WTUL consisted of some of the most prominent early twentieth-century activists, including Mrs. Walter Weyl, Mary Beard, Mrs. John Dewey, and Eleanor Roosevelt.[13]

Although the WTUL was never an official part of the AFL, the organization was heavily involved in much of the early twentieth-century strike activity. For example, the WTUL joined the "Uprising of the Twenty Thousand," a 1909 strike called against the Triangle Shirtwaist Factory and Leiserson's, two of the largest garment manufacturers in New York City. Spurred on by a rousing speech from a Russian immigrant named Clara Lemlich, the strike was in full swing by November 22, 1909. During the height of the strike over 500 shops were affected, and production in the garment industry was virtually halted. Over 75 percent of the strikers were women, most between the ages of sixteen and twenty-four.[14]

In the midst of 25,000 striking workers (the strike had quickly spread to other manufacturers), massive arrests, brutal police actions, and hired thugs, the WTUL organized a volunteer force of 275 "allies" and nine lawyers, and furnished almost $30,000 in bail money. The headquarters of the New York WTUL became a strike center where on short notice the volunteers could organize a parade of 10,000 workers. Moreover, the WTUL was aided by several leisure-class women activists, including

Ann Morgan (an heir to the J. P Morgan fortune) and J. Borden Harriman. In the end the strike cost $100,000, a fifth of which was raised by the New York WTUL. As a result of the "Uprising of the Twenty Thousand," the International Ladies Garment Workers Union (ILGWU) became the third largest union in the AFL.[15]

In 1910 the WTUL became embroiled in Chicago's huge Hart, Schaffner, and Marx clothing strike. By October 1910, 40,000 workers had walked out, and the garment district of Chicago was immobilized. Margaret Drier Robbins, the head of the national office of the WTUL, was given a seat on the strike committee. When the strike ended fifty days later, the Chicago WTUL had raised $70,000 for strike relief.[16] By 1911, the WTUL had grown considerably: the New York branch had almost doubled, the Boston group had grown by one-third, and the Chicago chapter had become the largest with 725 members.[17]

In 1912 the WTUL became involved in the disastrous "Bread and Roses" strike in the textile mills of Lawrence, Massachusetts. Unlike earlier strikes, the Lawrence strike was organized by the Industrial Workers of the World (IWW) rather than the AFL. Nonetheless, the WTUL quickly established a strike headquarters which fed and clothed 8,000 workers. Working through John Golden's United Textile Workers (UTW), the AFL sabotaged the strike by having the UTW sign a separate agreement with the employers, and then ordering the strikers back to work. However, most strikers did not return, and Golden ordered the WTUL to end its relief efforts. The WTUL complied and the strike was lost. Although the league hated Golden, was sympathetic to the Lawrence strikers, and was impressed with the IWW's organizing ability, they nevertheless reaffirmed their policy of working only in AFL-sanctioned strikes.[18]

According to William O'Neill, the Lawrence strike illustrated the conservative nature of settlement leaders. Robert Woods, head resident of Boston's South End House, sided with Golden and harassed the workers, even going so far as to secure a court order forcing the strike committee to open its accounts. The only prominent settlement leader to endorse the IWW strike was Vida Scudder, by then no longer a settlement resident.[19]

Although several factors fueled the underlying tension between the WTUL and the AFL, a primary issue was socialism. The WTUL was not a socialist organization; however, many of its constituents and leaders were socialists. One such member was Lenora O'Reilly, resident of Henry Street Settlement, member of the WTUL's first national executive board, and vice-president of the New York WTUL. Although from a working-class background, O'Reilly had generous leisure-class friends who funded her education at Brooklyn's Pratt Institute.

In O'Reilly's capacity as vice-president of the New York WTUL, she recruited socialists such as Rose Schneiderman, Pauline Newman, Theresa Malkiel, Anna Maley, Bertha Mailly, and Meta Stern. O'Reilly and these younger Jewish radicals formed a militant bloc which played a major role in the New York WTUL.[20] For example, it was no coincidence that the WTUL experienced its greatest successes in the garment trades, an area where Jewish workers carried the political banner of socialism.

Committed socialists were always wary of the WTUL, a skepticism heightened by the organization's unswerving and often blind loyalty to Gompers and the antisocialist bureaucracy of the AFL. According to Mari Jo Buhle, despite their suspicions, female socialist trade unionists recognized the power of the WTUL in drawing public attention to working conditions. Moreover, Buhle maintains that industrial women were more comfortable in the WTUL than the often hostile socialist party or the misogynistic mainstream of the AFL.

An example of the disinterest of the AFL is illustrated by their refusal to provide the WTUL with a significant level of funding. In fact, the only money the AFL provided was $150 per month in 1912, and that was cut off when the league strayed from its position on the Lawrence strike.[21] Throughout its history, the fiscal situation of the league was characteristic of a shoe-string operation. Margaret Drier Robbins, WTUL National President from 1907 until her retirement in 1924, virtually supported the national office from her own personal funds. Her sister, Mary Drier, paid one-third of the expenses of the WTUL's New York office.[22]

Much of the strain between the AFL and the WTUL existed because the league was comparatively more progressive than the highly conservative, Gompers-led trade union movement. For example, in their second annual meeting, the WTUL refused to endorse oriental exclusion, a policy strongly favored by the AFL. Although the WTUL supported the involvement of the United States in World War I (as did Gompers), the postwar planks of the league were far to the left of the AFL. These planks included no intervention in Russia, compulsory health insurance, and public ownership of utilities, trains, communications, mines, packing houses, and grain elevators.[23] In 1955 the WTUL finally closed its national office.

Significant trade union gains that can be attributed solely to the efforts of the WTUL are difficult to ascertain. On a modest level, the league was responsible for training working-class women to occupy posts in labor and government. For example, 90 percent of WTUL's delegates in 1919, and all the officers except Robbins, were or had been workers.[24] In that same year, thirty-eight women affiliated with the WTUL held federal government posts.[25] Perhaps more importantly, the efforts of the WTUL may have convinced women that working in trade unions need not be an expression of voluntarism, but, instead, a bona fide career.

THE EMERGENCE OF THE NATIONAL CONSUMERS LEAGUE

Although the National Consumers League (NCL) was also a reform organization, its major goal was not trade unionism but the awakening of public consciousness to the deplorable industrial conditions in early-twentieth-century America.

The NCL was a small, elite organization of well-educated women that grew out of a 1897 mass meeting organized in New York to publicize the conditions of retail shop women, a group forced to endure low pay, long hours, and wretched working conditions. As a result of this meeting, a group of prominent citizens was formed to investigate the situation.

Established as a nonpartisan organization for middle-class consumers, the NCL bylaws forbade membership to employers and workers. The goal of the NCL was to reform working conditions through an emphasis on consumer education, investigation, moral suasion, and public pressure. The aim of the organization was to promote safe, wholesome products, made and sold by healthy, well-paid workers. In 1898 Florence Kelley came to New York from Hull House to lead the organization.

Kelley proved to be a dynamic and visionary leader of the organization. A complex individual, Kelley was a socialist and the first factory inspector in Illinois. Her father, William Darrah Kelley, was an attorney, an abolitionist, and a radical Pennsylvania Republican elected to serve fifteen terms in the House of Representatives. After graduating from Cornell in 1882 and then being rejected by the University of Pennsylvania because of her gender, Kelley went to study in Zurich. Converted to socialism while in Eurpe, Kelley subsequently married a left-wing Polish medical student, Lazare Wischnewetzky.

Kelley and Wischnewetzky moved to New York with their infant son in 1886. Upon arriving, both promptly joined the Socialist Labor Party (SLP), but were expelled because the German-speaking membership distrusted them. Despite her expulsion, Kelley maintained her long-standing friendship with Friedrich Engels, a friendship that began with her English translation of Engels's famous *Condition of the Working Class in England*. In fact, Engels wrote an angry letter to the chapter when he learned of Kelley's dismissal from the SLP. Between 1888 and 1892 Kelley made the transition from socialist politics to the world of women's reform organizations.

Kelley's relationshp with her husband deteriorated and in 1891 she moved to Hull House. She became involved in industrial reform while in Chicago, and in 1893 the radical governor John Peter Altgeld appointed her as the first Chief Factory Inspector of Illinois, an appointment which allowed her to employ a staff of twelve—five of whom the legislature mandated to be women.

Kelley was hired as the General Secretary of the National Consumers League in 1898, a poistion she held until her death in 1932. Upon returning to New York, Kelley took up residence in Henry Street Settlement and remained there until 1926.[26] Throughout her career, Florence Kelley led the fight for passage of major legislation affecting children and women workers, including the abolition of child labor, the eight- and ten-hour minimum workday, and minimum wage legislation.

The major strategy of the New York NCL was based on creating a White List of reputable employers and then encouraging the public to buy from them. Conversely, disreputable employers and shop abuses were also publicized. This tactic met with some success, and, by 1899, there were leagues in many of the larger cities. Kelley's leadership was so dynamic that by 1903 there were 90 local leagues, 20 state leagues, 35 auxiliaries, and numerous college branches. By 1914 the White List had been made national and seventy clothing manufacturers were using it.

After 1907 the NCL began to concentrate on maximum-hour and minimum-wage laws for women. The ensuing struggle attracted such notable reformers as Pauline and Josephine Goldmark (sisters-in-law of Supreme Court Justice Louis D. Brandeis) and Frances D. Perkins, later Franklin Roosevelt's Secretary of Labor. The chief counsel of the NCL was Louis D. Brandeis, who after being appointed to the Supreme Court, was replaced by Felix Frankfurter, also destined to become a Supreme Court Justice. Despite its ability to attract prominent reformers, the NCL never had a membership exceeding 2,000.[27]

World War I slowed the momentum of the organization. The conservative ethos of the period translated into attacks on labor laws and the possibility of new labor legislation appeared dim. Furthermore, several NCL leaders such as Pauline and Josephine Goldmark were appointed to government posts and were thus unavailable. Lastly, Kelley's virulent oppostion to America's entry into World War I eroded the credibility of the organization.

The major postwar issues of the NCL included the eight-hour day, the elimination of night work for women, the passage of a child labor bill, the establishment of minimum-wage commissions in all states, and compulsory health insurance in industry. The social turmoil of the postwar period saw the programs of the NCL attacked on two fronts: by the feminists who supported the Equal Rights Amendment and were thus opposed to protective legislation for women, and by the successful attack of the ultraconservative Supreme Court on the legality of minimum wage laws and child labor prohibitions.[28] In the end, the league was successful in establishing the constitutionality of maximum-hour laws of working women.

Although Florence Kelley did not live long enough to see the NCL programs enacted in the New Deal of the 1930s, the legacy of the league is clearly visible in the modern welfare state.

COMMON GROUND AND UNCOMMON TENSIONS

Progressive-era reformers and the conservative union movement led by Samuel Gompers had several positions in common. Allen F. Davis maintains that Progressives such as Jane Addams, Graham Taylor, and Robert Woods, "like most progressives advocated no drastic change in the economic system. Most opposed such organizations as the Industrial Workers of the World. Instead, they aligned themselves with the conservative labor movement to prevent the more radical elements from gaining control and to preserve the American system of free enterprise."[29]

In a similar vein, Margaret Drier Robbins, head of the WTUL, wrote:

[We] do not believe in the philosophy of the class struggle as an interpretation of past social history, nor as the method of future development in civilization. We [Margaret and her husband, Raymond] believe that the whole progress of social order has been toward individual freedom, rather than collective domination.[30]

O'Neill maintains that:

Social reformers . . . were determined to rationalize, not destroy, the class system. What they minded was not the existence of the proletariat and the bourgeoisie, but the dangerous gulf between them. . . . The more sophisticated accepted trade unions, despite their admitted class consciousness, as essential to industrial stability. In the long run, they believed, collective bargaining would reduce social tensions by providing an orderly means for resolving conflicts of interest. But this was as far as most progressives were willing to go.[31]

Progressives and the conservative leaders of the trade union movement possessed a common belief in the value of social stability and a fundamental faith in capitalism. Despite disagreements with the AFL on certain social and political issues, social work reformers believed in the omniscient quality of market relations and free contractual labor.

Despite their common positions, social work reformers and mainstream progressive-era union leaders had substantial differences. An example of this tension is evident in comparing the philosophy of Samuel Gompers to that of Jane Addams. Addams was neither a militant trade unionist, nor was she devoted to bread-and-butter union issues; instead, she believed that strikes and class warfare were barbaric and should be replaced by arbitration. Addams wrote that strikes were a "brutal and ineffective way for settling labor disputes."[32] She went on to write that "the cruelty and waste of the strike as an implement for securing the most reasonable demands, came to me."[33] According to Levine, Addams "favored labor organizing only as a temporary tactic in long range strategy, the aim of which was a society in which there would be no class struggle, nor even any consciousness of economic classes.... This reordering ... would have to be accomplished through a broad and rapid expansion of the federal government."[34]

Gompers believed that the non-working-class elements in the trade union movement were panacea peddlers. Moreover, the vision of Addams and others was naive and destructive to the future of the AFL. Gompers's philosophy was "unions, pure and simple." In sharp contrast to the almost utopian vision of Addams' cooperative society, Gompers's advice was to "study your union card ... and if the idea doesn't square with that, it ain't true."[35] Neither idealistic nor visionary, Gompers's programs were based on concrete shop concerns—union cards, speed-ups, seniority, and so forth. A hard-boiled pragmatist, Gompers was proud to have no greater social vision than to build membership in the AFL. Furthermore, the ideas of mediation and arbitration, which Addams considered a measure of civilized industrial relations, were anathema to the tough Gompers. Though allies in the short run, broad philosophical issues separated reformers from the mainstream of AFL leadership.

The essence of the reforms proposed by progressive-era social workers rested largely on greater federal intervention. For example, the WTUL advocated welfare measures that included minimum wage and maximum hours, social insurance, national health insurance, and labor-management arrangements that required federal mediation. Progressive reformers believed that the government had the responsibility to enforce social justice. Gompers, on the other hand, believed in "self-help" and, consistent with his laissez faire attitude toward labor relations, he opposed almost all forms of government intervention. In effect, Gompers believed that the rights of labor should not be guaranteed by the government, but, instead, by an organization of strong unions that could effectively compete with employers. His policy was to aid the small and elite minority of workers that were eligible for AFL membership. Given Gompers's philosophy, the fact that he opposed minimum wage and maximum hour laws for adult workers, the eight-hour day, and public health and unemployment insurance is not surprising. Perhaps more importantly, Gompers feared that if the government guaranteed the eight-hour day, unemployment coverage, and other benefits, workers would see no purpose in joining unions.

The Progressive Era was marked by social work reformers helping others, particularly women, to organize. Although social workers encouraged traditionally exploited groups to become unionized, little thought was given to organizing their own profession. Throughout the Progressive Era, social work was carried on almost exclusively in small agencies, using solidly middle-class volunteers and a few paid staff. That reality would change with the creation of the large bureaucracy necessary for the relief programs of the New Deal.

THE LEGACY OF THE RANK AND FILE IN SOCIAL WORK, 1934–1947

The depression of the 1930s ruptured social work as it did all of U.S. society. The country's illusions of reform, faith in the philanthropic elite, and naive trust in voluntary giving were profoundly shaken.

By 1932 it was obvious that the depression was severe and, moreover, that it was not going to be ephemeral. The social volatility of the middle 1930s, resulting in massive and often violent strikes; the polarization of Americans into opposing camps; and the mounting pressure for massive social change convinced Roosevelt that to save capitalism he would have to effect either social or political remedies. Roosevelt opted for social solutions, many of which took the form of public welfare.

Roosevelt's social welfare strategy necessitated the rapid creation of massive public welfare services requiring a virtual army of social workers. The existing supply of trained social workers fell far short of the demand; schools of social work had neither the time, money, nor the necessary resources to train this standing army. Moreover, trained social workers required a salary greater than either the state or federal welfare authorities could afford. Hence, the majority of social workers were untrained, many having been drawn from the ranks of the unemployed. In large measure, this group would later form the bulk of the rank and file movement in social work.

In 1931, a handful of practitioners (a majority of whom were caseworkers in the private Jewish agencies) formed the Social Worker's Discussion Club of New York (SWDC). The SWDC defined itself as an "open forum for the analysis of basic social problems and their relation to social work."[36] The club platform consisted of leaders of the unemployed, representatives of the Communist Party of America (CPUSA), left-wing writers and editors, and union leaders. Discussions ranged from employment relief, the dangers of war, psychiatry and society, unemployment insurance, and social aspects of literature, to the Negro and the new economic crisis. Despite claims about an open forum, SWDC discussions were clearly tilted to the left.

Contact between the New York SWDC and other left-wing social workers resulted in the formation of clubs in Boston, Philadelphia, and Chicago.[37] The Boston and Philadelphia clubs were frail, and in 1933 they ceased all activity. Unlike its New York counterpart, the Chicago SWDC

primary attracted public welfare workers. In addition, the Chicago group
stressed personnel problems as well as social issues, and organized against
payless vacations, salary cuts, uncompensated overtime, and unsatisfactory working conditions.[38]

The SWDC, unlike the more establishment-oriented American Association of Social Workers (AASW), often took action on issues considered outside the purview of professional social workers. For example,
the New York SWDC endorsed the 1932 March of the Unemployed on
City Hall, contributed to the National Hunger March in Washington,
and actively supported the Workers Unemployment Insurance Bill. The
Philadelphia SWDC elected two delegates to a radical committee of farm-
ers, milk drivers, and consumers. The Chicago SWDC made contributions in defense of Tom Mooney and the Scottsboro Boys, supported a
local dress strike, and actively protested the policies of Nazi Germany.[39]

Perhaps the most imporant feature of the SWDC was its insistence
that social workers be defined as "workers." Moreover, they believed that
the fate of social workers was interconnected with the general destiny
of working people. Although professionalism was important, SWDC
members believed that the concept could no longer be used as a guise
to cover up workplace inequities.

The social work union movement in the private sector was born in
late 1931. This nascent movement, called the Association of Federal
Workers (AFW), was an organization of senior caseworkers employed
by constituent agencies of the New York Federation for the Support of
Jewish Philanthropic Societies.[40] Spearheaded by the New York SWDC,
the AFW emerged as a response to the salary cuts imposed by the federation. For the first time, social workers employed trade union tactics
which included picket lines, strike activities, mass meetings, publicity,
petitions, and solicitation of other labor and community groups. Perhaps
most importantly, the AFW represented the first organized effort to
demand collective bargaining for social workers.[41] On February 5, 1934,
the New York AFW organized the first work stoppage in social work
history.

The earliest attempt to organize public welfare workers was begun by
the Chicago SWDC, a club composed largely of employees of the Cook
County Welfare Department and the Unemployment Relief Service.
Shortly after the institution of the National Industrial Recovery Act
(NIRA) of 1933, the Chicago SWDC announced that the standards of
the act could only be met by the creation of a union. On November 6,
1933, the Social Service Workers Union (SSWU), the first protective
union in public social services, was voted into existence.[42]

The problems addressed by the SSWU were similar to those found in
most depression-era relief agencies. The conditions experienced by relief
workers included the lack of desks, chairs, and stationery; crude sanitary

facilities; long hours with uncompensated overtime; nonexistent or in-adequate vacation periods; little or no compensated time for illness or injury; low salaries; arbitrary pay cuts; no job tenure; excessive case loads; and inadequate or nonexistent training. Chicago relief workers also resented the presence of armed guards in the welfare departments. The welfare supervisors, many of whom were trained social workers, were often viewed as oppressive agents of the administration.

The situation in public relief was exacerbated because few of the case-workers had any previous social work experience. In fact, most of the caseworkers were unemployed teachers, insurance salesmen, and former technicians and professionals who had been thrown into the labor market as a result of the Depression. At least initially, most relief workers viewed their employment as temporary and looked forward to an early return to their previous vocations. However, as the Depression wore on, many public welfare employees began to see social work as a permanent rather than a temporary career.[43] From this realization emerged a growing and immediate concern about work conditions and a demand for increased training. At that point, a new concept of labor-management relations entered the field of social work.

The SSWU responded to constituent concerns by drafting a Code For Social Service Workers which included demands for minimum salaries and maximum hours, provisions for adequate vacations and sick leaves, minimum working conditions, maximum caseloads, the right of em-ployees to get workmen's compensation, free medical care, and time off for social work courses. The code also opposed discrimination based on race or organizational activity and dictated a one-month notice for em-ployee termination.[44] Like the New York AFW, the SSWU was organized on the model of an industrial union and, hence, all categories of workers from senior caseworkers to clerical staff were included.[45]

The announcement of the formation of the SSWU resulted in a con-certed drive by welfare officials to crush the organization. Charges of communist domination were levied at the union and resulted in the termination of six of the organization's leaders. Although four union leaders were reinstated, the stridency of the antiunion attacks succeeded in driving away all but a handful of the membership.[46] The antiunion strategy of Cook County and other Illinois relief officials ensured that the SSWU would never develop beyond the blueprint stage, and, as such, protective organizations were temporarily stopped in Chicago.

The lessons of the Chicago debacle burned deep into the consciousness of the social-work union movement. The painful lesson was clear: when faced with union organization, public relief commissions would employ the same antiunion tactics as industry.

The setback in Chicago may have been somewhat counteracted by the successful union organizing drive in New York City. In 1933, over 100 workers of the New York Emergency Home Relief Bureau became one of the most effective social work unions of the 1930s. While the issues and working conditions were basically the same in New York as in Chicago, the Emergency Home Relief Bureau Employees Association of New York City had a unique grievance: all employees of Home Relief came from the welfare roles, and, as such, were subject to periodic check-ups to reestablish need.[47]

The Home Relief Employees Association was begun by a provisional committee representing six out of the forty districts in New York City. As a result of the first meeting on December 5, 1933, an executive committee was elected and a program established.[48] The union's successes were immediate and far-ranging. Immediately after the first meeting the Executive Committee sent a delegate to meet with the Director of the Temporary Emergency Relief Administration (TERA) to extract a promise that there would be no discrimination based on union activity. The TERA director provided the necessary assurance.[49] The association's wage demands were approved at the third meeting and accepted in total by the Civil Works Service. Workmen's Compensation was also approved. Perhaps most importantly, TERA administrators agreed not to look into the personal resources of employees, thus insuring workers an increased measure of job security.[50] Unlike the AFW, the Home Relief Employees Association restricted membership to persons on the work relief payroll, thereby excluding supervisors, administrators, and special workers. By virtue of their training, many of the professional social work staff were supervisors and thus excluded from union membership.[51]

By the end of 1933 the rank-and-file movement could claim thirteen organizations in eight cities. This included discussion clubs in Boston, Philadelphia, New York, St. Louis, and Cleveland, and protective organizations in New York, Chicago, Minneapolis, Brooklyn, Detroit, and Philadelphia. The total membership of the rank-and-file social work movement numbered around 1,000.[52]

Between 1934 and 1936 the Social Work Discussion Clubs began to transform themselves into protective associations. This transformation was not based on a diminution of interest—the New York City meetings usually drew from 400 to 600 persons, and on several occasions they drew over 1,000—but on the realization that protective associations represented a logical evolutionary growth of the discussion club movement.[53]

In 1934 the New York SWDC reorganized and became the Association of Workers in Social Agencies, a protective and educational association.[54] The Cleveland SWDC became the Cleveland Welfare Guild, also a protective association. In late 1934 the Chicago SWDC became the Joint Committee of Social Work Organizations.[55] In short, most of the SWDCs either assumed a trade union form of organization or they became educational auxiliaries to other social-work protective associations.

Although the rank-and-file movement had been active since 1931, it wasn't until 1934 that it really took shape. The event that triggered the growth of the rank and file occurred at the 1934 National Conference of Social Work. Mary van Kleeck, in two eloquent and powerful papers, swept the national conference off its feet.[56] Both her speeches filled the hall and were so successful that conferees who had not been present demanded a second reading. The following day the Kansas City newspapers put the van Kleeck story on the front page and sent reporters to interview William Hodson who was conference president and the New York City Commissioner of Welfare. In essence, Hodson attacked van Kleeck and her "call to revolution." A day later, 1,000 conferees voted to censure Hodson for attacking van Kleeck.[57] (Hodson's attack on van Kleeck can be attributed to her radical critique of the New Deal and to an attempt to save face for Harry Hopkins, the conference's keynote speaker.)

In "Our Illusions Regarding Government," van Kleeck charged that the strongest interests dominated government and, because of capitalism, government protected property rather than human rights. Mary van Kleeck believed that the New Deal was the saviour of capitalism rather than a symbol of the coming of a new and more equitable age.[58] In a rousing speech, she called on social workers to ask themselves whether private ownership and profit were compatible with the public good, and whether a planned and socialized economy was not the real answer to the economic crisis.[59] Van Kleeck's second paper, "The Common Goals of Labor and Social Work," called on social workers to cooperate with organized labor to eliminate unemployment and exploitation.[60]

In some measure, the strong reaction to van Kleeck's papers revolved around what she represented rather than on what she actually said. Van Kleeck's radical analysis of the New Deal was not an uncommon attitude in 1934. Furthermore, neither of her two papers posed any lines of inquiry that the left had not discussed and analyzed since the early 1930s. The threat that van Kleeck posed was based on the fact that she represented a mainstream thinker who, because of the Depression, had become converted to radical thought. Van Kleeck was an unlikely figure to be a radical. Born into an old and established Dutch family (her grandfather owned a half interest in the Ohio and Northern Railroad), Director of the Industrial Relations Division of the Russell Sage Foundation, and a graduate of Smith College, van Kleeck imbued radical thought with a legitimacy that status-quo social workers feared.

Although van Kleeck was the most forceful dissenter at the conference, she did not stand alone. Eduard C. Lindeman, a professor of social work at Columbia University, also called for a new social order characterized by a "high degree of collectivism in economics." Lindeman maintained that America faced two choices: a workers' government or fascism.[61] Bertha Reynolds, a professor of social work at Smith College, noted the futility of offering casework services given the present social order. Dissent was a mood that permeated the conference.

By the end of the 1934 conference, dissenting groups of social workers called on the editors of *Social Work Today*, the organ of the Social Work Discussion Club of New York City, to establish a National Coordinating Committee (NCC). The NCC's goal was to organize the activities of the various rank-and-file groups; to further that pursuit, a call was issued for a national convention.[62]

The 1935 NCC convention had delegates representing eighteen protective organizations, six discussion clubs, four practitioner groups, and three miscellaneous organizations. Areas represented included Baltimore, Boston, New York, Chicago, Cleveland, Cincinnati, Pittsburgh, Newark, Philadelphia, St. Louis, and two county delegations from Pennsylvania. The delegates represented slightly less than the 8,600-member constituency of the mainstream American Association of Social Workers.[63] The convention platform fell under three headings: (a) national social welfare programs, (b) personnel practices, and (c) professional standards. To promote the platform the NCC elected four officers and one representative from each affiliated group.[64] The new charge of the NCC included calling annual delegate meetings, setting up appropriate committees, dissemination and manufacture of discussion materials, making public statements, supporting social welfare legislation, establishing a means for organized participation at future National Conference of Social Work meetings, and engaging in public speaking.[65]

From 1935 to 1936 the NCC claimed affiliations from eighteen organizations representing a membership of over 12,000.[66] By February 1936 the NCC was the voice for all the larger national rank-and-file groups.

THE END OF AN ILLUSION

The NCC's weaknesses revolved around its loose-knit and tenuous structure as well as the absence of money, paid staff, and office space. Moreover, the NCC functioned more as a clearing house than a strong centralized organization providing leadership and direction. The NCC had no power of enforcement or censure upon its affiliate groups; it was thought of only as a provisional organization that would give way to a national membership organization. At least through 1935, this national membership organization was envisioned as a national union of social service employees.[67]

The dream of a national union of social workers was dead by 1936. After a brief but frustrating attempt at organizing a national social workers union under the American Federation of Labor (AFL), the NCC recommended that rank and filers join the American Federation of Government Employees (AFGE), at least until such time as AFGE could create an autonomous department, later known as the American Federation of State, County, and Municipal Employees (AFSCME).[68]

The NCC met for the last time at the National Conference of Social Work in 1937. At that meeting it voted to dissolve and recommended that its organ, *Social Work Today*, be incorporated as an independent publication. With the dissolution of the NCC, affiliate groups rushed to the AFL and the newly emerging AFSCME.[69]

Reasons for the demise of the NCC were manifold. With neither time, money, nor paid staff, the NCC could not adequately immerse itself in local New York City union struggles, much less support union organizing in other cities. In addition, the NCC's lack of resources did not encourage the trust of social service workers facing layoffs and other serious workplace problems. When faced with major labor problems, most social service workers turned to AFGE for assistance. Furthermore, several national unions had already claimed workplace jurisdiction over most of the social welfare field by 1937. The NCC's application for national union status would probably have been denied by both the AFL and the CIO.

Ten unions in the Committee for Industrial Organization (CIO) were purged by the AFL executive council in 1937.[70] By 1938 the CIO cut its last formal ties to the AFL. As a result of these developments, the State, County, and Municipal Workers of America (SCMWA) was formed through a CIO charter in 1937, a charter which allowed the new union to organize all nonfederal government workers.[71] In 1937 the CIO also issued a charter to the United Office and Professional Workers of America (UOPWA) to organize all white-collar workers not claimed by other CIO unions.[72]

Among the earliest subscribers to these new unions were most of the public welfare locals in the AFL's AFSCME, and all of the AFL-chartered social service unions in private agencies. SCMWA was headed by Abraham Flaxer, former president of the AFSCME local in the New York Department of Public Welfare. The UOPWA was headed by Lewis Merrill, former president of the AFL office workers union.

By 1937 SCMWA had signed up 35,000 members; 8,500 of whom were in twenty-eight public welfare locals.[73] The social work section of UOPWA was composed of seven locals and two divisions, with a total membership of about 2,000. By 1938 the New York SSEU (Social Service

Employees Union, a subunit of UOPWA) could claim several contracts, including the national office of the National Council of Jewish Women and the Russell Sage Foundation. In 1940 the UOPWA signed a contract with the National Refugee Service covering over 500 employees. These developments climaxed in 1941 when the UOPWA signed a contract with the Jewish Social Service Association, the largest Jewish family agency in the country.[74]

By 1942 the SSEU was in sixteen cities representing over 4,000 members. With the exception of Local 19 (New York) and Local 39 (Chicago), most locals contained less than 50 members. By 1948 the SSEU had expanded to cover thirty locals representing about 10,000 workers. Half of the membership, however, was centered in Local 19.[75] Although by 1940 the UOPWA had made its major gains in the Jewish agencies, 43 percent of the membership of Local 19 was in nonsectarian agencies.[76]

The success of UOPWA in collective bargaining was far less spectacular than its growth. By 1942 the UOPWA only had 25 written contracts, many informal agreements, and union recognition in roughly fifty agencies. Most of the formal written contracts were with Local 19.[77]

SOCIAL WORK TODAY: A JOURNAL OF THE RANK AND FILE

From 1937 to 1942 the main connection between social work and the unionization movement occurred through Social Work Today. In the fall of 1937 the magazine hired Frank Bancroft as its full-time managing editor. To stabilize the financially shaky journal, fund-raising activities were conducted that included theatre and dinner parties, benefit concerts, and the creation of a financial sponsorship system called Social Work Today Cooperators. Supporters of the journal included notables such as Bertha Reynolds, Mary van Kleeck, Grace Marcus, Kenneth Pray, Grace Coyle, Mary Simkhovitch, Ellen Potter, and T. Arnold Hill.[78] Although the fund-raising activities kept the magazine afloat, actual subscriptions never exceeded 6,000.

Though the content and editorial positions of Social Work Today were clearly to the left, its wide range of authors included faculty members of schools of social work, governmental figures such as Frances Perkins, Katherine Lenroot, and Thomas Parran, and generally well-known public figures such as Roger Baldwin, John L. Lewis, and A. Philip Randolph.

From 1935 to 1942 the editorial direction of Social Work Today followed a meandering and sometimes erratic path. While the journal was extremely critical of the New Deal programs of 1935, the thrust of the critique was basically leveled at the adequacy of public relief rather than its function as a captialist palliative. By 1938, Social Work Today's critique of the New Deal had turned into a glowing endorsement. In fact, the

1938 editorials characterized Harry Hopkins as a Progressive, and even William Hodson, an old enemy of the radical social work movement and New York's Commissioner of Public Welfare, was applauded for his abilities. The May 1938 issue asked readers to write to their Congressman and urge him to show support for the New Deal. Apart from its consistent coverage of the social-work union movement, *Social Work Today* was almost indistinguishable from mainline social work journals by 1942.

Social Work Today abruptly disappeared in May of 1942. Surprisingly, the last issue gave no indication that the magazine would discontinue publication, and, in fact, a new editor had been hired and the final editorial reflected a general optimism regarding future issues.

The reason why *Social Work Today* discontinued publication is unclear. There is some indication that the journal may have experienced severe financial difficulties, but some former rank-and-file leaders suggest that it died chiefly from a lack of interest by the directors.[79] Perhaps this erosion of interest was precipitated by the coming of World War II and the relative prosperity experienced in the war preparation of 1941.

Although this explanation appears plausible, there appears to be another compelling reason for the abandonment of the journal. Beginning in the late 1930s, *Social Work Today* became a glossy magazine that had achieved a certain degree of respectability. It may be precisely that respectability that insured its demise. Perhaps it lost the anger and rage that was the *raison d'être* for its existence. By becoming acceptable—and therefore indistinguishable from mainline journals such as the *Compass* and the *Survey*—*Social Work Today* may have sabotaged its future by muting its initial appeal to the readers' sense of injustice. Whatever the reasons, the death of *Social Work Today* left a vacuum in social work, and the one formal connection between professional social workers and the union movement was severed. Perhaps Bertha Reynolds stated it most succinctly when she observed that "with the death of *Social Work Today* a light has gone out of social work."[80]

THE FALL OF THE RANK AND FILE

The radical unionization movement in social work ended as quickly as it had begun. Both the UOPWA and SCMWA fell victim to the "red purges" of the CIO, and in 1947, the unions were disbanded.[81] Most social work locals organized by the UOPWA or SCMWA affiliated with AFSCME or AFGE.

The reason for the failure of the early social-work unionization movement continues to be an important question. Haynes has attributed the collapse of the rank-and-file movement to its domination by the Communist Party (CPUSA).[82] Specifically, Haynes charges that the editorial direction of *Social Work Today* mirrored the positions of the CPUSA.[83]

On foreign policy issues *Social Work Today* took what appears to be erratic positions. In 1938 the magazine called for a "Peace and Democracy Agenda" which urged U.S. military help for the countries invaded by Hitler. In November 1939, *Social Work Today* suggested a "Peace Agenda For Social Work" and called for an expansion of the New Deal. An editorial in January 1941, "Two Salients for Peace," asked social workers to concentrate on meeting clients needs rather than on war. A February 1941 editorial, "Social Workers Can Think For Themselves," again juxtaposed war and social welfare. In November 1941 *Social Work Today* did a flip-flop and supported the involvement of the United States in World War II.

Haynes appears to be correct in that *Social Work Today*'s vacillation on social and economic issues did mirror the platform of the CPUSA. However, the positions that the journal took on domestic and foreign issues also mirrored that of many non-CPUSA organizations. For example, from 1938 to 1941 isolationism was a common sentiment among both Progressives and Conservatives. Opposition to racism and a strident critique of New Deal programs were also common progressive positions. One is hard-pressed to discern the political differences on many of these questions between Progressives and CPUSA members.

Similarities between the foreign and domestic policies of *Social Work Today* and the CPUSA seem relatively unimportant, especially given the fact that the overwhelming majority of the journal's content revolved around unionization issues, social work practice, and general developments in social work. Although the journal addressed war and peace issues, it was often done through editorials rather than articles. The general content of the magazine rarely centered around the editorials, and, moreover, editorials that examined international issues were rare. It is clear from examining the content of *Social Work Today* that its primary mission involved reforming the profession of social work.

Although many of the principal actors in the rank-and-file movement were CPUSA members, this did not guarantee they would prostrate themselves before the party line.[84] Nor did their party membership ensure that the rank and file was merely a CPUSA-front group. One leader of the rank-and-file movement observed that "I was a party member [CPUSA] but not a revolutionary."[85] When asked why he joined the party he responded that "it was the in-thing to do."[86] Even attending neighborhood party meetings was to one informant "a nuisance that was tolerated to fulfill [party] membership requirements."[87] Indeed, CPUSA membership was viewed by many 1930s intellectuals as a requisite badge of the intelligentsia. For many people, the social role of party membership was more important than any political significance that may have been attached to it.

In contradistinction to Haynes's hypothesis, the failure of the rank and file may lie in the opposite direction; that is, the discipline and centralized nature of the CPUSA's organizational strategy was never fully incorporated into the rank-and-file movement. For example, a major reason for the NCC's dissolution was that it lacked the necessary centralization to provide real leadership to incipient groups of radical social workers. Affiliate defections, lack of a consistent strategy, and a fuzzy ideological perspective reduced the potential of the rank and file to that of "dissenters" rather than disciplined trade unionists. This does not suggest that communist ideology and tactics should have been adopted by the rank and file; but rather, the valuable tactical lessons that communist organizers had taught other trade unionists went unheeded by the rank and file. In that sense, the demise of the rank and file can be traced more to its democratic nature than its communist leanings.

The historical evidence suggests that the rank and file was not a creation of the CPUSA, but an indigenous movement that gave expression to the social and workplace concerns of large numbers of depression-era social workers. To attribute the demise of the radical social work movement to the influence of the CPUSA, or, for that matter, to the "machinations of hard political types," appears unfounded. Moreover, such a simple interpretation deflects the historian from the real causes of the movement's demise—a demise based more on the shifting political, social, and economic climate than on internal political disagreements.

THE LEGACY OF THE RANK AND FILE

Through their activities—literature, speeches, and direct action tactics—the rank-and-file movement exposed large numbers of social workers to the powerful concept of "organization."[88] Thousands of social workers exposed to the NCC, *Social Work Today*, and other activities of the rank and file were provided with a training ground and an educational experience that would be useful in later public-sector organizing. For social workers in the public and private sector, participating in job actions and learning the "language of power" would make the later call to unionization less distant a cry. Furthermore, the experience that social workers received in arbitrating grievances, making demands, organizing meetings and rallies, and walking a strike line were valuable skills that could be used in the labor movement as well as in the later civil rights and antiwar movements. In that sense, the rank and file trained social work leaders in the skills of confrontation and power: a job that schools of social work were ill-prepared to do. In short, the significance of the rank-and-file movement lay in its spadework—the breaking of ground to allow the seeds of social work unionization to take root.

Although it is obvious that social work leaders in the union movement made key strategic mistakes, it is also clear that even without those miscalculations they would have had a difficult time achieving their goals. In the main, trained social workers have always identified themselves as professionals rather than as workers. This sense of professionalism has been reinforced by schools of social work through an emphasis on self-determination and autonomy. Even when the real world of work suggests that autonomy is illusory, professional education continues to promulgate a bifurcated separation between professional autonomy and vocation.

Efforts at unionization were also impaired by the managerial aspirations of large numbers of trained social workers. In choosing managerial positions as their career goal, many professional social workers elected to identify with the objectives of management rather than with the goals of line workers. For these social workers, direct service was merely a brief stop on the road to management, and, hence, they often exhibited only a half-hearted commitment to their fellow workers.

Many social workers from ethnic and working-class backgrounds saw professionalism as a way out of the economically grim reality experienced by their parents. To achieve professional status, and then revert to the self-identity of a worker, may have touched the sensitive chords of class consciousness.

Reasons for the reluctance of large numbers of social workers to embrace unionism are complex. Antiunion sentiments in social work have always been strong, and to suggest that the rank and file could have created a massive union structure is to ignore the lure of professionalism. Nevertheless, despite antiunion feelings, greater numbers of social workers have joined and are actively participating in union activities.[89]

The post-1942 history of labor and social work is in many ways anticlimatic. While social workers continued to join unions such as AFSCME, the Service Employees International Union (SEIU), AFGE, the Communications Workers of America, and others, they did so as workers rather than as social workers possessing a distinct professional identity.

NOTES

1. Not all settlement houses provided aid and comfort to labor unions. For example, social settlement houses in Minneapolis were indifferent to organized labor. See Howard Jacob Karger, *The Sentinels of Order: Social Control and the Minneapolis Settlement House Movement, 1915–1950* (Latham, Md.: University Press of America, 1987). In the main, support for organized labor appears to have been forthcoming mainly in the large urban areas, and, in particular, in the more well-known settlement houses of the Northeast and Middle West.

2. Sarah Eisenstein, *Give Us Bread But Give Us Roses* (London: Routledge and Kegan Paul, 1983), p. 17.

3. Blake McKelvey, *The Urbanization of America, 1860–1915* (New Jersey: Rutgers University Press, 1963), p. 134.

4. Robert Bremner, *From the Depths* (New York: New York University Press, 1964), p. 232.

5. Mary Anderson, *Woman at Work* (Westport, Connecticut: Greenwood Press, 1973), p. 34.

6. Jane Addams, *Twenty Years At Hull House* (New York: Macmillan, 1951), p. 227.

7. Daniel Levine, *Jane Addams and the Liberal Tradition* (Madison, Wisconsin: State Historical Society of Wisconsin, 1971), p. 161.

8. Allen F. Davis, *Spearheads For Reform* (New York: Oxford University Press, 1967), p. 106.

9. Robert Woods (ed.), *The City Wilderness* (Boston: Houghton, Mifflin and Company, 1899), p. 282.

10. Quotation from Jacob S. Potofsky, "Happy Birthday to Ellen Gates Starr," *Advance*, 1939. Quoted in Davis, *Spearheads*, pp. 106–107.

11. Meredith Tax, *The Rising of the Women* (New York: Monthly Review Press, 1980), p. 96.

12. Philip Foner, *Women and the American Labor Movement* (New York: The Free Press, 1979), p. 305.

13. Ibid.

14. Mari Jo Buhle, *Women and American Socialism, 1870–1920* (Urbana, Illinois: University of Illinois Press, 1981), p. 191.

15. William L. O'Neill, *Everyone Was Brave* (Chicago: Quadrangle Books, 1969), p. 155.

16. Ibid.

17. Ibid., p. 156.

18. Ibid., pp. 157–160.

19. Ibid., p. 160.

20. Buhle, *Women and American Socialism*, p. 189.

21. Tax, *The Rising of the Women*, p. 102.

22. Ibid.

23. O'Neill, *Everyone Was Brave*, p. 162.

24. Ibid., p. 163.

25. Tax, *The Rising of the Women*, p. 121.

26. Florence Kelley, (edited by Kathryn Kish Sklar), *The Autobiography of Florence Kelley* (Chicago: Charles H. Kerr Publishing Company, 1986), pp. 1–16.

27. O'Neill, *Everyone Was Brave*, pp. 151–153.

28. Ibid., pp. 232–240.

29. Davis, *Spearheads*, p. 111.

30. Unsigned draft of letter to "Carrie," September 16, 1907. Robbins Family Papers, State Historical Society of Wisconsin. Quoted in O'Neill, *Everyone Was Brave*, p. 138.

31. Ibid., p. 139.

32. Addams, *Twenty Years at Hull House*, p. 218.

33. Ibid., pp. 218–219.

34. Levine, *Jane Addams*, p. 160.

35. John R. Commons, "Karl Marx and Samuel Gompers," *Political Science Quarterly*, 41 (June, 1926), p. 284.

36. Jacob Fisher, *The History of the Rank and File, 1931–6* (New York: New York School of Philanthropy, 1936), p. 7.

37. Ibid.

38. Ibid.

39. Ibid.

40. Leslie B. Alexander and Milton Speizman,"The Union Movement in Voluntary Social Work," *The Social Welfare Forum, 1979* (N.Y.: Columbia University Press, 1980), p. 184.

41. Fisher, *The History of the Rank and File*, pp. 8–9.

42. Ibid., p. 11.

43. Ibid., p. 15.

44. Ibid.

45. Ibid., p. 12.

46. Ibid.

47. Ibid., p. 13.

48. Ibid.

49. Ibid., p. 12.

50. Ibid., p. 14.

51. Ibid.

52. Ibid., pp. 15–16.

53. Ibid., pp. 17–18.

54. Ibid., p. 19.

55. Ibid., pp. 19–21.

56. Mary van Kleeck, "Our Illusions Regarding Government," and "Common Interests of Labor and Social Work," *Proceedings*, National Conference on Social Work, 1934 (Chicago, Ill.: University of Chicago Press, 1935).

57. Jacob Fisher, *The Response of Social Work to the Depression* (Boston: Schenkman, 1980), pp. 74–76.

58. van Kleeck, "Our Illusions," p. 376.

59. Ibid., p. 379.

60. Ibid., p. 383.

61. Eduard C. Lindeman, "Basic Unities in Social Work," *Proceedings*, National Conference on Social Work, 1934 (Chicago, Ill.: University of Chicago Press, 1935), p. 116.

62. Fisher, *The History of the Rank and File*, pp. 36–37.

63. Ibid.

64. Ibid., p. 38.

65. Ibid., pp. 39–40.

66. Twelve thousand members was a significant amount, especially since AASW only claimed 15,000 members. There may, however, be a tendency to overlook the fact that even with combined membership—probably overlapping—there were still only 27,000 social workers accounted for. This was not a significant number since, by 1935, there were about 130,000 social workers.

67. Fisher, *History of the Rank and File*, p. 41.

68. Ibid., pp. 41–43.

69. Fisher, *Response*, pp. 161–162.

70. The Committee for Industrial Organization (CIO) began in the 1930s as an attempt to fill the vacuum left by the American Federation of Labor (AFL).

The AFL tended to organize skilled workers, while the CIO organized both skilled and unskilled workers on an industry-wide rather than craft basis. The CIO was generally considered the more liberal union during the 1930s and early 1940s. A good description of the two unions and the ways in which they differed can be found in M. Derber and E. Young, *Labor and the New Deal* (Madison, Wisc.: University of Wisconsin Press, 1957); and David J. Sapass, *Communism in American Unions* (New York: McGraw Hill, 1959).

71. Fisher, *Response*, pp. 187–188.

72. Ibid.

73. Ibid., p. 197.

74. Ibid.

75. Alexander and Speizman, "The Union Movement," p. 185.

76. Ibid.

77. Ibid., pp. 185–186.

78. See *Social Work Today*'s list of cooperators from the years of 1937–1942.

79. Interview with Jacob Fisher, former leader in the social work rank and file movement, Sarasota, Florida, December 28, 1981.

80. Bertha Reynolds, *An Unchartered Journey* (New York: Citadel Press, 1961), p. 72.

81. "Report of the Joint Fact-Finding Committee on Un-American Activities to the 57th California Legislature," (Sacramento, California, 1948), p. 375.

82. John Earl Haynes, "The Rank and File Movement in Private Social Work," *Labor History*, 16 (Winter 1975), pp. 78–98.

83. Ibid., p. 84.

84. The fact that many of the rank and file leaders were members of the CPUSA was confirmed by the Jacob Fisher interview, and by a personal interview with George Wolfe, Sarasota, Florida, December 29, 1981. Both Fisher and Wolfe were principal leaders in the movement.

85. Interview conducted in 1980. Because of the current political climate, I have chosen to guard the anonymity of the informant.

86. Ibid.

87. Ibid.

88. The work of Bernard Karsh and Philip I. Garman, "The Impact of the Political Left," in Milton Derber and Edwin Young, (eds.), *Labor and the New Deal* (Madison, Wisconsin: University of Wisconsin Press, 1957), is used as the basis for my analysis of the significance of the rank and file movement.

89. There are over 72,000 unionized social workers in the United States. See H. Jacob Karger, "Reclassification and Social Work: Is There a Future for the Trained Social Worker?" *Social Work*, 28 (November-December 1983), p. 431.

II

COMMON AND CONFLICTING GOALS OF LABOR AND SOCIAL WORK

2

The Common Goals of Labor and Social Work

HOWARD JACOB KARGER

This chapter probes the common goals of labor and social work by examining their historical contexts, the similar struggles waged by the National Association of Social Work (NASW) and public-sector labor unions, and by analyzing issues that represent significant areas of agreement between professional social work associations and public service unions.

Questions involving the common goals of labor and social work have been salient since the 1930s. In a controversial paper delivered at the 1934 National Conference on Social Work, Mary van Kleeck, an important figure in social reform, observed that:

The immediate common goals of labor and social work . . . [are] maintenance of standards of living, both for individuals and for the community. Social work, particularly in these last few years, has repeatedly declared that it is not primarily an agency for relief in emergency, in disaster and industrial depressions, but that it is representative of the common good will of those who seek to bring expert knowledge to bear upon . . . the whole program of social legislation and public services. . . . Those have been characteristic activities of social workers which interest us all as permanent goals.

The labor groups have had the same general aim. They have sought to maintain the standards of living of the workers; to ask that the return in the pay envelope bear some proportion to the productivity of labor; to ask that there be leisure, growing also out of the increased productivity of labor.[1]

Van Kleeck saw the potential for a partnership between social work and labor unions whereby both groups could help forge a new society.

An idealist, van Kleeck saw the goals of social work and labor as the common goals of humanity.

Van Kleeck's positive view of labor unions was shared by the nascent group of social work rank and filers of the early 1930s. This group was concerned with fusing professional social work values with trade union values:

Readers of *Social Work Today* are fully aware of the genuine concerns of the trade union movement in social work with standards. . . .

Have the professional bodies and the trade union organizations common purposes? Is there a meeting ground for cooperative effort?

Any cursory examination of the program and demands of the trade union reveals their goals to be as clear and direct as those of the professional society— high standards of service and high standards of employment practices.[2]

Although the social work rank-and-file movement and *Social Work Today* were defunct by 1947, the legitimacy of union membership was becoming more widespread. A 1947 article in the mainstream *Social Work Yearbook* observed that "labor and social work make contact at many points and have much in common."[3] The article went on to note that "the ultimate goal of organized labor has always been improvement in the standards of living among the workers of the nation. . . . Social work, too, is concerned with action for long-range social progress."[4] Although not an endorsement, this tacit acceptance of organized labor represented a major shift in the attitude of the social work profession which, during the 1920s, would have been appalled at the prospect of unionization.

Apart from the important inroads made by the rank and filers of the 1930s, the relationship between professional social work associations and unions can be traced to organized labor's involvement in the public and private network of social services. Although the experience with social services of displaced workers in the 1930s was largely negative, the ordeal taught labor leaders that social services had the potential to affect more than just a small segment of society. The interest of organized labor in social services—often private, nonprofit agencies under the aegis of Community Chests—brought unions and social workers into closer contact. According to Wilbur F. Maxwell, this contact allowed social workers to "become aware of the labor movement as something other than merely a force dealing with economic and wage problems," and for unions to see "social work as something other than merely an agency for dispensing 'charity' and relief."[5]

Beginning in the early 1930s, the profession of social work and organized labor intersected at three major junctions: the election of labor leaders to social welfare boards, community chests, public welfare boards, and so forth; the initiation of social workers into labor unions; and the growing recognition by social work associations of the importance of organized labor.

Despite the absence of a formal relationship, in 1967 the NASW adopted a policy reaffirming the right of NASW members to "participate in the formulation of personnel policies and procedures through whatever instruments they choose." Revised in 1971 and again in 1975, this policy admonishes management to "accept and work with whatever means of representation is chosen by the employee group."[6]

A COMMON STRUGGLE AGAINST REACTION

Although on a national level there is little formal association between the NASW and public sector unions, they do nominally interact through the Coalition of American Public Employees (CAPE).[7] CAPE, an organization which includes NASW as well as the major public sector unions, lobbies on national public welfare issues. On the local level, however, there are several examples of active collaboration between professional social work associations and unions, often around issues of social service cuts and other domestic concerns.[8]

In an attempt to encourage a better relationship with professional social workers, Jerry Wurf, a former AFSCME president, wrote an article for the *NASW News* in which he maintained that:

AFSCME's involvement with . . . [social issues] is part of a larger commitment to improving public services and programs. But more importantly, these vital efforts prove the true mission of a labor organization to be closely linked to that of social work. AFSCME's growth in the last decade was due in large part to its role as a social missionary. This precious pursuit has undoubtedly been enhanced by the growing number of social workers in our ranks.

Union representation can serve as a compliment to the functions NASW provides: collective bargaining is the most concrete way of resolving workplace disputes such as case overloads, grievances, and other job-related problems.[9]

Since both organizations are liberal in their outlook, it is not surprising that the scorecard of agreement on national issues is nearly perfect. For example, both AFSCME and NASW support pay equity legislation, and both groups endorsed the Federal Pay Practices Act of 1985.

Agreement on federal budget issues is also widespread. Although both the NASW and AFSCME are concerned about the effects of the Gramm-Rudman-Hollings bill on social welfare financing, AFSCME has gone one step farther and has called for its repeal.[10] Both groups also agree on the necessity to refund the Title XX Social Services Block Grant to its higher, pre-1981 levels.[11]

AFSCME issues where NASW support is expected include opposition to Medicare cuts, the expansion of Medicare to cover all pregnant women, reduction of out-of-pocket costs to Medicare beneficiaries, modification of the Diagnostic Related Groups (DRG) to make them more sensitive to the severity of illness, the expansion of the WIC (Women, Infants, and Children) programs, increased funding for the WIN (Work Incentive Now) program, the elimination of Food Stamp cuts, and an increase in AFDC payment standards to 80 percent of the poverty level.[12]

Welfare reform represents another potential area of agreement between AFSCME and NASW. For example, the main principles in the NASW position on welfare reform include:

1. promotion of self-sufficiency
2. the need to address the economic and structural causes of poverty
3. promotion of family strength and stability
4. assurance to individuals of a decent standard of living in order to meet basic needs
5. addressing the needs of the whole person and the family by paying particular attention to the provision of needed social services
6. emphasizing transitional as well as preventive services[13]

In particular, NASW endorses providing welfare recipients with voluntary employment and adequate pay, opportunities for meaningful long-term work, and health insurance for children and adult family members. NASW is opposed to forced work programs. In addition, NASW advocates the creation of a full-employment policy, an increase in the minimum wage, elimination of all discrimination in hiring, a national minimum benefit level for AFDC (indexed for inflation), the institution of the AFDC-Unemployed Parent Program in all states, strengthening the enforcement of child support laws and increased support payments, providing adequate support services for working parents, furnishing "soft services" (such as counseling), and making ongoing services available for people after they have entered the work force.[14]

The AFSCME proposal for welfare reform is almost identical to that of NASW. For example, AFSCME strongly supports voluntary work and training programs, and like NASW, AFSCME proposals call for a substantial commitment of resources. In addition, AFSCME argues for strong support services in the areas of child care, health care, and transportation, and lastly, like NASW, AFSCME calls for an increase in the minimum wage, a policy of high employment, and an end to employer discrimination practices.[15]

A final area of agreement between public sector unions and NASW involves the issue of defense spending. In testimony given before the budget committee of the U.S. House of Representatives, NASW officials stated that:

NASW has two major concerns about the military budget: (1) it cannot be allowed to expand at the cost of domestic programs; and (2) the allocation of funds within the military should favor personnel needs and preparedness rather than strategic and nuclear weapons.

A prudent reduction in the Pentagon budget would permit the continuation of vital social services and would contribute to our efforts to curb the federal deficit [original emphasis].[16]

In substantial agreement with NASW, one AFSCME resolution called for an end to "the unwarranted, inflationary, and unjustified defense buildup proposed by the Reagan Administration."[17] Going one step further, the resolution demanded an "orderly, planned economic conversion," which entails "alternative uses for defense installations and plans for the redevelopment of communities adversely affected by such closings."[18]

Although NASW and public sector unions have minor differences on national domestic policy, for the most part, a substantial level of agreement prevails. It is clearly in the interests of both groups to advocate for increased public spending, more comprehensive social welfare programs, and less defense spending (inevitably coming at the expense of social programs), and to maintain a belief in the need for the continued growth of the welfare state.

The parting of company, if there is one, occurs at the level of workplace issues. Barriers that separate unions and social work organizations do not involve war and peace issues, domestic spending concerns, or other major public policy debates. Instead, divisive issues revolve around nitty-gritty job issues such as reclassification and licensure.

NOTES

1. Mary van Kleeck, "The Common Goals of Labor and Social Work," *Proceedings*, National Conference of Social Work, 1934 (Chicago, Ill.: University of Chicago Press, 1935), p. 295.

2. Quoted in Milton Tambor, "The Social Worker as Worker: A Union Perspective," in Simon Slavin, (ed.), *Managing Finances, Personnel, and Information in Human Services* (New York: Haworth Press, 1985), p. 267.

3. Wilbur F. Maxwell, "Labor and Social Work," in *Social Work Yearbook, 1947* (New York: Russell Sage, 1947), p. 277.

4. Ibid., p. 278.

5. Ibid.

6. Elma Phillipson Cole, "Unions in Social Work," in *Encyclopedia of Social Work* (New York: National Association of Social Workers, 1977), p. 1559.

7. The lack of sustained formal contact between NASW and public-sector labor unions was affirmed in telephone conversations with Thomas Gauthier, Senior Staff Associate, NASW, November 10, 1986, and with Albert Russo, Community Services Department, AFSCME, November 12, 1986.

8. Leslie B. Alexander, "Unions: Social Work," in *Encyclopedia of Social Work* (New York: National Association of Social Workers, 1987), p. 798.

9. Jerry Wurf, "Labor Movement, Social Work Fighting Similar Battles," *NASW News*, 25 (December 1980), p. 7.

10. AFSCME, "Resolution on Gramm-Rudman-Hollings Bill," 27th International Convention, June 23–27, 1986, Chicago, Ill.

11. See "Legislative Agenda, 1986" (Silver Spring, Md.: National Association of Social Workers). Also see Resolution, "Funding of Social Services," 27th International Convention, June 23–27, 1986, Chicago, Ill. (Washington, D.C.: AFSCME). See also National Association of Social Workers, "Testimony Before the Committee on the Budget of the U.S. House of Representatives on the Fiscal Year 1988 Federal Budget," Silver Spring, Md.: NASW, February 19, 1987.

12. AFSCME, Resolutions, "Funding of Social Services," 27th International Convention.

13. Dorothy V. Harris, President, NASW, "Testimony Before the Committee on Finance of the United States Senate on Welfare Reform," Silver Spring, Md.: National Association of Social Workers, February 2, 1987, p. 3.

14. Ibid., pp. 16–20.

15. Gerald W. McEntee, International President, American Federation of State and County Municipal Employees, Testimony Before the Subcommittee on Social Security and Family Policy of the Senate Committee on Finance, "Welfare: Reform or Replacement?" Washington, D.C., 1986.

16. National Association of Social Workers, "Testimony on the Fiscal Year 1988 Federal Budget," Silver Spring, Md.: NASW, February 23, 1987, p. 5.

17. AFSCME, Resolution, "Defense Spending," 27th International Convention.

18. Ibid.

3

Unions and Social Work Licensure

HOWARD JACOB KARGER

The licensing of social workers is a divisive issue separating professional social work organizations and public sector unions. This chapter will provide a description of legal regulation, examine the National Association of Social Workers' (NASW's) support of licensure, explore the union position on the legal regulation of social workers, and probe the potential conflict between NASW and public sector unions over licensure.

State regulation of professions may include the licensing of practice, titles, or both. In most cases where the title of Social Worker is protected, it is preceded by an identifying term, such as Registered Social Worker (often used at the BSW-level), Master or Certified Social Worker (usually referring to the MSW-level), or Clinical Social Worker (an independent level of practice).

In 1986, thirty-seven states and territories had laws regulating the social work profession. Twenty-six of those states recognized three levels of practice: baccalaureate (BSW), master's degree (MSW), and the independent practice level (MSW plus two years of experience). Most states that license social workers do so at one or more of the above levels; only thirteen states regulate just a single level of social work practice.[1]

THE HISTORICAL BACKGROUND OF SOCIAL WORK LICENSURE

The majority of state laws regulating social workers are recent. However, Puerto Rico enacted a licensure act in 1934 using the qualifications of the American Association of Social Workers. Shortly afterward, California and Missouri enacted a voluntary system of certification managed by their state conferences of social work. In 1945 California became the first state to pass a regulatory act requiring the MSW degree for use of the title "Registered Social Worker." Seven states followed California's lead and passed similar title protection bills.[2]

Internal rifts over licensing began in the late 1960s. In 1968 the California chapter of NASW vetoed attempts by private-practice social workers to pass a licensing act requiring the MSW plus two years of supervised clinical practice. This squabble over licensure spurred on the formation of the State Societies of Clinical Social Work, an organization still in conflict with NASW over the requirements for licensure.

Three state legislatures enacted social work regulation in 1972. Of those states, Michigan ratified a title protection act with several levels; Louisiana passed a single-level clinical-social-work law; and Utah approved an act which followed the NASW model statute almost verbatim. From 1972 to 1980, NASW chapters successfully lobbied for the passage of nine licensure and two title protection acts.

Beginning in 1971 licensing acts became harder to shepherd through state legislatures as antiregulatory forces began to pick up momentum. A 1971 HEW report viewed with alarm the proliferation of licensing in the allied health professions, and called for a two-year moratorium. The antiregulatory mood of the nation was illustrated in the creation of self-rescinding "Sunset Laws." By 1982, thirty-five states had adopted some form of "Sunset" legislation, at least some of which affected the social work licensing acts passed in the middle 1970s.

Despite the erratic nature of licensure legislation (three acts were passed in 1977 while none was successful in 1978–1979), eight new acts were passed from 1980 to 1984, and two previous state regulations were amended to include multilevel licensure. In 1984 NASW reported that nearly all chapters in states without social work regulation had developed a program for action.[3]

THE JUSTIFICATION FOR LICENSURE

NASW's justification for licensure encompasses a myriad of rationales. Foremost among them is a concern about the quality of social services and the personnel that provide them. A statement by the Minnesota Coalition for the Legal Regulation of Social Workers sums up the argument:

Without legal protection, consumers do not have the assurance that individuals using the title social workers and practicing social work have met the standards of the profession. Licensure would screen out untrained individuals and ensure that those practicing as social workers have met educational and ethical standards. When these standards are not met, individuals will not be permitted to continue practicing. This will reduce the incidence of harm from incompetent and unethical practitioners and thereby improve the quality of services.[4]

A NASW lobbying pamphlet further clarifies the need for licensure:

1. Clients in public programs receiving social work services are often vulnerable populations requiring protective services. These clients literally have no choice about who serves them and rarely would they have the ability to assess the qualifications or competence of the provider. Thus, without licensing—establishing criteria for competent service provision—these vulnerable clients are put at even further risk.

2. Non-social work programs in human services have been proliferating in recent years. Many of these university-based programs are not accredited professional programs, and many do not even require a practicum. Social work programs are accredited by the federally sanctioned Council on Social Work Education, and like the major helping disciplines (medicine, social work, psychology), they require an extensive practicum.

3. A large number of persons employed as social workers lack the necessary training and have little or no awareness of the profession's ethical and practice standards. The only way to ensure the accountability of persons practicing social work is through state regulation.

4. There is no certification for the great majority of persons employed as social workers. Most civil service workers are not required to be trained social workers, and the public has no way of knowing whether they are qualified.

5. Licensing will end the confusion caused by the proliferation of job titles through recognizing standards for which social workers, regardless of background or training, will be held accountable.

6. Licensing will create an easily accessible forum in which a client can raise charges of malpractice and unethical conduct.

7. Licensing will establish standards which can be recognized by other state agencies, thereby reducing wasteful studies and concerns about social work activities in state related agencies.[5]

Proponents of licensure cite evidence of a link between training and the provision of competent services:

There are two studies...that specifically address this issue [the BSW degree as a more effective preparation for social work practice than a BA in another discipline].

The results showed significant differences in the educational backgrounds of workers and the kinds of services received by children and their families. The study [Olsen and Holmes] demonstrated that *non-professionally trained (BAs) did not perform as effectively as professional staff (BSWs) in several areas of service* [original emphasis]. They were less successful in providing substitute and supportive services to children, and environmental support services to families. They also had more difficulty in planning for sustained contact among families whose children had been removed from their homes.

The dominant finding of the Bailey study is that *BSW staff perform in their social service positions at significantly higher levels than do undifferentiated staff* [original emphasis].[6, 7]

THE OPPONENTS OF LICENSURE

Criticism of social work licensure comes from both internal and external sources. Perhaps the chief internal critic is the National Association of Black Social Workers (NABSW), an organization representing 140 national chapters:

The ongoing efforts of NASW in concert with the Society of Clinical Social Workers to secure licensing for social workers must be stopped. This movement represents an attempt to establish an elitist hierarchy within the social work profession which will significantly change the racial structure of not only the human service job market but also job mobility, the kind of quality of services, the allocation of resources and the number of black service agencies....

What it [licensing] will do ... is to limit the job market and discriminate against Blacks entering the profession by way of a framework in institutional racism.[8]

For the most part, the NASW has dismissed the concerns of the NABSW. In one position paper, the NASW stated that, "Suffice it to say, NASW disagrees with their assessment, and NABSW opposition has not been a major problem in most states."[9] A lobbying document prepared by the Minnesota Coalition for Legal Regulation of Social Workers addressed those same concerns by maintaining that:

Licensure should help to solidify the gains made by women and minorities and expand their opportunities in the future [original emphasis]. ... Schools of social work have better records than other disciplines in actively recruiting and supporting women and minority students. Nationally, in 1983–84, ethnic minorities comprised 29 percent of juniors and seniors enrolled in BSW programs, 16 percent of MSW students, and 22 percent of social work doctoral students.[10]

A second internal critic is the Federation of State Societies of Clinical Social Work (Clinical Society). Unlike the NABSW, the Clinical Society is fervently in favor of licensure. Even more zealous than NASW, the Clinical Society supports a single-level independent practice certification requiring clinical education, and, in most states, a minimum of five years of supervised clinical experience.

External forces opposed to licensure encompass many groups and viewpoints. Antiregulatory zealots believe that licensing social workers means greater governmental intervention in marketplace relations.

Many legislators—and much of the public—neither understand nor appreciate the value of professional social work. Furthermore, some public administrators see no special value in social work training, and others fear that licensing will result in greater salary costs.

Perhaps the strongest opposition to licensure comes from public sector unions. Although AFSCME is the largest public sector union (representing the majority of unionized social workers), it has no explicit national policy on social work licensure.[11] Nevertheless, AFSCME's implicit position is illustrated in a letter written by Albert Russo, Coordinator of Social Service Programs:

Historically, AFSCME's position has been that we object to the imposition of licensing requirements upon social workers and caseworkers employed in the public sector.

Public social workers and caseworkers at the state and local level are required, prior to employment, to meet specified merit system standards for their positions. . . . The same rigid requirements apply to any and all promotional opportunities which may be available to them. Moreover, once employed, their work performance is reviewed regularly and periodically. . . .

AFSCME maintains that it is patently redundant and unnecessary to subject public social workers and caseworkers to the additional burden of meeting state licensing or registration demands.

On the other hand, we see merit in State laws on this subject which limit coverage to social workers and caseworkers who are employed by private, nonprofit agencies or who are in private practice. . . .

For those engaged in private practice, State licensure or certification conveys a clear message to the private individuals who purchase these services that the provider is qualified and competent. . . .

I would recommend that the AFSCME Councils . . . band together and support a Bill only if it is limited to social workers and caseworkers who are employed by private, nonprofit agencies or who are in private practice.[12]

A CRITIQUE OF LICENSURE

Opponents maintain that NASW is promoting licensure to satisfy the demands of private practitioners seeking third-party reimbursement from medical/mental health insurance companies.[13] In fact, NASW acknowledges that:

One of the major changes in our society has been the increasing use of insurance as a primary means of providing personal services . . . insurance companies demand that providers, such as social workers, have some objective form of certifying their competence. State licensing is the primary way in which all such professions are certified for practice, and therefore social work should be regulated.[14]

Critics argue that third-party insurance reimbursement only affects the elite group of social workers in private practice, thus having little effect on the vast majority of salaried social workers.

Another criticism involves the potential of NASW to use licensure as a lever to restrict entry into the profession during times of economic adversity. Moreover, opponents fear that licensure may result in enforced conformity to the often limited views held by licensing board members. In the end, some adversaries believe that the NASW objective in licensure is to allow it to acquire the kind of pervasive influence currently held by the American Medical Association, the American Bar Association, and the American Psychological Association.[15]

Gross argues that attempts at licensing

do not seem to be providing the structure for effective solutions to the problems of delivering quality care in the health and helping services. Instead, the evidence overwhelmingly supports the conclusion that licensing maintains a structure that is in the self-interest of the service giver and in opposition to the public interest. Licensing actually results in a lack of accountability to the public. This information may cause some to question a collusion between the state and the professions which is justified in altruistic terms but which appears not to merit public confidence.[16]

In one sense Gross is correct: little evidence exists to support the charge that licensure protects consumers against incompetent practitioners or insures the delivery of quality services. Moreover, one need only look at the rates of malpractice cases in medicine and law to see how much protection licensing actually affords the consumer. Lastly, state governments are not deluged with requests by the public for the regulation of social workers, nor do they report significant numbers of consumer complaints and law suits against social service providers.

Another dilemma facing social workers' attempts to gain licensure is their inability to lay claim to a specific practice domain. Since social workers are employed in a variety of settings, often working under sundry titles, what constitutes a social worker and what basic skills is he or she expected to possess? Unlike the prescribed knowledge base of law and medicine, the domain of social work knowledge is widely diffused. Therefore, questions arise as to the validity of the knowledge base used to test social workers. Perhaps this explains why Herman Borenzweig found that the only variable correlated with passing the California licensing examination for clinical social work was the applicant's involvement in personal therapy.[17]

The inherent restrictions in licensure may also provide a formidable barrier for minorities. In large measure, much of the employment gain for blacks has been in public employment. As such, the public sector has been an avenue for blacks and other minorities to enter middle-class economic life. Since public employment has been historically based on civil service examinations and only secondarily on educational credentials, blacks have been able to make significant inroads despite their educational handicaps. Moreover, since promotions in public service are often based more on tenure and performance than on educational credentials, blacks have been able to rise through the public hierarchy, especially in the large urban areas. By emphasizing educational degrees at the expense of experience and on-the-job training, licensure may well retard the significant gains made by blacks in public welfare.

Licensure may also result in a brain drain from the public to the private sector. For example, if as the unions demand, licensure is restricted only to the private welfare sector, and if this creates a shortage of licensable social workers, it can be expected that those eligible for licensing will gravitate to private agencies. This status-based migration may occur in spite of the fact that no evidence exists that licensure increases the wages of social workers.[18]

The desire for licensure has a marked class bias. For many years the social work profession has been gravitating away from its historical responsibility to the poor. The present emphasis on private practice, industrial social work, family therapy, and so forth, is an attempt to diminish the stigma of working with the poor. Hungry for status and recognition, many social workers see licensure as a means to increase professional status and to achieve public recognition through the right to display a state license.

Faced with a growing competitive disadvantage in relationship to other licensed human service professionals, and confronting a diminishing social service field increasingly colonized by competing disciplines (community psychology, applied sociology, counseling programs, and so forth), social workers are forced to consider licensure as a means for their future survival.

LICENSURE, UNIONS AND COMPROMISE

The AFSCME stance on licensure is premised on the idea that it should only include the private sector; public employees require no regulation because of extensive supervision. However, if that supervision is provided by untrained social workers—as is often the case—then its adequacy must be questioned. Moreover, AFSCME's position on licensure is plagued by a fundamental contradiction: if as the previously cited Russo letter states, "licensure or certification conveys to the private individual who purchases these services that the provider is qualified and competent," then how will the public welfare client be assured of the same competence on the part of his or her service provider?

Exempting state employees from licensure is a two-edged sword. Although exemption eliminates conflict between social work organizations and public sector unions, it also helps to form a two-tiered system in which the public is informed that two classes of social workers exist: those that have passed the licensing examination and are deemed competent; and those employed in public welfare.

It is likely that the public perception will be that unlicensed social workers are inferior, and that agencies that use them are relegating their clients to second-class services. Services provided by unlicensed social workers will ultimately be identified as services earmarked for the poor.

Private agencies serving all social and economic classes will be forced by consumer pressure to hire only licensed social workers. On the other hand, because of economic exigencies, agencies that serve only the poor will retain unlicensed social workers. In short, middle-class social service consumers will see licensed social workers, while the poor will see unlicensed public welfare workers.

Although exemption from licensure will not necessarily reduce the ranks of public-sector social workers, it will diminish their currency within the human service community. Already viewed by some social workers as the proletariat of human services, public welfare workers may experience more opprobrium as their inferior status is codified through licensing laws. Exemption from licensing may eventually become a liability rather than a benefit.

Demands for exempting public welfare workers from licensing laws represent a short-sighted objective for public sector unions. Although this position may protect current members, the ramifications for clients and future social workers and the responsibility of the public sector to provide high-quality services may be significant.

Competence, unfortunately, is all too often judged solely on the merit of educational credentials. An alternative union strategy would be to not insist on exemption, but, instead, to demand that public welfare personnel receive the necessary training to qualify for licensure. This would entail that public welfare administrators, in conjunction with unions, formulate ongoing continuing education plans to prepare workers for licensing examinations.

Professional social work organizations must also be willing to compromise, and, where appropriate, licensing laws should have a grandfather clause. NASW must recognize experience and on-the-job training as valid indicators of professional competence. Moreover, the Council on Social Work Education must ease its restrictions and allow schools of social work to grant academic credit for work-related experience.

Licensure is an important issue for professional social work associations and labor unions. Although it initially appears that a victory on licensing means a loss for public sector unions, on closer examination, licensing social workers can provide benefits for both groups.

NOTES

1. See Myles Johnson, "Background Information on the Licensure of Social Workers," Silver Spring, Maryland: National Association of Social Workers, October, 1985, p. 1.; and "Chapter Action Guide for Identification and Retention of Baccalaureate Social Workers," Silver Spring, Maryland: National Association of Social Workers, 1986, p. 2.

2. Myles Johnson, "A Brief Review of the Legal Regulation of Social Work," Silver Spring, Maryland: National Association of Social Workers, circa 1984, n.p.

3. Ibid.

4. Minnesota Coalition for Legal Regulation of Social Workers, "Social Worker's Application for Licensure, Review Factor of Cost Effectiveness and Economic Impact," St. Paul, Minnesota: Minnesota Coalition for Legal Regulation of Social Workers, February 27, 1986, p. 19.

5. National Association of Social Workers, "Answers to Questions State Legislators Ask About Social Work Licensing," Silver Spring, Maryland: National Association of Social Workers, circa 1980, n.p.

6. The studies referred to in this quotation are Lenore Olsen and William M. Holmes, "Educating Child Welfare Workers," *Social Service Review*, 35 (March 1985), pp. 32–43, and Walter Hampton Bailey, "Comparison of Performance Levels Between BSW and BA Social Workers," unpublished DSW dissertation, Catholic University of America, 1978.

7. Minnesota Coalition, "Social Workers' Application for Licensure," p. 19.

8. "NABSW Position on Licensing," exhibit 4, "NASW: A Brief Review of the Legal Regulation of Social Work," Silver Spring, Maryland: National Association of Social Workers, circa 1984, n.p.

9. "NASW: A Brief Review of the Legal Regulation of Social Work," circa 1984, n.p.

10. Minnesota Coalition, "Social Workers' Application for Licensure," p. 3.

11. This was confirmed by an October 1, 1986 telephone conversation with Albert T. Russo, Coordinator, Social Service Programs, Department of Public Policy, AFSCME, Washington, D.C.

12. Letter from Albert Russo, Coordinator, Social Service Programs, Political and Legislative Affairs, AFSCME, to Tom Cronin, AFSCME District Council 47, AFL-CIO, dated November 16, 1982, pp. 1–2.

13. Letter from Fredrick P. Smith, Ph.D., President, St. Louis Chapter, National Association of Black Social Workers, Inc., January 28, 1986, to Henry A. Panethiere, Chairman, Missouri Senate Committee on State Departments and Governmental Affairs, Jefferson City, Missouri.

14. National Association of Social Workers, "Answers to Questions State Legislators Ask About Social Work Licensing," n.p.

15. Ibid.

16. Stanley J. Gross, "The Myth of Professional Licensing," *American Psychologist* 33 (November 1978), p. 1015.

17. Herman Borenzweig, "Who Passes the California Licensing Examinations," *Social Work*, 22 (May 1977), pp. 173–177.

18. The lack of evidence to prove that licensure increases social work salaries is noted in a letter from Myles Johnson, Senior Staff Associate, NASW, to David Dempsey, Executive Director, NASW Missouri Chapter, June 27, 1983.

4

Reclassification: NASW and the Unions

HOWARD JACOB KARGER

Several areas of conflict exist between professional social work organizations and public sector unions. For the most part, these areas of friction do not involve domestic or international policies, but revolve around workplace concerns. This chapter examines reclassification, a major area of disagreement between public sector unions and professional social work organizations. As part of that examination, the chapter probes the issue of reclassification; explores the positions of the National Association of Social Workers (NASW), the American Federation of State and County Municipal Workers (AFSCME), and the hypothetical public; and attempts to understand the policy implications of reclassification attempts. The Michigan reclassification plan is used as a case study.

The scope of the reclassification problem is significant. In 1981 NASW reported that over 50 percent of its chapters were coping with reclassification attempts by state civil service commissions.[1] In 1978 the Public Employee Department of the AFL-CIO estimated that 375,000 of the 800,000 human service workers in the United States were employed as social workers.[2] By 1985 there were 448,000 persons employed as social workers: out of that number only about 200,000 held social work degrees; about 140,000 had an MSW or higher degree; and about 60,000 had BSW degrees. Over half of the social service labor force has no formal social work training.

In a further breakdown of social service personnel, the National Center for Social Statistics counted 241,000 employees in public assistance and child welfare in 1973.[3] By 1981 almost 80 percent of the social work labor force was employed in public agencies.[4]

Although not generally understood by the social work profession, current reclassification attempts in many states pose a serious dilemma for social work.[5] T. Kahn, in a report for the Michigan Chapter of the National Association of Social Workers, defines reclassification as "a term that has been coined to describe the reduction of educational standards for public service jobs."[6] According to Kahn, reclassification trends include the reduction of educational requirements for entry-level jobs, the assumption of an interchangeability of bachelor's degrees, reorganization of jobs to reduce educational requirements, nonrecognition of the exclusivity of Bachelor's of Social Work (BSW) and Master's of Social Work (MSW) skills, and equating education with experience.

Although reclassification appears to be a new issue, the underutilization of professional social workers and the refusal of public agencies to exclusively recognize the MSW are not new problems. Rino J. Patti and Charles Maynard found that 70 percent of the positions in social services and 76 percent of the positions in mental health required a master's degree, but in only 33 percent of those job specifications could the requirement be satisfied exclusively by an MSW degree.[7] However, according to Kahn, the background of reclassification can be traced to several key Supreme Court decisions on affirmative action. For example, the *Griggs vs. Duke Power Company* case (1971) stated that employers did not have to discriminate intentionally to be in violation of Title VII of the Civil Rights Act of 1964.[8] Once a *prima facie* case is established, the employer must provide evidence that its employment criteria (test scores, educational credentials, and so forth) are job related. The results of *Griggs vs. Duke* and other key decisions led many civil service systems to alter job entry requirements under the aegis of expanding affirmative action.[9] Although these court cases form a historical basis for reclassification, fiscal savings also figure prominently in a state's reorganization plan.

Regardless of the historical background and the justification for reclassification, little doubt exists that this trend poses a serious challenge to standards of social work personnel, and, in general, to the entire profession.

RECLASSIFICATION IN MICHIGAN

Statements on the reclassification plan in Michigan contain few objective positions, but, instead, are advocacy-based. Moreover, these statements emanate from special interest groups that include NASW, the Michigan Civil Service Commission, and AFSCME.[10]

The remainder of this chapter focuses on the reclassification attempts of the Michigan Civil Service Commission. The reasons for selecting Michigan as a site for a case study include the following:

1. Michigan represents a northern, politically liberal, industrial state with a well-developed social-welfare delivery system.

2. The struggle involving reclassification reached the greatest clarity in Michigan. The Michigan Civil Service Commission has been specific in its reclassification plan, the Michigan Chapter of NASW has been active and visible, and AFSCME has been heavily involved in the dispute.

3. The Benchmark Plan—as it is known by the Michigan Civil Service Commission and the involved parties—has resulted in an articulated national response from NASW.

4. The time and energy expended by NASW on reclassification in Michigan suggests that the issue may be seen as a proving ground for NASW, as well as setting an important national precedent in the area of civil service reform and social services.

THE BENCHMARK PLAN

The reclassification study was begun by the Michigan Civil Service Commission in 1975, and by 1979 the study had been completed and the plan implemented.[11] Contrary to what many Michigan social workers thought, the Civil Service Commission maintained that Benchmark was scientifically administered and part of the overall responsibility of the civil service commission.[12] Although civil service had changed in a piecemeal fashion, Benchmark was the only thorough civil-service reform undertaken in Michigan since 1938.

The purpose of Benchmark was to provide a systematic grouping of occupations based on duties, responsibilities, and the qualifications necessary to fill individual positions. It serves as a basis for an equitable pay plan, a recruitment and testing program, and budgeting and other personnel services such as planning and training the workforce. Although Benchmark affected all areas of civil service classifications, of the 43,900 employees in Michigan Civil Service, over half (23,000) were classified as human service workers.[13]

The principal methodology used by the Michigan Civil Service Commission included a comprehensive job analysis to determine the differences, if any, in the tasks performed by workers in different classes and with different educational backgrounds and experiences. The purpose of the study was also to determine what entry-level skills were needed in social service positions.[14] A summary of the specific recommendations of Benchmark include:

1. Master's degree-level workers are underutilized and often do the same work as bachelor's degree-level workers. The pay differential is thus unwarranted.
2. Education is the most important variable in determining whether a beginning-level social service employee has the necessary knowledge and abilities de-

manded at the entry level of practice. Experience is an unreliable indicator of job performance. Job selection should therefore be based on a screening that demands at least a bachelor's degree for beginning-level practice. The report stated that a BSW is the most desirable degree for entry-level practice, and that no alternatives should be allowed in lieu of the bachelor's degree in human services. One year of experience beyond the bachelor's degree is a substitute for the MSW.

3. The plan also developed four levels of job classifications for social service workers:

a) Trainee—entry-level position requiring a bachelor's degree. Promotions to the next level are based on knowledge of the job and tenure. After one year the trainee is promoted to the second level.

b) Developing Worker—requires a bachelor's degree and one year of experience or an MSW. The new employee who recently received an MSW would enter at this level, thereby joining the social worker with a bachelor's degree and one year of experience.

c) Journeyman—employees with bachelor's degrees and MSW social workers can move into this promotional level based on job knowledge and experience.

d) Special Technical Worker—a special category that utilizes workers with MSWs or other master's degrees as special resource persons for management, as supervisors of lower-level social service workers, and for serving difficult clients.

The Benchmark Plan essentially equalizes the Developing Worker-level employees with MSW- and bachelor-degreed workers, thereby eradicating differences between those workers at the middle of the personnel range. This equalization also extends to the upper, but not to the top level of job classification, which is reserved only for master's-level workers—although not exclusively for workers with MSWs. It is doubtful that this last level will encompass enough available positions to allow easy access to the upper classificiation rungs for MSW-degreed employees. Clearly, Benchmark most strongly recognizes educational achievement at the beginning level of practice. In the end, Benchmark increases access to the upper levels of public social service for the bachelor's degree-level worker, thereby enlarging the real and potential career ladder of the noncredentialed social worker.

RESPONSE OF NASW

NASW responded to Benchmark through its Michigan chapter and at the national level. A national NASW policy statement maintained that, "Social work education is a unique combination of knowledge, skills, abilities, values and ethics for which there is no exact equivalent and that cannot be acquired either by on-the-job training or by possession of a related degree."[15] This policy statement went on to note that, "In the design of programs, the division of labor, and the allocation of authority and responsibility, it is the profession of social work that must be held responsible for the provision and quality of social services."[16]

Sheldon Siegel and Michael Sherraden, in basic agreement with NASW, support the establishment of a specialist class. They also call for social service classes for which professional social work education is the mandatory entrance requirement.[17] These social work educators, however, also acknowledge the need for "partializing" social service functions to nontrained social service employees. Siegel and Sherraden criticize the Benchmark Plan for recognizing educational achievement only at the entry level, with the corresponding assumption that on-the-job training will function as an alternative to the advanced social work degree.

As an alternative to Benchmark, Siegel and Sherraden recommended a division of labor that places the MSW-degreed employee at the top. Moreover, they suggest that social workers with MSWs should provide specialized expertise and assume responsibility for social service delivery as well as the supervision of nontrained social work personnel.

The official position on reclassification of the Michigan Chapter of NASW stated:

1. Personnel offering professional social work services must have a professional social work education.

2. There is no exact equivalent to social work education. On-the-job training and an allied degree do not equal a social work education.

3. All social services must have a career ladder that extends to both preprofessional and professional social work positions.

4. The profession of social work and the professional social worker must be held accountable for the provision and qualilty of social services.

5. Clients have the right to receive the high-quality social work skills that are expected from trained social workers.[18]

The NASW position can be summarized by three demands: (1) upper-level and key line personnel must have social work degrees, (2) social workers should direct and control public social services, and (3) there is no equivalent to professional social work education.

AFSCME'S POSITION

AFSCME's position on Michigan's reclassification plan was hard to identify, because much of it was based on implication. With no written national position on reclassification, the matter presumably was to be handled on a local or council level.[19] However, Peter Weidenaar, Director of NASW's Michigan Chapter, believes that AFSCME favored reclassification.[20] Kahn stated that

The union philosophy has generally advocated the *least restrictive standards for entry* [original emphasis] to higher level jobs, as well as promotion based on experience rather than education.... In the dispute over education versus experience, unions usually favor on-the-job training over the "esoteric" educational model.[21]

NASW concern about the acceptance of key elements of reclassification was validated by the AFSCME testimony at the Benchmark hearings. AFSCME representative Michael McCain stated that:

The entry level Child Welfare Worker I [the implementation of a special class titled Child Welfare Worker]... shall be based on the possession of an MSW or related degree in Guidance and Counseling, Sociology, Psychology, etc., or a bachelor's degree with some experience as a Social Service Worker V.[22]

The union's recommendations for the intermediate-level child welfare worker was one year of experience at the entry level, and for the journeyman child welfare worker, one year of experience at the intermediate level. AFSCME's position therefore fit well within the spirit of Michigan's reclassification attempts by subordinating a master's level education to on-the-job training. NASW's suspicion about AFSCME's support of key points in the reclassification plan appears valid.

An attempt to bridge NASW's and AFSCME's concerns was made by Milton Tambor, a professional social worker and AFSCME employee. Tambor noted that NASW and AFSCME had worked together through the Coalition of American Public Employees, and had jointly lobbied on health and welfare issues.[23] Tambor suggested that through working with unions, professional social workers could translate professional concerns into bargaining issues. In addition, social work education could be advanced by including educational leaves as part of contract negotiations. In the light of AFSCME's position on reclassification—a position based on the need to protect its present constituency in which over 50 percent of social service workers have no professional social work training—issues that separate the union from NASW are problematic. Although both groups have shared interests on a national level, deep contradictions exist when it comes to the organization of the social service workplace.

THE POSITION OF THE PUBLIC

The public's position on Benchmark was perhaps best summed up by columnist Pat McCarthy in a 1979 editorial for *The State Journal*. McCarthy noted that the state's higher education industry may be producing a more refined product than the state needs.[24] He observed that although the state is pouring money into graduate programs, the civil service commission is simultaneously removing educationally based job restrictions. McCarthy's position suggests a threat exists not only to the reduction of MSW positions in public welfare, but also to the reduction in state funding for MSW programs. The problem in public welfare therefore extends, albeit indirectly, into the private voluntary sector. McCarthy attributes the reclassification problem to decades of overspecialization in which higher education's perception of society's needs was exaggerated, and the emphasis on higher degrees ignored the real needs of public welfare for competent, beginning-level practitioners.

IMPLICATIONS AND POLICY ALTERNATIVES

To categorize reclassification as abhorrent ignores the benefits provided to the BSW-degreed worker, especially the benefit of a wider career ladder that could culminate in higher pay and greater professional challenge. For the minority member victimized by differential access to higher education, reclassification may translate into a more meaningful affirmative action program, and as the commission maintains, Benchmark may remove artificial barriers to job advancement. Needless to say, most state civil service systems are in dire need of reform.

As to whether reclassification will prove injurious to clients, even Siegel and Sherraden maintain that the case for the benefits of professional social work education has yet to be proven beyond a doubt.[25] Moreover, as Kahn notes, the preponderance of service given to clients in public welfare has always been delivered by personnel not trained as social workers.[26] This fact, in combination with the historic lack of interest of MSW-degreed social workers in public welfare, suggests that the problem of reclassification may be blown out of proportion.

Despite communication problems, the interests of each group emerged with some clarity.[27] For the state, the central issues appeared to be the streamlining of civil service and the resulting budgetary savings. Union concerns seemed to encompass constituent protection and increased pay and opportunities for the majority of their social service members. The central issues for NASW appeared to be increased opportunities and preferred treatment for MSW-degreed social workers, the exclusive recognition of professional social work education, and the expropriation of public welfare as an exclusive field for social work.

The successful replication of reclassification in other states could have profound consequences for social welfare, including:

1. Paving the way for cuts in state funding to social work graduate programs.

2. Decisions by public agencies to hire workers with less expensive bachelor's

or BSW degrees in lieu of workers with MSWs, thereby increasing the disadvantage to those workers in a shrinking job market.

3. The decision by private agencies to imitate public agencies and also reduce entry-level job qualifications.

4. A reduction in the quality of client services resulting from the hiring of less qualified public welfare workers, and in the promotion of employees with little social work training.

Should the social work profession lose the reclassification fight, and should reclassification be widely implemented in other states, the loss of professional power would be substantial.

RETAINING SOCIAL WORK IN PUBLIC WELFARE

The following section will present a series of alternative measures for NASW to consider in its fight against reclassification.

NASW's present national strategy on reclassification includes the following measures: (a) public relations and educational campaigns to teach the worth of social work, (b) encouraging the Council on Social Work Education (CSWE) and schools of social work to recruit and train non-degreed social service employees, (c) the support of affinity groups as a way to accommodate professional diversity, (d) support for state licensure of social workers, (e) technical assistance to chapters facing reclassification, (f) cooperation with schools of social work to study personnel requirements and to analyze existing studies, and (g) cooperation with other organizations.[28] In addition, a major thrust of the NASW strategy involves the use of job analysis evaluations designed to isolate key knowledge, skills, and abilities of given social service positions.

The present strategy of NASW is flawed in several ways. First, this strategy is heavily dependent on "research thinking," a belief that if research is produced to prove the necessity of hiring workers with BSW and MSW degrees, state civil service commissions will be swayed. This strategy might be possible if the evidence existed to prove NASW's claim about a positive relationship between quality of services and professional training. The risk, however, is that further research might ultimately reveal little difference between the skills of workers with BSWs, other bachelor-degreed employees, and MSW-degreed social workers. Moreover, even if supportive evidence were found, this would undoubtedly lead to further research that might counter the claims of the original studies. A circular process of research is begun, and the essentially political argument over reclassification is reduced to a methodological one. The last thing that the public or civil service commissions want is to get embroiled in an argument over research methodology. "Research thinking" is only productive when the evidence is available—something that

NASW presently lacks. Moreover, research in a political struggle is not a strategy, but a tool that complements the strategy. To believe that research has the power to change a political situation is to imbue it with a potency it doesn't possess. Therefore, the time, energy, and fiscal resources that NASW has invested in job analysis may prove to have been misguided. While NASW is busily engaged in research, civil service commissions may have already made their decisions.

Nevertheless, research, public education, and interorganizational co-operation can be useful strategies. However, without an organized constituent base—a group of employees ready to apply political power, and, if necessary, to withhold their services—a strategy based solely on awareness is doomed to failure. Given the fiscal crises experienced by many states, in combination with the current antiwelfare feeling, any social policy strategy that seeks to educate and persuade without any real or implied power will be ineffective. If NASW continues its present strategy without the backing of an organized power base such as a public sector union, the result will be wasted money, staff time, and energy.

Giving Up the Fight

The second option for NASW involves abandoning the reclassification issue. This would necessitate admitting that public sector unions support key aspects of reclassification, and that acting alone, NASW has little chance of success. This decision would mandate the removal of all funds and staff time from the issue. Moreover, NASW would be forced to concede that public welfare was never a stronghold of the organization, and that since so few public welfare workers are members of NASW, continued involvement in the reclassification fight will only deplete resources that could be better used elsewhere.

This strategy would result in a net loss of public welfare positions for professionally trained social workers, a two-tiered system of service whereby the poor see untrained social workers and the middle and upper-class receive professional social work services, and the diminution of social work influence in public welfare. On the positive side, NASW could assign increased resources to areas that have a better prognosis for success. This strategy, however, would be an abdication of social work's historic responsibility to the poor. Given the current job market for MSW-degreed social workers and the profession's commitment to the poor, the implementation of this option may prove too costly.

NASW as a Collective Bargaining Agent

The third option for NASW involves adopting a quasi-collective bargaining stance similar to that of the American Association of University

Professors, the National Education Association, and the American Nursing Association. This strategy would entail the transformation of NASW from a professional association to a hybrid professional and trade union. NASW could undertake collective bargaining in a statewide or regional area with technical assistance and support from the national office. Reclassification would therefore become an appropriate item in the collective bargaining process.

Several factors contribute to the difficulty in implementing this strategy. Foremost among them is the negative feeling that many social workers have toward NASW becoming a collective bargaining agent. Gary Shaffer and Kathleen Ahearn, in a study of the attitudes of trained social workers toward unions, found that two-thirds of the respondents were opposed to NASW becoming a collective bargaining agent.[29] This finding may illustrate a lack of faith in NASW rather than a blanket refusal to be covered by a professional union, especially since most respondents believed that social workers have a right to join unions, and most were unhappy with the protection offered by civil service. The general pro-union sentiment was also observed by Leslie P. Alexander, Philip Lichtenberg, and Dennis Brunn when they reported that only 38.3 percent of the social workers in their study perceived a conflict between being a professional and a union member.[30]

The scope of current social work unionization is broad. Of the 448,000 social workers in the United States, about 15 to 20 percent (approximately 72,000) are unionized.[31] There would obviously be a significant gain in membership and power were NASW to become a collective bargaining agent. NASW's role as a collective bargaining agent would not necessarily supersede its role as a professional organization because it would not act exclusively as a union, but would function as a hybrid— a professional association complemented by a collective bargaining component. The emphasis of NASW on professionalization would be enhanced by the inclusion of autonomy and professional regulation as items in the collective bargaining process.

Nevertheless, several obstacles preclude the possibility of NASW becoming a collective bargaining agent. Foremost among them would be the competition with existing public sector unions. For example, out of the 1.1 million AFSCME members, approximately 50,000 are in public welfare and another 10,000 in private agencies.[32] The prospect of successfully competing with AFSCME for the bargaining rights of public welfare workers appears dim, especially since 50 percent of those employees are not even eligible for NASW membership.

In addition, NASW presently lacks the administrative machinery and the technical expertise to engage in collective bargaining. Such an attempt might well create an organizational debacle resulting in even greater losses in the reclassification fight. The identification and aspiration of social workers with management, their frequent denial of their status as workers, and unfavorable union stereotypes—at least in some quarters of the profession—contribute to strong antiunion feelings. In the event that NASW became a collective bargaining agent, the accommodation of those forces might well prove impossible. In short, the prospect of NASW becoming an exclusive bargaining agent for social workers appears remote.

Achieving a Middle Ground

NASW has little interaction with public sector unions over questions involving professional standards and on-the-job issues.[33] However, NASW and AFSCME have coalesced around issues of social welfare expenditures and national social policy issues. This liaison could be exploited to provide a forum for the discussion of an alliance around workplace issues, especially reclassification.

The difficulty in forming an alliance between NASW and public sector unions involves the problem of reciprocity. If NASW were somehow able to compromise its demands on reclassification and form an alliance with public sector unions, it would gain the combined strength and political clout of the American union movement. In terms of numbers, organization, and its connection to the powerful AFL-CIO network, the strength of unions is formidable. However, while public sector unions would bring their power and connections to the bargaining table, NASW must also be able to offer tangible benefits to such an alliance. The power of NASW is certainly limited, and, although it has supported social work unionization since its inception in 1955, it has not actively encouraged it. Within that context, NASW's vigorous encouragement of unionization would show good faith to the public sector unions. Unfortunately, that alone may not be enough to bring to the coalition table.

Given the variable geographic strength of public sector unions, and the often fierce competition between them, an exclusive alliance between NASW and one designated union would alienate competing unions. For example, if on a national level, NASW had a firm alliance with AFSCME, the Communications Workers of America (CWA)—which now represents significant numbers of social workers—might easily be provoked. For NASW to enter internecine union fights would be an act of insanity.

An alternative to becoming embroiled in interunion fights is for NASW, on a local level, to actively encourage the unionization of its members. On the national level, NASW could continue its liaisons with progressive unions. On the chapter level, however, NASW could develop a subcontract that authorizes the strongest union amenable to its concerns to receive its sole backing and endorsement. The compatibility of goals would be negotiated and assessed on the local level, and the union that best reflected NASW's concerns would be endorsed as the collective bargaining agent for social workers in a state or region. In this way NASW would subcontract out—at no cost to the organization—representation for its interests and the responsibility for monitoring on-the-job concerns of social workers.

NASW would thus form the prototype of the hybrid professional organization: an organization that is concerned with workplace activities as well as the overall professional concerns of its members.[34] As part of the *quid pro quo*, NASW would facilitate union organizing by volunteering the time and resources of its members.

Forming an alliance with union represents the best alternative for NASW in its fight against reclassification. Only through a professional–union alliance can reclassification become an appropriate item for collective bargaining, and be seen for what it is—a political and economic issue.

CONCLUSION

It is clear that issues such as reclassification are not temporary problems, but structural obstacles resulting from a set of fiscal dilemmas that are currently part of the social welfare landscape. Reclassification strategies that appeal to concerns for the poor, professional standards, the right of recipients to receive quality services, and other noble virtues have diminished currency for both states and the public at large. To develop strategies that fail to recognize the current climate of cynicism and antiwelfare feeling is to circumvent success. Moreover, to refuse to view reclassification as a political and fiscal struggle is to deny the essential characteristic of the issue.

NASW's present strategy of research, education, and political lobbying has limited utility in the reclassification struggle. The limitations of NASW are reflected in the size of the organization and its political influence. Approximately 90,000 members spread throughout fifty states is obviously not enough clout to intimidate politicians.

If professional social work associations are to succeed in stopping the erosion of public welfare services and the reduction of professional qualifications in the public sector, they must do so as part of a larger movement. At this point, the only group that may have the power to counter the reclassification trend is the union movement. Only by transforming professional issues into collective bargaining items does the profession of social work stand a chance to stem the tide in public welfare.

NOTES

1. NASW, "Relationships With Other Social Work Organizations and Other Human Service Disciplines," working draft of policy statement, NASW General Assembly, Philadelphia, Pennsylvania, 1981, p. 2.

2. AFL-CIO Public Employee Department, draft paper for *Data Book*, December 1978, cited in Gary Shaffer and Kathleen Ahearn, "Unionization of Professional Social Workers: Practice and Training Development and Implications," p. 2. Unpublished manuscript, School of Social Work, University of Illinois, Urbana-Champaign, September 1981.

3. National Center for Social Statistics, Social and Rehabilitation Service, *Report on Personnel in Public Welfare*, E–2 (FY #73), Washington, D.C.: U.S. Department of Health, Education and Welfare, 1975, cited in Miriam Dinerman, "Options in Social Work Manpower and Education," *Social Work*, 20 (September 1975), p. 349.

4. Shaffer and Ahearn, "Unionization of Professional Social Workers," p. 2.

5. This paper uses the term "reclassification" instead of "declassification." Most civil service systems engaged in manpower reclassification are not proposing the total declassification of social work positions, but rather, that educational job restrictions (e.g., an MSW degree) be eased in favor of a BA or BSW degree.

6. T. Kahn, "Chapter Action Guide on Declassification," Lansing: Michigan Chapter, National Association of Social Workers, 1981, p. 3.

7. Rino J. Patti and Charles Maynard, "Qualifying for Managerial Jobs in Public Welfare," *Social Work* 23 (July 1978), p. 292.

8. See Kahn, "Chapter Action Guide on Declassification," p. 22.

9. Two other court suits, *Albermarle Paper Company vs. Moody* (1975) and *Washington vs. Davis* (1976), are discussed in Hubert S. Feild and Robert J. Teare, "A Conceptual Framework for Validation of Social Services Job Requirements: General Concepts and Background," working draft, NASW, Washington, D.C.: National Association of Social Workers, August 1980, pp. 9–10.

10. American Federation of State and County Municipal Employees (AFSCME), an affiliate of the AFL-CIO, is the largest public sector union with a membership of about 1.1 million. AFSCME also represents over 50,000 social workers, the largest number represented by any U.S. union.

11. Michigan Department of Civil Service, "Benchmark Factor Rating System of Classification," Lansing, July 1981, pp. 1–2.

12. Peter Weidenaar, Executive Director of the Michigan Chapter, NASW, Lansing, Michigan, March 17, 1982, stated in a telephone conversation that many Michigan social workers incorrectly perceived the Benchmark Plan as almost a conspiracy against them. Weidenaar conceded that creating the Benchmark Plan was simply a responsibility of the Michigan Civil Service Commission. This was affirmed by a telephone conversation with Martha Bibbs, Michigan Department of Civil Service, Lansing, March 10, 1982.

13. Michigan Department of Civil Service, "Benchmark Factor Ranking System of Classification," pp. 1 and 6.

14. Michigan Department of Civil Service, Planning and Research Section, "Technical Report of the Job Analysis of the Social Service Workers Positions (Summary)," Lansing, May 1978, pp. 2–3, 5–6, and 11.

15. National Association of Social Workers, "Declassification: A Policy Statement of the National Association of Social Workers," in *NASW Delegate Assembly Guidebook*, Silver Spring, Maryland: National Association of Social Workers, p. 12.

16. Ibid.

17. Sheldon Siegel and Michael Sherraden, "Perspectives on Education and Training for Social Service Work: A Position Statement." Unpublished paper, University of Michigan, November 1978, pp. 1, 8, 11, and 12.

18. NASW, Michigan Chapter, "Proposed Policy Statement: Declassification," n.d., p. 3. This policy statement was approved by the NASW Delegate Assembly, Philadelphia, Pennsylvania, November 1981. This policy statement therefore represents the NASW official position on reclassification.

19. Telephone conversation with Marilyn Depoy, AFSCME Director of Research, International Office, Washington, D.C., February 19, 1982.

20. Weidenaar conversation.

21. Kahn, "Chapter Action Guide," p. 8.

22. Testimony of Michael McCain, "A Public Hearing in the Matter of the Human Services Group in the Benchmark Classification System," State of Michigan, Department of Civil Service, Lansing, June 23, 1979, p. 27.

23. Milton Tambor, "Declassification and Divisiveness in Human Services," *Administration in Social Work* 7 (Summer 1983), p. 63.

24. Pat McCarthy, "State Down Plays Degrees," *The State Journal*, April 29, 1979, p. A–13.

25. Siegel and Sherraden, "Perspective on Education," p. 7.

26. Kahn, "Chapter Action Guide," p. 6.

27. This lack of communication was confirmed by a personal conversation with Thomas Gauthier, Senior Research Associate, NASW, February 22, 1982. Gauthier also acknowledged that NASW had little communication with AFSCME concerning the reclassification issue. Peter Weidenaar, in the previously cited conversation, also stated that he had little interaction with AFSCME.

28. NASW, "Relationships With Other Social Work Organizations and Other Human Service Disciplines," p. 3.

29. Shaffer and Ahearn, "Unionization of Professional Social Workers," pp. 3, 7.

30. Leslie P. Alexander, Philip Lichtenberg, and Dennis Brunn, "Social Workers in Unions: A Survey," *Social Work*, 25 (May 1980), p. 22.

31. Bureau of National Affairs, "Labor Management Relations in State and Local Governments: 1978," *Government Employee Relations Report*, Reference File 197, Washington, D.C., Bureau of National Affairs, September 8, 1980, pp. 71:4091.

32. Milton Tambor,"Unions and Voluntary Agencies," *Social Work*, 18 (July 1973), p. 42.

33. This was confirmed by previously cited conversations with Peter Weidenaar and Thomas Gauthier.

34. For a fuller discussion of the hybrid organization, see Leslie P. Alexander, "Professionalization and Unionization: Compatible After All?" *Social Work*, 25 (November 1980), pp. 476–482.

5

The Compatibility of Labor and Social Work

HOWARD JACOB KARGER

Any examination of the common and conflicting goals of labor and social work must inevitably be reduced to a fundamental question: Are unionism and professional social work compatible? This chapter will address both the negative and positive views of social work unionism, the reasons for antiunionism, and the position of NASW on collective bargaining.

ANTIUNIONISM AND SOCIAL WORK

In general, opponents of unionism maintain that:

1. unions cost employees money,
2. strike losses are never retrieved,
3. union members have little voice in union affairs and often they are kept ignorant,
4. bureaucratic union hierarchies control the economic destiny of employees,
5. union corruption is rampant,
6. the consistent opposition of unions to increases in productivity arrests agency growth,
7. union "featherbedding" results in unneeded employees and unnecessary payroll expenses,
8. union membership campaigns foster conflict rather than collaboration,
9. the right of managers to strive for greater productivity is curtailed by union rules, and

10. unions have little consideration for the effects of increased wages on future
     employment, inflation, and tax increases.[1]

The antiunion bias in social work is focused around issues of professionalism, bureaucracy, and what could be called social work "exceptionalism." Dena Fisher, writing in *Social Work*, examined a 1984 strike
by Local 1199 of the Retail Drug Employees Union, which involved over
fifty institutions and virtually all the social work staff in hospitals and
nursing homes covered by the union. Fisher concluded that:

Standards for professional practice conflict with the [NASW] Code of Ethics
with regard to behavior during a labor strike when the prescribed behavior
includes withholding service, failing to terminate clients properly, and picketing
activity directed toward consumers of health care.... The problem is that participation in a strike is a nonprofessional activity. . . . Standards of professional
behavior conflict with union membership requirements.[2]

In 1957 Ernest Greenwood listed five elements characterizing an "ideal
type profession," including a code of ethics that specified that a professional must "render his service upon request even at the sacrifice of his
personal convenience."[3] Harold L. Wilensky and Charles H. Lebeaux
claim that in addition to technical skills, professional status requires
adherence to certain moral norms, including: the provision of technically
competent, high-quality service; the development of an impersonal, im-
partial, and objective self; and altruistic motives predicated on a service
ideal with represents a devotion to the best interests of the client.[4] Therefore, a true professional must possess both technical ability and an adherence to a prescribed set of professional norms.

Apart from fears that clients will be endangered by union-coordinated
job actions, apprehension about the impact of unionism also centers
around an uneasiness that social workers, when organized, will become
like other workers; that is, professional concerns will become subordinated to union issues. When social workers perceive themselves primarily
as "workers," they are in turn viewed by management in that same light.
For those social workers insecure about their professional status, the
"commonness" of social work portends a diminution in prestige, and,
ultimately, a devaluation of the individual self.

A belief in the "exceptionalism" of social work forms a superstructure
underlying the debate on professionalism. This exceptionalism implies
that tasks performed by social workers are vastly more important than
those performed by other workers, especially nonprofessionals. Therefore, while a strike of orderlies is disturbing, a social work strike is
catastrophic. This sense of importance is characteristic of a professional
mission. Moreover, the conviction that a particular profession is inval-

uable to the social fabric of society can provide solace when the professional feels overburdened by intense responsibilities and what presents itself as endless work.

The embellished sense of social work's importance is often juxtaposed to nagging questions about its relative worth. The tension between self-importance and self-doubt is illustrated by Fisher:

Social workers in unions should consider the impact of their actions on the existence of their jobs. . . . If management [in the 1984 strike of Local 1199 of the Retail Drug Employees Union] could survive seven weeks without professional social work service, it could be concluded that social workers do not provide essential services. Many hospital administrators drew that conclusion and cut back on social work staff.[5]

Fisher has depicted a paradoxical conundrum. If the work performed by social workers is as important as Fisher and others maintain, and if its interruption during a strike clearly endangers clients, then the withholding of services should only make administrators more actuely aware of the importance of social work services. In that sense, a social work strike should increase rather than devalue the currency of the profession. If, on the other hand, administrators find that social work services are not as essential as they originally thought, the exceptionalism argument is shattered and social workers must therefore be seen as important but not irreplaceable. One cannot have it both ways: either social work services are so essential that withholding them will paralyze an institution, or they are not as important to major social welfare institutions as social workers maintain. The best way for social workers to avoid disappointment is to leave the question untested.

Perhaps a more important consideration than the indispensability of social work services is the question of whether those services can be administered by other than trained social workers. Beneath notions of exceptionalism lies an anxiety that basic social services can be competently executed by nonprofessionally trained employees. The specter of "replaceability" haunts all professions whose skills base is considered within the domain of "soft knowledge."

Caricatured assumptions about the exceptionalism of social work often lead to overstated moral and ethical standards. For example, when teachers choose to strike they rarely put each through the mental torture that often marks social work strikes. Is teaching less important than social work? Is social work so exceptional that laws ought to be promulgated to specifically forbid social workers to strike? The belief in the exceptionalism of social work has been in the service, albeit unwitting, of the societal forces that have conspired to keep social work salaries well below those of other professions. For most social workers, the appellation of "worker" is more of a reality than the preceding "social."

A second concern of the antiunion forces in social work revolves around the issue of bureaucracy. Although most social workers operate within the context of a bureaucratic setting, that same setting is often seen as interfering with professional priorities and autonomy by introducing rules, regulations, and an administrative hierarchy that superimposes authority of office over authority of expertise.[6] In the eyes of many people, including social workers, bureaucracies are associated with rigidity and authoritarian procedures.

Therefore, it is not surprising that some social workers view unions as representing the same bureaucratic constraints that they despise in their organizational life. This situation becomes exacerbated when the union is not seen as part of an existing bureaucracy, but, instead, as a new bureaucratic mechanism introduced into the workplace which will further diminish professional autonomy and discretion.[7] Lightman succinctly summarizes the dilemma:

The power-based language and processes of the union are alien to the experience of most social workers, whether management or line, and its different goals and priorities can be expected to result in yet another bureaucratic layer. The norm of altruistic service is challenged not only by the general bureaucratic context but also by the overt goals of personal gain and the language of confrontation which are assumed to characterize the union.[8]

Although rarely mentioned, opponents of unionization harbor a major concern regarding the issue of management prerogatives. Early social work unions promoted two ideals: to better the salaries and working conditions of social service workers, and to improve benefits and services offered to clients. This approach implies that social workers function as both employees championing their own self-interest, and as advocates for their clients.[9] This situation is unique among trade unions and may be the basis for much of management's resistance to unionization. A statement by Fred Steininger, a former official of the Department of Health, Education, and Welfare, summarizes the dilemma of management:

Some public welfare administrators have found themselves buffeted by the vigor of their employees' thrust and the tenacity of the Board's resistance. Employee unions have argued for a voice in management. Management has stood on its prerogatives. Some administrators have been seduced by the union's cause when it argued for decent housing, respect for the individual, and opportunity for the hopeless. They have backed the union only to find that they came to a parting of the ways when the employees' voice in management seemed louder than their own.[10]

NASW'S POSITION ON UNIONISM

NASW's position on social work unionism is both straightforward and vague. A letter written in 1959 by the chairperson of the New York City chapter of NASW declared:

The New York City Chapter of the National Association of Social Workers . . . is increasingly concerned about the current hospital situation—specifically, the impasse between the hospitals and the unions which are seeking recognition.

Among our concerns are matters immediately affecting social workers employed in your hospital. I have been requested by our Board of Directors to write to you . . . that it is the position of this professional organization that in the event of a strike [the 1959 strike by Local 1199 of the Retail Drug Employees Union], which is currently scheduled, each employee has a right to determine for himself whether or not to report to work and any action taken by an employer which penalizes an employee for exercising this right violates the employment rights of the employee. It is also our position that any employee who reports to work during a strike should not be required to assume duties other than professional social work duties for which he is employed.

It is the stated position of the National Association of Social Workers that employees have a right to belong to a union of their choice for purposes of collective bargaining.[11]

According to Fisher, NASW issued a virtually identical statement in response to a 1984 strike initiated by the same union.[12]

In an article commenting on the 1959 strike by Local 1199, Helen Rehr claimed that the "encouragement given to workers by their professional organization to act on an individual's civil right at the cost of the patient's welfare was anathema to the other professions."[13] Both Rehr and Fisher strongly believe that NASW encourages and supports the unionization of social workers.

Ernie S. Lightman, on the other hand, maintains that NASW views collective bargaining as "one means of providing a rational and coherent method of solving problems, but the NASW fails to denote trade unionism explicitly as a preferred alternative, and by implication suggests that other approaches may be more desirable."[14] According to Lightman, the posture of NASW toward social work unionization can be best described as neutral. By explicitly stating in the *Code of Ethics* that the social worker's primary responsibility is to clients, NASW has indicated that the service norm must take precedence over all bureaucratic processes and goals.[15] How the emphasis on a service norm plays out in relation to a strike situation is a question that remains unanswered.

Despite any ambivalence, NASW is caught in a philosophical bind. Since NASW aggressively endorses the rights of clients to self-determination, how can it then allow that right to be denied to social workers?

Moreover, social work values such as advocacy, empowerment, and self-determination cannot be endorsed for clients while at the same time abridged for those who serve them. Such philosophical arguments require that NASW tolerate, if not actively support, social work unionization.

THE COMPATIBILITY OF PROFESSIONALISM AND UNIONISM

Although relatively few studies have examined the compatibility of unionism and professional social work, all have found that most unionized social workers perceive little incongruity between the two loyalties.[16] For example, Alexander, Lichtenberg, and Brunn studied 84 MSW-degreed union members and found that "they view their work as solidly professional and, for the most part, do not see unionism and professionalism as incompatible."[17] Lightman had similar findings when studying 121 randomly chosen professional social workers in Toronto. According to Lightman, "The vast majority saw no incompatibility; indeed, many felt unionization may facilitate service goals, offsetting work place bureaucracy."[18] Lastly, reporting on exploratory research using two child welfare agencies, one in Pennsylvania and the other in Illinois, Shaffer found that "workers did not find unionism incompatible with their educational or professional goals."[19]

While the research suggests that the majority of social workers perceive little incongruity between being a professional social worker and a union member, the studies also hint at a bifurcated attitude toward unions and professional associations. For example, Alexander, Lichtenberg, and Brunn found that social workers clearly preferred a job-conscious or instrumental form of unionism over an approach that stressed professional or political concerns.[20] A similar finding was reported by Lightman.[21]

It appears that unionized social workers may bifurcate their professional and workplace concerns: unions are viewed by these social workers as best representing their workplace interests—pay, seniority, and job security issues; professional associations are seen as best embodying their professional concerns. This perspective is logical since professional social work associations possess little actual clout in the workplace. For example, although NASW can censure an agency and thus publish its name in the *NASW News*, beyond that, there is little other power of enforcement. On the other hand, unions can pursue grievance procedures, National Labor Relations Board (NLRB) hearings, law suits, and other remedies in an attempt to secure an employee's rights.

Issues involving the compatibility of social work and unionism—often based on views of social work exceptionalism—appear bogus. Although social work is a profession imbued with ideals of autonomy and self-directed practice, most social workers are employed by bureaucratic structures that relate to them as workers. Moreover, notions of professionalism do not function as effective forms of protection in workplace disputes over wages and working conditions, and, in the final analysis, social workers are as vulnerable to unfair employment practices as other workers. To believe that professional associations which lack mechanisms for collective bargaining can provide real protection in bureaucracies is to opt for naivete over realism.

NOTES

1. See Rene Laliberty and W. I. Christopher, *Health Care Labor Relations: A Guide for the '80s* (Owings Mills, Maryland: National Health Publishing, 1986), p. 57.

2. Dena Fisher, "Problems for Social Work in a Strike Situation: Professional, Ethical, and Value Considerations," *Social Work*, (32), 3 (May-June 1987), pp. 253–254.

3. Ernest Greenwood, "Attributes of a Profession," *Social Work* 2 (1957), pp. 44–55.

4. Harold L. Wilensky and Charles H. Lebeaux, *Industrial Society and Social Welfare* (New York: Russell Sage Foundation, 1958), pp. 283–334.

5. Fisher, "Problems for Social Work in a Strike Situation," p. 254.

6. See Ernie S. Lightman, "Professionalization, Bureaucratization, and Unionization in Social Work," *Social Service Review*, (56), 1 (March 1982), p. 131.

7. Ibid., p. 132.

8. Ibid.

9. Milton Tambor, "Unions and Voluntary Agencies," *Social Work*, 18 (July 1973), pp. 41–47.

10. Fred H. Steininger, "Employee Unions in Public Welfare." Paper presented in the *National Conference on Public Administration*, American Society of Public Administration, Boston, Massachusetts, 1968. Quoted in Elma Phillipson Cole's "Unions in Social Work," *Encyclopedia of Social Work* (New York: National Association of Social Workers, 1977), pp. 1560–1561.

11. Helen Rehr, "Problems for a Profession in a Strike Situation," *Social Work*, (5), 2 (April 1960), pp. 24–25.

12. Fisher, "Problems for Social Work in a Strike Situation," p. 253.

13. Rehr, "Problems for a Profession in a Strike Situation," p. 25.

14. Ernie S. Lightman, "An Imbalance of Power: Social Workers in Unions," *Administration in Social Work*, (2), 1 (Spring 1978), p. 76.

15. Lightman, "Professionalization, Bureaucratization, and Unionization in Social Work," pp. 133–134.

16. See for example, Leslie B. Alexander, Philip Lichtenberg, and Dennis Brunn, "Social Workers in Unions: A Survey," *Social Work*, (25), 3 (May 1980), pp. 216–223; Gary L. Shaffer and Kathleen Ahearn, "Current Perceptions, Opinions, and Attitudes Held by Professional Social Workers Toward Unionization and the Collective Bargaining Process." Unpublished paper, School of Social Work, University of Illinois, Champaign-Urbana, 1982; Ernie S. Light-

man, "Professionalization, Bureaucratization, and Unionization in Social Work"; Ernie S. Lightman, "Social Workers, Strikes and Service to Clients," *Social Work*, (28), 2 (1983), pp. 142–147; and M. L. Kirzner, *Public Welfare Unions and Public Assistance Policy: A Case Study of the Pennsylvania Social Services Union.* Unpublished doctoral dissertation, University of Pennsylvania, 1985.

17. Alexander, Lichtenberg; and Brunn, "Social Workers in Unions," p. 222.

18. Lightman, "Professionalization, Bureaucratization, and Unionization in Social Work," p. 130.

19. Gary Shaffer, "Labor Relations and the Unionization of Professional Social Workers: A Neglected Area in Social Work Education," *Journal of Education for Social Work*, 15 (1979), pp. 80–86.

20. Alexander, Lichtenberg, and Brunn, "Social Workers in Unions," p. 222.

21. Lightman, "Professionalization, Bureaucratization, and Unionization in Social Work," pp. 136–140.

III

UNIONS AND SOCIAL SERVICE AGENCIES

6

Labor Relations Laws and Social Workers

HOWARD JACOB KARGER

The legal matrix for governmental labor relations is a cornucopia of statutes, court decisions, ordinances, and attorney general opinions. The federal government lacks a single policy governing all of its employees, and state and local labor-management policies run the gamut from encouraging collective bargaining to being openly antiunion. The legal environment of public-sector labor-management policies is diffuse, non-standardized and, in most states, seriously in need of reform.

Before beginning this chapter a caveat is necessary. Although some states single out police, fire fighters, or teachers in their labor relations laws, no state labor-management policies address social workers as a specific occupational group. Therefore, federal and state labor relations policies treat social workers as merely another group of public workers and it must be presumed that general public-sector laws apply. Moreover, most social workers in the private sector are covered under the National Labor Relations Act (NLRA), and public-sector labor laws are thus inapplicable.

Given that caveat, the majority of this chapter will focus on the relationship between labor relations laws and public sector social workers. A discussion of federal labor laws pertaining to social workers will review the various Executive Orders and the Civil Service Reform Act of 1978. An overview of state and local labor relations laws will be provided, including the Garcia Decision, which led to the Fair Labor Standards Amendment of 1985.

FEDERAL EMPLOYEES AND LABOR RELATIONS LAW

Although the majority (62 percent) of unionized social workers are employed in state and local agencies, a significant number (7 percent) of social workers are also hired by the federal government and therefore under the aegis of federal labor-management regulations.[1]

Organizations of federal employees have been in existence since the 1840s. As a result of strikes and agitation, in 1840 the federal government granted its employees the ten-hour day with no reduction in wages. In 1868 all federally employed laborers and mechanics were awarded the eight-hour day.[2] Apart from these reforms, the major development affecting federal workers was the Civil Service Act of 1883, which established the Civil Service Commission. The purpose of the commission was to institute a merit system to be used in the selection of government workers—a landmark activity which eventually led to the discontinuation of the spoils system in the federal government. Under the Civil Service Act of 1883, Congress was to regulate the wages, hours, and conditions of employment for federal workers.[3] The Civil Service Act did not allow for a collective voice on the part of federal employees.

During the early nineteenth-century, federal workers began to intensively organize and lobby. Their demands, centering around wages and working conditions, led Presidents Theodore Roosevelt and William Howard Taft to thwart their political activities by imposing a series of executive orders known as "gag rules." Through the efforts of the organized federal postal employees, Congress passed the Lloyd-LaFollette Act in 1912, guaranteeing federal employees the right to petition Congress, and, more importantly, the right to join unions.[4]

Despite successful organizing efforts, elected officials disapproved of public sector unionism. Many elected officials believed that the federal government was a sovereign employer, and, as such, it should not delegate any occupational authority to unions. Even President Franklin D. Roosevelt, usually considered a friend to labor, wrote of the incipient dangers of collective bargaining for federal employees:

All government employees should realize that the process of collective bargaining... cannot be transplanted into the public service.... The very nature and purposes of government make it impossible for administrative officials to represent fully or to bind the employer in mutual discussions with government employee organizations. The employer is the whole people, who speak by means of laws enacted by their representatives in Congress. Accordingly, administrative officials and employees alike are governed and guided, and in many cases restricted, by laws which establish policies, procedures, or rules in personnel matters.[5]

Denied Roosevelt's support, federal employees were not granted coverage under the National Labor Relations Act of 1935 (also known as the Wagner Act), the major statute governing private-sector labor-management relations.

The federal government's position stiffened in the Post–New Deal Era, and in 1947 the Taft-Hartley Act was passed, which included a provision (Section 305) that made it unlawful for federal employees to engage in strike activity. Penalties for striking under Section 305 were severe and could result in immediate discharge, loss of status, and a three-year prohibition against reemployment. The enactment of Public Law 330 in 1955 overrode Section 305, substituting even more punitive language: "Federal employees who strike or knowingly belong to an organization that takes such action are liable to felony prosecution (punishable by a fine of up to $1,000 and a year and a day in jail)."

Numerous federal labor relations bills were introduced into every congressional session from 1949 to 1961. All of them failed. Despite executive and legal obstacles to unionization, well over 1 million federal employees are covered by bargaining agreements—about 60 percent of the nonpostal workforce.[6]

The recognition of federal unions was in large part achieved through Executive Order 10988. Shortly after being elected, President John F. Kennedy organized a Task Force on Employee-Management Relations in the Federal Service. Chaired by Arthur Goldberg, Secretary of Labor, the purpose of the task force was to study existing governmental and union relationships. Accepting the task force recommendations in full, Kennedy signed Executive Order 10987 (Agency Systems for Appeals from Adverse Actions) and Executive Order 10988 (Employee-Management Cooperation in the Federal Service) on January 17, 1962.

Executive Order 10988—covering all federal workers except the FBI, CIA, and the other employees whose work involved high-security positions—was a landmark act based on the following precedents:

1. It established for the first time the right of federal employees to form and join unions—without management interference—and to bargain. As part of that precedent, the order provided for three levels of union recognition: informal, formal, and exclusive. The criteria for these levels of recognition were based on the representative strength of a union. Informal recognition was given to a union that could claim some employee representation, formal recognition was given to a union that could claim 10 percent of the workforce, and exclusive recognition—the only kind of recognition presently allowed under federal policy—was given to an organization which had the support of the majority of the bargaining unit.

2. Concepts such as "exclusive bargaining unit" and "negotiated agreement" were introduced into governmental labor relations.

3. Although the negotiation of a union shop agreement was prohibited, a mea-

sure of union security was afforded through establishing a dues checkoff system.

4. Advisory arbitration was permitted for the settlement of labor disputes.
5. Management rights were more clearly delineated.
6. A Code of Fair Labor Practices was established to regulate the interactions between unions and management.

Executive Order 10988 was in effect until 1969 at which time it was superseded by President Nixon's Executive Order 11491. Nixon's new policy abolished formal and informal recognition, retaining only exclusive recognition. While management bargaining power was unchanged, the scope of bargaining permissible for employees was restricted. Financial disclosure and reporting requirements (similar to those imposed on private unions under the Landrum-Griffin Act of 1959) were made mandatory. In addition, binding grievance arbitration was made negotiable for the first time, and also for the first time, agency heads could be overruled by third-party impasse procedures.

Several other executive orders followed. For example, Nixon revised his earlier order of 1971. In 1975 President Gerald Ford further modified federal labor relations by signing Executive Order 11838. Until the Civil Service Reform Act of 1978, a significant legislative victory for the Carter administration, most labor-management reforms in the federal sector were accomplished through a series of incremental Executive Orders rather than through statutes. As such, these orders were prone to constant modifications by succeeding presidents or to being annulled by Congress. Federal employees were offered little continuity and security by their involuntary reliance on executive orders.

The Civil Service Reform Act of 1978 represented the single most important federal employee-management reform since the Civil Service Act of 1883. The act covered all federal employees except for members of the military, foreign service workers, Government Accounting Office employees, the TVA, the U.S. Postal Service, and employees of the various security agencies. The Civil Service Reform Act provided for:

1. A statutory guarantee of labor rights for federal employees.
2. The creation of a Federal Labor Relations Authority to administer the program, and the establishment of the Office of Labor-Management Relations within the Office of Personnel Management.
3. Expansion of the scope of negotiated grievance procedures.

Excluded from the scope of bargaining were wages and fringe benefits, Hatch Act prohibitions on political activities, and position classifications. The scope of bargaining remained virtually unchanged from the earlier executive orders.

Labor-management relations in the federal sector are characterized by statutory limitations that in many cases are greater than those imposed on public workers by individual states. In any case, despite recent progressive reforms, important issues such as wages and fringe benefits are still closed to collective bargaining. As such, federal employees lack the legal rights as private-sector workers.

LABOR RELATIONS IN STATE AND LOCAL GOVERNMENT

If the federal system of labor relations is characterized by fragmentation, the legal basis for labor-management relations in the state and local sector is one of diversity bordering on chaos. For example, each state is considered a sovereign entity within its own physical borders, and more than 100 separate state statutes currently regulate public-sector labor relations. These statutes are aided by local ordinances, court decisions, attorney general opinions, and other policy mechanisms.

State laws run the gamut from liberal policies in Minnesota, where certain classes of employees have the right to strike, to highly conservative attitudes such as prevail in states like North Carolina, where collective bargaining is outlawed. No states grant public employees the extent of coverage allowed private sector workers covered under the NLRA.

A Sketch of State and Local Labor Relations Policies

Many of the public-sector labor laws were enacted between the middle 1960s and the middle 1970s. According to Kearney, a variety of decisions had to be faced by state lawmakers, including: (1) whether each jurisdiction should be allowed to establish its own policy, or whether the whole state should be made to conform to one central policy: (2) whether one statute should apply to all occupations, or whether separate policies should be created for each functional classification: (3) the determination of who should administer the policy; and (4) the determination of which labor principals should be adopted.[7]

Apart from the wide variations in state policies, for the most part, the trend has been to liberalize labor-management relations and to extend greater coverage to state employees. According to Richard Freeman, thirty-nine states had no explicit labor relations policy in 1959. By 1984 only four states reported no public-sector labor relations policy. Moreover, only one state required collective bargaining in 1959; by 1984 twenty states required it.[8] Furthermore, according to a study done by Robert G. Valletta and Freeman, the number of states considered pro-bargaining climbed from five in 1969 to twenty-one in 1984.[9] Conversely, seven states had penalties prohibiting strikes in 1969, while in 1984 that number rose to twenty-one.[10]

In 1981, forty-three state governments reported having some form of labor relations policy. At present, forty states cover at least one group of public workers, and all states except Arkansas, Arizona, Colorado, Louisiana, Mississippi, North Carolina, South Carolina, Utah, Virginia, and West Virginia lack statutory bargaining rights for public employees. States that permit negotiations to take place in public include California, Florida, Kansas, Minnesota, and Texas.[11]

Many states define the scope of public employee bargaining in terms of wages, hours, and other terms and conditions of employment. Merit-pay policies and retirement benefits are frequently excluded from the scope of bargaining. Some states dictate the specific items to be included in bargaining clauses. For example, Nevada has a detailed list of what is open for public employee bargaining. Other states that specify negotiable items include Delaware, the District of Columbia, Iowa, Maine, Minnesota, Oklahoma, Oregon, Rhode Island, Tennessee, Vermont, and Washington.[12]

Although grievance and arbitration procedures are generally permitted in many states, they are mandatory in Alaska, Delaware, Florida, Illinois, Oklahoma, Minnesota, Pennsylvania, New Hampshire, New Jersey, New Mexico, South Dakota, and Vermont.[13] Some measures of union security (such as the mandatory dues checkoff) are allowed in almost half of the states with public-sector bargaining laws. The agency shop, a system requiring nonunion members to pay the equivalent of union dues to a charitable cause, is permitted for some employees in fourteen states and the District of Columbia.[14]

The affluent and industrialized states, with the exception of the South, generally have labor relations policies which provide the most comprehensive coverage. An early study by Thomas W. Kochan found that one-third of the variance in public-sector bargaining laws could be explained by per capita state government expenditures, per capita change in personal income, and by previous innovations attempted by state legislatures.[15]

LABOR RELATIONS IN THE PRIVATE SOCIAL-SERVICE SECTOR

Unlike the public sector, many social workers in the private sector are covered under the National Labor Relations Act (NLRA), depending upon how the agency is funded and affected by interstate commerce. Coverage under the NLRA was broadened on August 25, 1974, and the right to strike was extended to about 1.4 million employees in the private social-service sector, including hospitals, health maintenance organizations, nursing homes, health clinics, extended care facilities, and other social welfare institutions.

Protected by the National Labor Relations Act, private-sector social workers have the right to select a labor union as their exclusive bargaining agent. Procedures for representation involve filing a union petition demonstrating a show of interest by at least 30 percent of the employees in an eligible unit. This interest is based on authorization cards signed by workers to acknowledge a particular union as their bargaining representative. In nearly all cases, the National Labor Relations Board (NLRB), a state employment commission, or a quasi-judicial body conducts a secret ballot election to determine whether the majority of workers desire a specific labor organization to be their bargaining agent. Prior to the election, a consensual agreement is usually reached by the employer and the union determining the appropriate unit of eligible employees and how the election is to be held. (Supervisors with the authority to hire, fire, or discipline workers are normally excluded from a bargaining unit of line workers.)

The NLRA requires that a union which has a majority of the signed authorization cards in an appropriate bargaining unit can request voluntary recognition from the employer. Once union recognition is granted, bargaining can quickly begin.

NLRA laws distinctly prohibit the employer from interfering or coercing employees in the exercise of their rights to join a labor organization. Conversely, it is also illegal for the union to interfere with employees in the exercise of their rights to refrain from union activity. Upon certification, the employer is legally obligated to bargain with the union. Disputes concerning the election or the composition of the bargaining unit and failure to bargain can be litigated in formal hearings conducted by state employment relations commissions and the National Labor Relations Board.[16] In all cases, private-sector workers covered under the NLRA have significantly broader rights than public sector employees.

ATTEMPTS AT FEDERAL LEGISLATION

The variegated, diffuse, and almost chaotic nature of state labor laws has not gone unnoticed by Congress. During the 1970s, a number of bills were introduced into Congress which incorporated three basic approaches to the problem. One such approach is illustrated by legislation introduced by Representative Frank Thompson (D-NJ), which would have amended the NLRA to cover state and local government employees. The authority of the NLRB would have been enlarged to cover nonfederal public employees, thereby usurping existing state and local labor relations laws.

A second aproach would have created a new federal labor authority to cover public employees. The proposed National Public Employment Relations Act, introduced by Representatives William Clay (D-MO) and Carl Perkins (D-KY), would have been administered by a National Public Employment Relations Committee. This proposed legislation, commonly called the Clay-Perkins Bill, would have guaranteed the rights of public employees to bargain collectively and would have stipulated unfair labor practices, unit determination, representation, impasse procedures, scope of bargaining, and other NLRA principals. In addition, the Clay-Perkins Act would have authorized dues checkoff and the agency shop, made the union shop a compulsory bargaining issue, conceded a limited right to strike, and given supervisory employees representation rights. All preexisting state labor legislation would have been superceded by the Clay-Perkins bill. Not surprisingly, the bill received unqualified support from the Coalition of American Public Employees (CAPE) unions.

The third approach represented a compromise. This scheme called for a federal-state partnership, with the federal government establishing minimum standards for labor relations. State conformity would be assured by the threat of withholding federal funds. Supported by the American Federation of Government Employees (AFGE), this approach promised to avoid total federal control of state labor relations, thereby permitting some state or local experimentation. Passage of this bill would have assured public employees the rights to join and form unions and engage in collective bargaining. This bill also included a definition of unfair labor practices, procedures for determining representation, and other measures designed to ensure good-faith bargaining. States which already conformed to the minimum federal guidelines could administer their own labor relations programs. None of the proposed bills passed.

A chill crept through public-sector labor relations from the middle 1970s to the 1980s. In 1976, the United States Supreme Court held unconstitutional a 1974 amendment to the Fair Labor Standards Act (FLSA). The court's ruling in *National League of Cities v. Usery* 44 USLW 4974 (1976) overturned an earlier 1968 decision which extended key FLSA provisions to certain state and local workers. The arguments raised by the National League of Cities, the National Governors' Conference, and other state and local authorities charged that FLSA rules mandating federal wage and hour requirements interfered with state sovereignty and disrupted the structure of state and local management relations. According to Richard C. Kearney, "*Usery* [original emphasis] has had the undeniable effect of squelching federal legislation designed to regulate state and local government labor relations."[17]

In 1985 the U.S. Supreme Court reversed itself in *Garcia v. San Antonio Metropolitan Transit Authority* and ruled that state and local government employees were covered under the FLSA statute, thereby requiring that they receive cash overtime for all work beyond 40 hours per week. The

Garcia decision prompted an outcry from public employers that the costs of paying overtime, and the subsequent removal of compensatory time as an option, would result in a multibillion dollar tax increase as well as a reduction in services.[18]

With uncharacteristic speed, Congress passed the 1985 Amendment to the Fair Labor Standards Act, requiring state and local employers to grant compensatory time for all work beyond 40 hours a week at the FLSA rate of time and one-half. The bill, which became effective on April 15, 1986, also limited the number of compensatory hours that may be accrued—480 hours for a public safety or emergency activity and 240 hours for all other workers. The bill also set standards for converting compensatory time to dollars, and exempted special detail work, occasional employment, substitute work, and volunteer work.[19] The 1985 FLSA Amendment is binding for all classes of public workers and supercedes all agreements between employees and employers.[20]

CONCLUSION

Most supporters of standardizing state and local labor relations policies believe that this must occur under the auspices of federal legislation. Opponents of federalizing public-sector labor relations, Harry K. Wellington and Ralph K. Winter argue that:

Federal legislation or regulation necessarily tends to a uniform rule. In the case of public employee unionism, uniformity is most undesirable and diversity in rules and structures virtually a necessity. . . .

State regulation, moreover, promises a more flexible approach than national legislation. State officials are likely to be more sensitive to problems of local government than federal officials, and legislation that proves inappropriate can be modified more easily at the state level than at the national level.[21]

Other foes of federal legislation invoke the sovereignty argument, claiming that federal laws that regulate public sector labor-management relations violate the autonomy of state and local governments. This "states' rights" argument has found increased currency in the conservative spirit of the Reagan years.

Advocates of federal legislation argue that a uniform labor relations policy would: (1) diminish the incidence of recognition strikes by making union recognition mandatory, (2) preclude strikes by stipulating impasse procedures, (3) provide equal treatment for all state and local government employees, and (4) increase the overall efficacy of labor relations by encouraging a common approach for training labor-management personnel.[22]

At least for social workers, and by implication other public-sector workers, the arguments for standardization appear compelling. Despite debates about the uniqueness of working conditions in various states, there appears to be relatively little difference between what a public welfare social worker does in Alabama and in Massachusetts. Social work job requirements and skills—many of which are mandated by federal AFDC rules—are virtually identical throughout the states. So, too, are the pressures and responsibilities that all social workers experience.

Social workers employed in states that have restrictive labor relations policies are penalized. Laboring in a work environment characterized by little opportunity for grievance resolution, no collective bargaining, and no procedures for impasse resolution often causes better-trained social workers to look for employment elsewhere, usually in the private voluntary or for-profit sector.

The common perception among many social workers, regardless of the accuracy, is that working conditions in the private sector are better than in public employment. This assumption is fueled by what some social workers believe to be punitive public-sector labor relations policies. In the end, some of the most qualified social workers are discouraged from entering public service.

NOTES

1. Steven G. Brint and Martin H. Dodd, *Professional Workers and Unionization: A Data Handbook*, Washington, D.C.: Department of Professional Employees, AFL-CIO, 1984, p. 57.

2. Marvin J. Levine and Eugene C. Hagburg, *Public Sector Labor Relations* (St. Paul, Minnesota: West Publishing Company, 1979), p. 13.

3. Ibid., pp. 13–14.

4. Ibid., p. 14.

5. Quoted in David Ziskind, *One Thousand Strikes of Government Employees* (New York: Columbia University Press, 1940), p. 187.

6. Richard C. Kearney, *Labor Relations in the Public Sector* (New York: Marcel Dekker, Inc., 1984), p. 42.

7. Ibid., p. 54.

8. Richard B. Freeman, "Unionism Comes to the Public Sector," *Journal of Economic Literature*, 24 (March 1986), p. 47.

9. Robert G. Valletta and Richard B. Freeman, "The NBER Public Sector Collective Bargaining Law Data Set," Boston, Massachusetts: National Bureau of Economic Research, June 1986, n.p.

10. Ibid.

11. The Bureau of National Affairs, "Government Employee Relations Report," Washington, D.C.: Bureau of National Affairs, October 10, 1985, p. 51:101.

12. Ibid.

13. Ibid.

14. Ibid.

15. Thomas W. Kochan, "Correlates of State Public Employee Bargaining Laws," *Industrial Relations* 12 (October 1973), pp. 322–337.

16. Much of this section is gleaned from Milton Tambor, "The Social Worker as Worker: A Union Perspective," in Simon Slavin (ed.), *Managing Finances, Personnel, and Information in Human Services* (New York: Haworth Press, 1985), p. 263, and from an earlier draft of "The Social Service Union in the Workplace." See also Rene Laliberty and W. I. Christopher, *Health Care Labor Relations: A Guide for the '80s* (Owings Mills, Maryland: National Health Publishing, 1986), p. ix.

17. Kearney, *Labor Relations in the Public Sector*, p. 53.

18. The Bureau of National Affairs, "Government Employee Relations Report," p. A–10.

19. Al Bilik, "Memorandum: Fair Labor Standards Coverage," Washington, D.C.: Public Employee Department, AFL-CIO, November 20, 1985, p. 2.

20. Ibid., p. 1.

21. Harry K. Wellington and Ralph K. Winter, Jr., *The Unions and the Cities* (Washington, D.C.: The Brookings Institution, 1971), pp. 53–54.

22. Kearney, *Labor Relations in the Public Sector*, p. 51.

7

The Social Service Union in the Workplace

MILTON TAMBOR

This chapter looks at overall social service workplace issues including collective bargaining, union organizing, the reaction of management to unionization, negotiation of the labor contract, and the administration of the labor agreement.

According to the Bureau of Labor Statistics Reports for 1986, union membership as a proportion of the U.S. labor force stood at 17.5 percent. The proportion of the organized labor force peaked at 35 percent in 1945, and since 1954 a general decline has followed. Much of that decrease has been attributed to structural changes in the U.S. economy. Specifically, manufacturing jobs, where union representation has been strong, have been sharply reduced, while lower paid nonunion jobs in the service sector have been greatly expanded.

However, within the public sector and among specific occupational groupings, the trend has been reversed. The last twenty years have witnessed a dramatic growth in the unionization of federal, state, and local government employees. Among the approximately 16 million government employees, 6 million or nearly 36 percent are represented by unions. Among protective services occupations, including police and fire fighters, and within professional specialty groups such as teachers and nurses, the unionization rate is also above 30 percent. Social work unionization has occurred within the context of the increased unionization of human service professionals.

SOCIAL WORK UNIONIZATION: GROWTH AND DISPERSION

While there are no precise figures on union membership among social workers, estimates range from 22 to 33 percent of the approximately 250,000 member social service workforce.[1] In Canada, the estimate is that a majority of social workers are covered by bargaining agreements, and in British Columbia, the proportion is above 90 percent.[2] In public welfare departments—where the majority of social srvice workers are employed—U.S. figures cited are as high as 69 percent.[3] The American Federation of State, County, and Municipal Employees, the largest AFL-CIO union with a membership of 1.1 million, represents 50,000 social service workers in city and county welfare departments, and another 10,000 in voluntary agencies. The Social Service Employees Union, with a membership of 500,000, represents more than 40,000 social service workers in California, Pennsylvania, New York, and the New England states. In smaller numbers, social workers belong to Local 1199 of the National Hospital Union, the National Union of Hospital and Health Care Employees (10,000 members), United Office and Professional Workers of America, the Communications Workers of America (10,000 members), the American Federation of Teachers, the United Automobile Workers, as well as being members of faculty labor organizations and independent staff associations.

The relatively large number of unionized social workers is reflective of the steady increase in white-collar union membership experienced in recent years. Although comprising only 24 percent of the members of collective bargaining units in 1973, white-collar workers increased to 37 percent by 1985.[4]

As an occupational grouping, social workers are located in both the public and private nonprofit sectors, and within a diverse range of institutions, such as hospitals, schools, mental health clinics, public welfare departments, and voluntary agencies. Further, in contrast to nurses and teachers, most bargaining units—those employee groups represented by a union—are not confined exclusively to professional social workers. As a result of a mutuality of interests, human service unions often represent other service and support workers in addition to professional social workers. The dispersion of social workers into heterogeneous bargaining units may explain why there has been no complete study of social work unionization. As a result, much of the experience of social service unions is communicated in-house or through union newspapers.

CURRENT EMPLOYMENT CONDITIONS

Significant changes in the nature of social work practice, and in the working conditions affecting social workers, are increasingly being noted. The standardization of professional tools, the increasing pressure toward greater productivity, and a lessening influence in policy-making decisions are cited as indications of a decline in the professional autonomy and status within social work.[5] This industrialization of social work practice is reflected in the erosion of craft elements relating to professional judgment and skills and the emergence of repetitive and mechanistic work.[6] According to some observers, the introduction of "Taylorism" into social services has distorted the nature of human service work.[7] For social workers, the dismantling of human service programs under the Reagan administration has also resulted in greater job insecurity, higher unemployment, declines in real wages, and the occupational displacement of higher- and lower-degreed social service workers.[8]

For the social worker who must cope as an individual with the worst of these employment conditions, the prognosis is not good. Job stress increases as job control decreases. A sense of powerlessness and impotence in the workplace is internalized as "burnout."[9] Professionalism, with its emphasis on individualism, personal excellence, and the service ethos, provides no solace but only contributes further to a sense of alienation.[10] In all too many instances, the despondent social worker is likely to take a leave of absence, pursue another career, or quit.

Unionization, on the other hand, provides a vehicle for both defending professional autonomy and improving working conditions. As the collective voice of the workers, the union is built upon mutual support. Workers act together as agents of change on the basis of their own interests and within their own work settings. By advocating actively for themselves as workers, social workers can also be more effective in helping their clients gain a greater measure of power and control over their lives.[11]

Besides negotiating job security and bread-and-butter issues, the social service union—along with labor organizations representing nurses and teachers—seeks to expand the scope of bargaining to include agency-level policy and decision-making processes. One union leader observed that: "To the professional—the teacher or case worker—things like class size and caseload size become as important as the number of hours in a shift is to the blue collar worker."[12] The interest of social service unions in bargaining about an agency's mission and standard of service is attributable to the professional's concern with job satisfaction, the centrality of professional judgment, and identification with clients.[13]

ORGANIZING A UNION IN THE WORKPLACE

In 1926, social workers in New York City hospitals and agencies organized the Associated Federation of Social Workers and demanded a collective bargaining agreement with the Federation of Jewish Philanthropies.[14] The issues that prompted those social workers to form a labor organization included: regular salary increments; caseload size; health insurance, salary scales related to training, experience, and job requirements; and standardization of promotional procedures. Sixty years later, these same workplace issues continue to generate union interest. In one community mental health agency the flashpoint for an organizing drive was a unilateral reduction in hours and arbitrary layoffs. In another agency, the unfairness of merit salary increases and the favoritism shown in awarding promotions became key organizing issues. The distribution of salaries and salary increments, rather than low pay *per se*, may sometimes be the central concern. For example, new workers may be hired at higher salaries than those currently employed, or sharp disparities in salaries may exist between administration and line staff. For one agency director, being a male employee who was the primary breadwinner constituted sufficient grounds for determining basic salary differences.[15]

In another agency, an unfair discharge demonstrated to staff that the agency's grievance procedure—with its decision making residing exclusively within the agency board—could not provide for due process. Rather, a union grievance procedure incorporating final and binding arbitration by a neutral third party was seen as the critical element in job protection. In the local and state employment sectors, caseload size, salaries and pay equity, physical working conditions, downgrading of services, career ladders, and training opportunities may constitute major organizing issues. Where state and local civil service rules provide some protection, less importance may be attached to areas of job security and promotions.

Doubts regarding the legitimacy of existing staff personnel practices can also spark union interest. When an agency board announced to the staff personnel committee that other priorities compelled the agency to suspend further discussion for six months, the staff committee recognized their powerlessness and formed a union. In the public sector, workers may experience a civil service system that restricts bargaining to certain subject matters, or allows only for a meet-and-confer mechanism that falls far short of collective bargaining.

During the initial phase, a core organizing group emerges who then begins to articulate the grievances and concerns of staff. As the process unfolds, the committee assumes responsibility for developing communication networks, arranging for meetings and meeting places, planning agendas, and chairing meetings. In the process of gathering information, other unionized social workers in the community may be contacted. Representatives from various international unions may be invited to attend staff organizing meetings prior to the selection of a union. In the selection of a labor organization, primary considerations involve the union's experience in that service sector, its resources, its reputation, its influence both locally and nationally, and its commitment to democratic processes.

Since a representation election is dependent upon signed authorization cards from the majority of the employees in a bargaining unit—those workers having a "community of interest" in the performance of their work—the definition of an appropriate bargaining unit is particularly important. Broad bargaining units that include professional, paraprofessional, and clerical workers, generally increase the collective strength of all workers. The fragmentation of bargaining units, on the other hand, or the exclusion of eligible employees from union representation, dilutes that collective strength. In some cases, the size and diversity of the workforce, the separate interests of employee groups, or local statutes and regulations may mandate separate occupational bargaining units.

The success of a union organizing campaign can usually be linked to the effectiveness of the organizers. Effective organizers project credibility in the workplace through their job performance, knowledge of the agency, and rapport with co-workers. They know how to listen and be responsible to the way co-workers experience their working conditions. If some workers are fearful, the organizer must acknowledge the potential for tension and conflict, but must also posit the value of unity and mutual support. For those workers who are unfamiliar with collective bargaining, or even personally opposed to unions, the organizer needs to be accepting while continually educating these workers about the true function of unions and the bargaining process.

As organizers, these workers are not only visible to their co-workers, but they are also known to management representatives. As such, they may be the targets of ostracism, petty harassment, or even overt intimidation. Organizers who have a background as political or community activists often understand the nature of confrontation in power relationships. Those organizers from union family backgrounds similarly understand the threat that an organizing drive can pose to a nonunion employer and the various forms of antiunion response. Organizers who may neither be radicalized, politicized, or union-oriented, may simply experience a raising and a dashing of promises and expectations.[16] The recognition of an individual's powerlessness to bring about real changes in salaries and working conditions, and the subsequent embracing of union principles, may deepen an organizer's commitment to fight for employee rights even under adverse conditions. In public-sector bargaining units, or in voluntary agencies where union support is strong among workers or where unions exercise significant political influence, this risk taking will not be present. As a consequence of exercising union leadership in the workplace, union organizers and officers may be considered by management as prime candidates for administrative and supervisory positions.

MANAGEMENT OPPOSITION

Managerial opposition to unions has increased dramatically since the 1970s. Labor management consultants specializing in union busting are routinely employed to run antiunion campaigns. If such a campaign were conducted in the social service workplace, the management strategy would involve frequent written and verbal communications with workers—usually through their immediate supervisor—explaining why they would be better off voting against the union. The union is likely to be portrayed as an interloper, an outside third party, who would disrupt cordial relationships and impose external demands unrelated to the needs of workers. The union would be cast as a dues-hungry organization responsible for unnecessary strikes. Unionization would be characterized as promoting rigidity and formality in staff relationships and working conditions. One agency director suggested that a fifteen-minute rest period under a union contract could require possible disciplinary action if a minute more or less was taken. Workers may also be told that after unionization existing benefits could no longer be assured and would therefore need to be renegotiated.[17]

The employer may also initiate or retract changes in salaries and employment conditions. If "the carrot" is offered, an unexpected salary increase may be promised or even delivered. If "the stick" is applied, prior commitments to wage increases and benefit improvements will be withdrawn.

Management may also erect legal obstacles that can delay either the bargaining unit determination, the conduct of the election, or the certification of the union. For example, following a vote for union representation, the agency filed charges against the union, claiming that one of the union organizers had harassed and intimidated workers into voting for the union. At the formal hearing the agency contended that the organizer, by virtue of his position as a psychiatrist possessing extensive credentials, qualifications, and high status, had exercised subtle intimidation upon his co-workers. Although the charge was dismissed, the union certification and the onset of bargaining were delayed by more than three months.

Union organizers can respond to management charges, threats, and actions in a variety of ways. In one campaign, the organizing committee drafted an open letter to the administration which was signed by nearly all the workers. The letter announced strong support for union representation and a readiness to face any agency tactic, and effectively served to halt the employer's campaign. In another campaign, when management began to discuss the negative aspects of unionization at a staff meeting, an organizer demanded equal time and proposed a debate format. The employer denied the request, and as such, suffered a serious loss of credibility.

Internally, the organizers can demonstrate how collective bargaining leads to economic improvements by using wage and benefit comparisons between unionized and nonunionized social service agencies. Similarly, a grievance procedure providing steward representation and arbitration can be characterized as empowering the worker. Countering the negative stereotypes of unions, organizers can introduce labor history materials describing how unions have acted as the primary defensive organization of working people in their struggle for dignity and justice.

In the industrialized states where bargaining units are large, unions and associations may compete for representation. In such an organizing drive, the state employer may not actively campaign against the union. The choice for most workers will not be between union and nonunion representation, but between which union will provide the better representation. This competition among unions is seen as wasteful, and under the AFL-CIO's newly established mechanism for solving intra-union conflicts, is less likely to occur in the future.

COLLECTIVE BARGAINING

After the majority of the employees vote for union representation, or when the employer agrees to union recognition, the process of collective bargaining begins. For the workers, the first step entails the election of officers and a negotiatng committee. The committee should be representative of all the job classifications within the bargaining unit. In preparing the contract proposals, the committee will usually meet with the membership to solicit ideas and suggestions. The same process is followed by unions in renegotiating their contracts. The union normally submits a letter requesting that the contract be reopened sixty or seventy days prior to the termination of the agreement. The types of grievances and workplace problems arising under the existing labor agreement provide an important framework for preparing new contract proposals.

In larger units, information about bargaining issue priorities can be gathered from membership surveys. The International Union representative may also provide specific contractual language from other union contracts. During this early phase, management likewise makes plans. A management negotiating committee and/or legal counsel will be designated, and negotiating positions will be developed. The first negotiation session generally provides the opportunity for the members of each team to meet and jointly establish the ground rules for bargaining. Ground rules typically involve the time, place, and frequency of meetings, the payment of committee time in negotiations, and the process of exchanging and agreeing to contract proposals.

The climate in bargaining is usually shaped by the events preceding the election and the experience of the existing labor-management relationship. If the social service employer cannot accept the union's legitimacy and rejects accommodation, then "hardball" bargaining will take place. Union proposals will be summarily rejected and concession proposals will be made. In response, the unions may lobby agency board members or public policy makers, seek support from neighborhood groups or power blocs within the community, file unfair labor practice charges, or engage in picketing or strike activity.

Even when a labor-management relationship has been in place for a period of time, major conflicts may remain unresolved. In one community health and social service agency, the union had repeatedly proposed third-party grievance arbitration in each of the negotiations conducted during a ten-year period. The employer consistently rejected the union proposal claiming that arbitration would undermine the authority of the board. The union maintained that a grievance appeal process without arbitration could neither be fair nor objective. No agreement could be reached in mediation, and the employer terminated the agreement. The employees went out on strike with grievance arbitration being the major issue in the dispute.

Though the strike may represent a harsh and undesirable consequence of the failure to reach an agreement, it is fundamental to the bargaining process. In strike situations, arrangements can be made to provide emergency client services by mutual agreement between the parties or independently of each other. The strike, as well as the management lockout, is the most direct means available to the parties to break through an impasse and compel the other party to agree to their terms. The potential threat of these tactics forces the parties to constantly reassess their positions, seek new means of compromise, and exhaust every avenue available to reach an agreement.

When an accommodation between the social service employer and the union is reached, bargaining takes on a different face. The bargaining process provides an education to both parties. Problems can be discussed and important information may be shared. Initial proposals are followed by mutual exploration and the sorting out of priorities by the respective parties. After first resolving the minor issues, the parties may then table the more difficult subjects. Package proposals may be made, and the parameters of a settlement acceptable to both sides may emerge. Moreover, a tentative agreement can be reached within a reasonable time frame. This tentative agreement is then brought before both the union membership and the employer's policy-making body for final ratification.

THE LABOR AGREEMENT

The collective bargaining agreement encompasses a broad range of economic and noneconomic provisions. Job security and protection issues are considered by the union as central features of any labor agreement. The grievance process and steward representation serve to defend employee rights. The system allows the steward time off to investigate and process grievances and includes the right of employee representation at the point of discipline. The grievance procedure also specifies the time limit for grievances to be heard at different levels of management. The grievance procedure will normally terminate with binding arbitration, and 95 percent of U.S. labor agreements include that provision.[18]

Union security provisions are also important components of the labor agreement. The union will propose that all employees in the bargaining unit either join the union or pay a service fee. The union's rationale for negotiating such a requirement is that the union is legally obligated to represent all employees in a given bargaining unit. Without such a provision, employees choosing not to pay either union dues or the service fee would still receive the same representation as union members. In right-to-work states where union security provisions may be prohibited, the resentment of union members to "freeloaders" is likely to develop.

The union will also propose that the labor agreement link seniority to job security. Under such provisions, pending layoffs would be based strictly on the criteria of seniority, as long as the seniority employee could perform the available work. Transfer rights would guarantee that the seniority employee be given preference toward a comparable job before a new hire or lesser seniority employee. Promotions would be based on seniority among workers with similar qualifications, or where the seniority employees met the necessary job requirements.

Job security would also be protected under the contract through provisions for leaves of absence (for example, health, education, or military) that would provide for job reinstatement. (Paternity, as well as maternity leaves, are increasingly becoming prevalent in labor agreements.)

The handling of personnel files is another subject receiving more attention in the labor agreement. A contract provision could limit the content and use of personnel files by guaranteeing their confidentiality, requiring employee notification, assuring employee rights to grieve or disagree with the contents, and by restricting the use of disciplinary records and counseling memoranda to a specific time period.

The labor agreement might also include policy statements prohibiting sexual harassment, affirming nondiscrimination, restricting polygraph and drug testing, permitting supplemental employment, promoting health and safety, and limiting the contracting-out of services.

Economic provisions of the labor agreement often include hours of work (length of work week, compensatory time, overtime), paid time off (holidays, sick leave, vacations, personal and funeral leave), insurance benfits (hospitalization, disability, life insurance, dental and retirement), and salaries. Besides specifying across-the-board increases, cost of living allowances, and annual step increments, the agreement could also designate the impact on salaries of education and experience within job classification.

Pay equity has become an important subject of salary negotiations in the public sector. Studies comparing dissimilar jobs, but using the same evaluation factors (for example, skill, effort, and responsibility), have concluded that jobs held predominantly by women pay less than male-dominated jobs of comparable value. In San Jose, the first major collective bargaining agreement addressing pay equity provided for the up-grading of wage rates for clerical workers, librarians, and other traditionally female jobs. These discriminatory wage disparities similarly exist in social work job classifications, and unions representing social service workers are advocating for pay equity in the courts and state legislatures, as well as across the bargaining table.

The social service union also uses the collective bargaining agreement to address professional and policy issues. Benefits relating to professional interests may include tuition reimbursement, sabbatical and educational leaves, conference time and costs, payment for professional dues and subscriptions, and flexible hours of work. A summary of possible contract items appropriate for collective bargaining includes:

—hours of work

—overtime (paid and/or compensatory time)

—holidays

—vacation

—sick leave

—other leaves (emergency, personal, military, jury duty, union, and so on)

—seniority rights

—retrenchment/layoffs/transfers/reorganization

—health benefits

—disciplinary procedures/terminations/suspensions

—grievance procedures (including arbitration)

—contract extension provision

—agency shop

—dues checkoff

—salary structure

—job titles and descriptions

—probation

—evaluations

—promotions.

An inventory of less traditional contract items may include:

—malpractice and professional liability insurance

—legal representation of workers

—automobile insurance reimbursement

—hazardous weather pay

—employee assistance programs

—sabbatical leaves

—minimum required training

—adequate work space

—medical reimbursement for communicable diseases contracted on the job

—parental leaves (including paternity)

—alternative work arrangements (flexible time, job sharing, and so forth)

—workload issues

—advanced training, including in-service training, conferences, courses, degree programs, licensing examination assistance, scholarships

—staff participation in policy making

—reimbursement for job and professional expenses

—remuneration for enhanced education.[19]

Gary Shaffer, in a study of sixty-nine social service, education, and fund-raising voluntary agencies, found that union and management representatives held strongly opposing views regarding the appropriateness of policy issues as proper subjects for bargaining. In the areas of work load, job duties, employee evaluations, representation on agency committees, staff development, and agency policies and proposals, 79 percent of the union officers considered those subjects as appropriate items for collective bargaining. In contrast, only 28 percent of the management representatives considered these issues as appropriate bargaining subjects. Within the collective bargaining agreements analyzed in the study, most included provisions relating to job duties and employee evaluations. Work load provisions were found in 33 percent of the agreements, while only 10 percent dealt with policy and program issues.[20]

The opposition of social work management to an expanded scope of bargaining may explain why some observers view social work bargaining as less developed than teacher bargaining.[21] Teacher work loads, including preparation periods and relief from extracurricular activities, are accepted as proper subjects for bargaining. Class size, once considered a policy issue, is now accepted as a working condition. Teacher consultation rights provide for a variety of labor management committees. Social service labor agreements, on the other hand, rarely specify actual caseload size. Instead, work loads are subject to reasonable standards, and if deemed unreasonable, the standard can be challenged through the grievance process. In many agreements, joint labor-management committees are established for the specific purpose of evaluating staff caseloads. If social workers experience continued pressure for greater accountability and productivity, then their unions may make stronger demands in the areas of policy and work load issues.

ADMINISTRATION OF THE AGREEMENT

The New York City Chapter of the National Association of Social Workers hosted a conference in 1986 on social workers as professionals and union members. Representatives from AFSCME, SEIU, District 1199, and the United Federation of Teachers discussed a range of issues facing their unions. Contractual disputes focused on productivity requirements linked to a rating system, contracting out of services, overlapping job titles in lieu of social work titles, education differentials in pay, mass shift changes, involuntary job assignments, and health hazards associated with video display terminals. Some of the disputes were processed as grievances, while other issues were being discussed at labor-management meetings and in *ad hoc* committees.

The administration of collective bargaining agreement is as important as the actual contract negotiations. What kinds of problems and disputes arise under the agreement? Which contractual provisions are subject to varying interpretations? Are provisions of the agreement applied consistently and uniformly? How are disputes settled? The answers to these questions will likely indicate the usefulness and relevance of the labor agreement on a day-to-day basis.

In general, grievance settlements and arbitration awards serve to elaborate upon the meaning and intent of the agreement. In one local union, arbitration decisions in five separate discharge cases defined more explicit guidelines in disciplining for just cause. These five discharges were predicated upon unsatisfactory job performance, verbal abuse of co-workers, and failure to report to work. In each case the grievant was reinstated with back pay. In their awards, the arbitrators cited the employers' failure to follow progressive discipline, their disregard for due process procedures, and their inability to use the employee evaluation forms, as evidence of poor performance.

Within one family service agency, a dispute in contract negotiations regarding merit increases prompted the formation of a joint labor-management committee. The employer argued that merit increases could be applied fairly and objectively based upon specific performance standards. The union rejected that claim, criticizing the system for promoting staff divisions and a speedup of work. The labor-management committee subsequently shifted its attention to broader and more substantive concerns about improving the quality of work life and labor-management relations within the agency.

Funding reductions in another agency brought the union and employer together in a special conference about possible layoffs. During these discussions, the union agreed to waive the layoff provision, and both parties, line staff and administration, accepted a short-term salary reduction.

Experiences in administering the contract attest to the continuity of the collective bargaining process and the vibrancy of the labor agreement.

CONCLUSION

As an institution representing working people, the trade union movement has traditionally acted as the catalyst for progressive change in the larger society. Acting beyond the immediate interests of their membership, unions have fought for improvements in economic and social welfare programs (such as full employment, progressive tax reform, National Health Insurance, minimum wage protection, civil rights legislation, and so forth), and opposed regressive utility hikes, cuts in welfare spending, and proposition-13 style initiatives. More recently, in the area of foreign policy, progressive unions have lobbied against increases in defense spending and opposed interventionist policies in Central America. Unions such as SEIU and AFSCME have also brought to the public attention serious gaps in our social service system, among them, inadequate nursing home care and deinstitutionalization.

As trade unionists, social workers can find expression for their political commitments and values within their unions. Through union involvement at a local level—apart from the collective bargaining process—social workers can use their labor organization's resources to improve client services and join in progressive coalitions with the neighborhood and community groups.

NOTES

1. Jeffry Galper, *Social Work Practice: A Radical Perspective* (Englewood Cliffs, N.J.: Prentice Hall, 1980), pp. 167 and 170.

2. Gilbert Levine, "Collective Bargaining For Social Workers in Voluntary Agencies," Toronto, Ontario: Association of Professional Social Workers, 1975.

3. Jack Stieber, *Public Employee Unionism: Structure, Growth, Policy* (Washington, D.C.: Brookings Institution, 1973), pp. 232–233.

4. Bureau of National Affairs, AFL-CIO Department for Professional Employees, *Union Labor Report*, Vol. 40, No. 31, July 31, 1986. Quoted in Gary Shaffer, "Professional Social Worker Unionization: Current Contract Developments and Implications for Managers." Paper presented at the National Association of Social Workers, Annual Conference, New Orleans, La., September 12, 1987.

5. See Neil Tudiver, "Business Ideology and Management in Social Work: The Limits of Cost Control," *Catalyst*, 4 (1982), pp. 25–48; and David Wagner and Marcia Cohen, "Social Workers Class, and Professionalism," *Catalyst*, 1 (1978), pp. 25–53.

6. Michael Fabricant, "The Industrialization of Social Work Practice," *Social Work*, (30), 5 (September-October 1985), pp. 393–394.

7. Bill Patry, "Taylorism Comes to the Social Services," *Monthly Review*, 30 (October 1978).

8. Linda Ratner, "Understanding and Moving Beyond Social Workers' Resistance to Unionization," *Catalyst*, 5 (1985), p. 81.

9. Howard Karger, "Burnout as Alienation," *Social Service Review*, (55), 2 (June 1981), pp. 270–283.

10. Joan Arches, "Don't Burn, Organize: A Structural Analysis of Burnout in the Human Services,"*Catalyst*, 5 (1985), p. 17.

11. Wendy Sherman and Stanley Wenocur, "Empowering Public Welfare Workers Through Mutual Support," *Social Work*, (28), 5 (September-October 1983), p. 375.

12. Joan Weitzman, *The Scope of Bargaining in Public Employment*, (New York: Praeger, 1975), p. 201.

13. Jerome Lefkowitz, "Unionism in the Human Services Industries," *Albany Law Review*, 36 (1972), p. 609.

14. Jacob Fisher, *The Response of Social Work to the Depression* (Cambridge, Mass.: Shenkman Publishing Company, 1980), pp. 105–106.

15. Milton Tambor, "The Social Worker as Worker," *Administration in Social Work*, (3), 3 (Fall 1979), pp. 289–300.

16. Eda DiBicarri, "Organizing in the Massachusetts Purchase of Service System," *Catalyst*, 5 (1985), p. 48.

17. Milton Tambor, "Unions and Voluntary Agencies," *Social Work*, (18), 4 (July 1973), pp. 41–47.

18. Lee Balliet, *Survey of Labor Relations*, (Washington, D.C.: Bureau of National Affairs, 1981), p. 157.

19. Much of this list came from Dena Fliegel and Bobbie Rabinowitz, *Contract Items Language*, handout presented in "Social Workers in Trade Unions," National Association of Social Workers, Annual Meeting, New Orleans, La., September 11, 1987; and from Gary Shaffer, "Professional Social Worker Unionization," p. 5.

20. Shaffer, "Professional Social Worker Unionization," p. 6.

21. Gary Shaffer, "Labor Relations and the Unionization of Professional Social Workers," *Journal of Education for Social Work* 15 (Winter 1979), pp. 83–84.

8

Privatization: Prospects for Unionizing Social Workers

DAVID STOESZ

Any consideration of unionizing social workers must address the issue of privatization. By privatization, I do not necessarily mean the cashiering of public resources as a way to generate revenues without raising taxes. While this is fashionable thinking in some circles in Washington, D.C., it has somewhat less relevance for social workers.[1] It is doubtful, after all, that anyone would seriously consider laying out substantial sums to acquire the local welfare department.

On the other hand, it is conceivable that some public welfare functions could become private welfare functions through the swift execution of legislation or executive decree that changes programmatic auspice. It is this connotation that has alarmed organizers of employees who work in public welfare—with the transfer of auspice goes the prospect of unionizing social workers, or so the thinking seems to go.

I would argue that this fear is symptomatic of a strategic error in approaching the goal of unionizing social workers for two reasons. First, a large number of social workers practice in the private sector, the implications of which will be addressed momentarily. To focus on public-sector social workers, while disregarding private-sector social workers, is to write off a large number of prospective union members. This consideration is magnified when many professionals work in both the public and private sectors at some time during the course of their careers. "Why," these professionals must wonder, "should I not have the benefits of union membership when I elect to practice in the private sector for what I believe to be valid reasons?"

Second, if the trade union movement is a model for unionizing social

workers, organizers should begin with the private sector. A fair gener-
alization is that private sector social workers receive lower wages and
have fewer rights and benfits as employees than do public-sector workers
who are protected by civil service. It may be argued that the decentralized
nature of the private sector makes organizing more difficult; if so, that
is the very reason it is more necessary. Social workers in the private
sector need the solidarity a union provides. Another justification for
focusing on the private sector is that job actions, probably the most
effective method for getting concessions from management, are illegal
in the public sector—but not necessarily in the private sector.

From my perspective, privatization presents a reality with which organizers must contend if social workers will ever be unionized. The key,
as David Donnison has pointed out in his examination of social welfare
in Great Britain, is to recognize "the progressive potential of privatization."[2]

THE PRIVATE SECTOR OF AMERICAN SOCIAL WELFARE

Social welfare in the United States is a remarkably varied institution.
Unlike its European counterparts, the American welfare state is less
complete—meaning that government has assumed less responsibility for
the needs of citizens. In the absence of government programs, private
nonprofit agencies have become an important source of welfare, and,
more recently, for-profit firms have entered the human services market.
However, the development that most differentiates the United States
from the European welfare states is that many American social workers
engage in independent practice. To European social workers—and some
leftists in this country—I suspect this borders on heresy. However dis-
agreeable independent practice may be, it is becoming an unavoidable
part of welfare in the United States. Like the nonprofit and for-profit
sectors, independent practice is private.

Voluntary Agencies

The private sector has a long history, preceding the intervention of
the federal government in American welfare. The first organized expression of private sector activity appeared with the Buffalo (New York)
Charity Organization Society in 1877. Before the end of the nineteenth
century, Charity Organization Societies were evident in virtually every
metropolitan area. The Charity Organization Society of Baltimore
achieved prominence by hiring Mary Richmond as its bookkeeper and
then director. Richmond was to write *Social Diagnosis*, a book which
established an empirical basis for social work practice.[3] Charity Orga-

nization Societies, and similar fraternal and sectarian aid societies, functioned well after the federal government established a dominant role in social welfare with passage of the Social Security Act of 1935. It is worth noting that the Social Security Act expressly excluded domestic and agricultural workers—many of whom were Black—and that workers in these occupational groups continued to rely on private sector agencies when government benefits were denied them.

Settlement houses emerged contemporaneously with Charity Organization Societies, and as Howard Karger has noted, they served a similar function—to socialize European immigrants to become upstanding Americans.[4] Settlements engaged in a range of activities that were somewhat different from those of the Charity Organization Societies, such as educating children, engaging in urban research studies, promoting public hygiene, and advocating for voter education and registration. Hull House, established by Jane Addams in 1889, served as a model settlement, not only providing important service to the Chicago neighborhood in which it was located, but also providing residence to a long list of bourgeois altruists, many of whom would later attain prominent positions in the New Deal.[5]

The proliferation of Charity Organization Societies and settlements eventually led to a competition for funding from philanthropic sources. The problem of multiple appeals to philanthropic sources was solved, initially in Denver, when agencies collaborated in a fund-raising campaign to be held at one time each year. The Federation Movement, as this approach became known, was a precursor of the United Way campaign, which is immediately recognizable by most American workers.

As nonprofit agencies became part of the social fabric of cities in the United States, the social workers employed by them gained an appreciation for the commonality of their work. This shared understanding of agency function became codified in 1926 when executives of the larger agencies contributed to a document, *Social Casework: Generic and Specific*— or the Milford Conference report, which described the model social service agency.[6] The agency model outlined in the Milford Conference report is essentially intact today. The form and function of sectarian agencies, such as Catholic Charities, Lutheran Social Services, Jewish Family and Community Services, and the Salvation Army, along with secular agencies, such as the Red Cross, the YMCA, and the YWCA, can be traced to the Milford Conference report.

How important is the voluntary sector today, even though government programs are dominant in social welfare? In their classic text, *Social Welfare and Industrial Society*, Harold Wilensky and Charles Lebeaux observed that a majority of social services were provided through the social service agency.[7] Approaching the end of the twentieth century the voluntary agency is anything but an artifact. While its roots are deep in

American history, the freedom of association fostered by our national culture continually prompts the formation of new agencies. In fact, most progressive initiatives in social welfare emerge first as voluntary associations. Current examples of this include rape crisis and domestic violence centers for women, hospices for the terminally ill, shelters for the homeless, and even more recently, support programs for victims of acquired immune deficiency syndrome (AIDS).

Voluntary agencies respond to new human needs and the people who establish them tend to be articulate, assertive and, in some instances, charismatic. It is not so surprising then, that under effective leadership, such agencies would become desirable places for social workers to practice, even though salaries may be lower and working conditions less comfortable than in more established institutions. That is often the case. Many professional social workers have an affinity for voluntary agencies because they are offered the opportunity to engage in service-provision to previously neglected populations in need. Many social workers recognize that newer voluntary agencies are manifestations of social change, and continue to support them even when they are no longer formally associated with the agency, and some social workers, despite other employment opportunities, continue the commitment they made as fresh graduates of social work training programs, and work for these agencies recognizing that doing so is a direct subsidy to a fiscally fragile organization. This group of social workers, more than any other, deserves the support and benefits of a union.

Private Practice

The private practice of social work was not officially sanctioned by the National Association of Social Workers until 1964. Before then, practitioners engaged in private practice were not considered to be practicing social work *per se*, since social work, properly speaking, occurred under the purview of the social casework agency. Such was the legacy of the Milford Conference report. This little bit of history is instructive, and I shall return to it in a moment. Nevertheless, the examples of psychiatry and psychology proved irresistible to many social workers who were applying methods derived from those disciplines. "If psychiatrists and psychologists practice privately," they seemed to ask, "why can't social workers?"

If the logic of the private-practice social workers wasn't persuasive, their numbers were. By the mid–1980s perhaps 30,000 social workers were engaged in private practice to some degree.[8] Issues important to private practitioners—state licensure of social workers, professional certification of clinical expertise, and third-party payments—have become prominent in the priorities established by professional associations. Anyone familiar with graduate education in social work will acknowledge that as many as half of all students entering master's programs do so with the expressed intent of becoming private practitioners. Clearly, a knowledge of private practice has become unavoidable if one is to understand the employment circumstances of social workers.

There is a strong temptation among people who have established careers in public welfare to look askance at private practice, associating it with the full-status professions such as medicine and law, and concluding that it does not necessarily serve the public interest (at least as it is broadly understood). From this perspective, social workers engaged in private practice are in it for financial reward and the pleasantness of sorting out relatively superficial client difficulties. Critics of private practice cite social workers in business for themselves as preferring clients who evidence a "YAVIS" syndrome. Their clients, so the allegation goes, tend to be Young, Attractive, Verbal, Intelligent, and Successful—almost the opposite of clients who are served by agency-bound social workers.[9] Quite naturally, agency-bound social workers may tolerate the plush offices of private practitioners, but draw the line at the subscription to *Psychotherapy Finances*.

In large measure the ambivalence about the private practice of social work is due to the quite personal experiences of social workers. To put private social work practice into perspective it is necessary to understand the context of traditional social work practice. According to the Milford Conference report, social work practice occurred within the social casework agency. The model casework agency was a small bureaucracy— although some of them became moderately large—and derived its values and priorities from the community in which it was located. Significantly, the social work practitioner was responsible to a supervisor who regularly reviewed the practitioner's work. The social worker who stayed with the agency typically assumed supervisory, then administrative responsibilities, which meant a corresponding lessening of contact with clients. There was, in the traditional casework agency, no provision for the master clinician. To be an agency veteran meant continuing to function under supervision, which must have been annoying, or to move up the organization and away from the clientele, which must have been frustrating.

However, the social casework agency of the voluntary sector was not the only structure that inhibited the expression of more independent-minded practitioners. The bureaucratic model of the social casework agency was easily inserted into the governmental bureaucratic structure when the American welfare state was installed. There, conditions for the veteran clinician were no better.[10] The public welfare bureaucracy derived its priorities from actors even more removed from direct services than had been true in the casework agency; namely, the legislature or department chiefs in cities, states, or levels of government. The chain of command typical of the welfare bureaucracy slowed decision making and reinforced routine performance. Supervision, still evident in a superior to whom the practitioner reported, took on another meaning with the addition of paperwork necessitated by elaborate reporting requirements. This institutionalized lethargy was labeled "red tape"—an expression synonymous with not getting things done. The red tape of the public welfare bureaucracy places a particularly heavy burden on social workers who are serving people with exceptional problems that demand wide discretion in intervention, and who need assistance urgently. To get an accurate description of the incongruence imposed on social workers in the public bureaucracy, I direct you to Fred Wiseman's documentary film, *Welfare*,[11] or George Konrad's book, *The Caseworker*.[12]

Under conditions such as these, it is no wonder that many social workers left the traditional context of social work practice, the voluntary agency. In the case of the public welfare department, the response was somewhat different—they fled. Either way, private practice proved a viable alternative through which to practice social work.

Another factor that makes private practice appealing for many social workers is that a majority of them are women. Moreover, they are women who consider themselves professionals. The vast majority of these are feminists who understand fully the political implications of their gender. Many of them have come to recognize how social welfare has exploited them and chafe at the prospect of working in an institution that replicates patriarchal culture. The patriarchal nature of social welfare organizations is probably more subtle than other social institutions simply because women have dominated the social-work labor force. Still, social welfare organizations are not particularly receptive to the needs of female professionals. Is this surprising considering that social welfare institutions expect employees to work a full thirty-five to forty-hour week, have a set schedule during which those hours must be worked, provide no benefits for workers who work part-time or on a contract basis, and place a premium on continuous work with the organization for promotional purposes? The consequences of these are serious. Not only do social welfare agencies fail to recognize the needs of female professionals to work less than full-time and interrupt their careers occasionally, but agencies also reward employees who do not make such demands on the conditions of employment. Traditionally, this is one of the reasons why the relatively small number of males have floated to the top of the welfare bureaucracy, leaving women in lower positions. Given this set of circumstances, the only way women can achieve status and income for comparable experience is not to make special demands on the organization. Since many of these demands are family-related, the easiest way to avoid the problem is not to have a family or, if professional women do have children, to go to extraordinary ends to convince a spouse or other care-giver to provide child care in order to minimize the interference that family life may present for a woman's career.

A popular literature has emerged to help women deal with the profes-sional-parent role conflict, but why should professional women have to subject themselves to the continual stress and never-ending negotiations inherent in that role conflict if an alternative work format is available? I believe that private practice is attractive to many female social workers for this very reason. In private practice the practitioner has a great deal of freedom in setting the hours of her employment, including the days she may choose to work. She is free to construct a benefit package to meet her needs; and, although these benefits may cost more than if she were a government employee, the cost is probably not that much higher than the benefit package of the voluntary agency. Significantly, the higher income generated by a private practitioner—usually for less than a forty-hour workweek—compensates for any higher benefit costs. Pri-vate practice allows the professional woman an opportunity to demon-strate her competence in many more dimensions than does the traditional context of social work practice. For this quite positive reason, I suspect private practice will continue to be a popular career choice for female social workers.

The Corporate Sector

Perhaps no development in social welfare since the New Deal is as significant as the proliferation of for-profit human service corporations. Virtually nonexistent twenty years ago, human service corporations have prominent—if not dominant—positions in several human service mar-kets: nursing homes, hospital management, health maintenance orga-nizations, child care, home care, and, more recently, life care and corrections.[13] To get an idea of the magnitude of this development, consider this—in 1984 the annual revenues of the Hospital Corporation of America eclipsed all of the contributions to the United Way of Amer-ica—more than $2 billion. In 1985 Humana accomplished the same feat. Between 1981 and 1986 the number of human service corporations reporting annual revenues above $10 million increased from thirty-four to sixty-seven, practically doubling.

The corporate sector presents employment opportunities for social workers—particularly in the nursing home, home care, and child care industries—and a growing number of social workers are working for human service corporations. What potential this presents for unionizing social workers is unclear. This sector is relatively new by institutional standards, and little attention has been directed at organizing employees of human service corporations—at least as compared to other industrial sectors. Another factor is that none of these corporations specialize in social welfare *per se* (although that term is notoriously vague) and social workers in the corporate sector seem to function in an ancillary capacity to workers of other professions. Given these considerations, unionizing social workers makes sense within a context of organizing all employees of human service corporations.

Another instance of social workers entering the corporate sector is the rapid emergence of industrial social work as a practice specialization. Programmatically, industrial social work services are provided through Employee Assistance Plans (EAPs).[14] EAPs are even more recent than the human service corporations in American social welfare, so relatively little is known about them. Furthermore, since the concept is in its formative stage, what is known may not be a good predictor of how the idea will eventually become institutionalized.

EAPs exist in a variety of forms. Some are extensions of corporate personnel offices and function to enhance the adjustment of the employee to corporate structure and procedures. This type of EAP is understandably met with considerable suspicion by proponents of unionization since it smacks of employee control via another guise for the scientific management of workers. EAPs have also been established under union auspices, and in these cases, the EAP is more acceptable to unionists since it includes, at least, the capacity to advocate for employees, both individually and collectively. Many EAPs function under joint sponsorship of management and labor.

EAPs simulate the conditions closest to the trade union, as regards the prospect for organizing social workers. EAPs are associated with corporations large enough to make the expenditure of funds necessary to establish an EAP, and who possess the work force that is sufficiently large and troubled enough to justify its continuance. In EAPs social workers are consolidated within one unit—as opposed to other instances of corporate employment where they seem more dispersed. The central question about organizing social workers in an EAP is to what extent their services are essential to corporate operations.[15] So far, EAP advocates have made that case to the extent that the majority of Fortune 500 firms have established EAPs, but the inexpendability of any one EAP is another question. Corporations are free to subcontract for this service and probably would if an in-house EAP became too difficult to manage. A better case could be made for unionizing social workers who are a part of union-established EAPs. Even then, however, the question of effectiveness arises. If data are inconclusive about the usefulness of EAP services, why should a union support a costly EAP program any more than management would? Nevertheless, EAPs seem the best candidates for unionizing social workers in the private sector, although it is too early to make the argument conclusively. Clearer prospects in this regard will probably emerge in the future. If, as seems the case, the corporate sector is beginning to rationalize the delivery of human services—much as it had rationalized the production of industrial goods—then the prospect of unionizing social workers, among other human service workers, is bright indeed.

CONCLUSION

The private sector presents real prospects for unionizing social work-ers. In fact, considering the role of the private sector in American social welfare, the inhospitableness of public institutions toward the needs of professional social workers, and the expansion of employment oppor-tunities in private practice and the corporate sector, organizers of social workers are remiss in not focusing on employees of the private sector. From this perspective, privatization is less a phenomenon to be alarmed about, and more a development that presents new—if not ignored—opportunities for organizing.

So, what should be done? My suggestions are derived from the above discussion. These suggestions will probably differ from prescriptions for organizing that are derived from the ideology and history of the Amer-ican labor movement. Most of this incongruence is due to the transition from an industrial economy to a service economy, and the special re-quirements imposed by that transition.

First, organizers must find ways in which to make unions relevant to the experience of private-sector social workers. This is not particularly difficult to do, even though the methods and objectives may be at var-iance with those associated with the trade union movement. As noted earlier, social workers employed by nonprofit agencies and some in pri-vate practice have great difficulty obtaining adequate health and pension benefits through their work. For a relatively modest investment, estab-lished unions could gain the loyalty of many social workers by offering a good benefit package to voluntary-sector social workers.

Second, unions need to recognize the transformation in the work environment that is characteristic of the service sector, and assist social workers in developing work contexts more consistent with the needs of professionals and clients. The bureaucratic edifices of the industrial era, whether corporate or governmental, are inadequate structures for the human service sector of a postindustrial economy. If that is the case, unions could be instrumental in pioneering innovative service delivery organizations that better meet the needs of social workers, their clients, and the community. Several years ago I proposed an alternative model for mental health services—the Family Life Center—which met this re-quirement.[16] Following the logic that has generated Employee Stock Ownership Plans and other forms of worker ownership, it is tantalizing to speculate on the consequences of social workers owning the means of service delivery. With the recent exception of private practice, social workers have always worked under conditions established by others. The popularity of private practice suggests that this is no longer acceptable for younger professionals. I suspect that an organizational model in which social workers manage their own work—similar to a co-op—would be attractive to social workers.

It is unlikely that the governmental or corporate sectors would promote such a concept since it would compete with programs controlled by them. As a result, something of a vacuum exists at the community level, with voluntary sector agencies having to contend with the bureaucratic behemoths. I think unions could attract the support of community groups and social workers by helping the voluntary sector—or independent sector, as it is sometimes called—to become more competitive.

Third, unions need to approach professional associations of social workers and reach agreement on the complementarity of functions. Recently, unions and professional associations have not worked together. This is an error. While the full-status professions, such as medicine and law, have been able to use their professional associations very effectively, the semiprofessions—social work, nursing, and teaching—have been less successful in this regard. A distinguishing characteristic of the semiprofessions is that their professionals function within an organizational context controlled by others. Because a primary purpose of professional education is not to attain and maintain control over the delivery of professional services (but serve a clientele, instead), the professional associations of the semiprofessions have not placed a high priority on controlling the means of service delivery. Unions, on the other hand, understand this more clearly and act accordingly.

Another advantage for unions to work directly with a professional association of social workers is that these professional associations attract members, many of whom work in the nonprofit, governmental, and for-profit sectors. If unions want exposure to social workers across auspices of service delivery, professional associations provide that. As noted earlier, the fact that a professional is likely to work in more than one sector—and possibly all three during her career—raises a question of continuity of benefits. For unions to ignore this type of career mobility (a likelihood if assumptions about unionizing are derived from the trade union experience) is to be out of sync with social work as it is currently practiced. The easiest way to address the problem of career mobility for social workers is to work jointly with a professional association.

Fourth, unions need to pay attention to what happens in the corporate sector. To the extent the human service corporations expand, they will serve as natural sites for unionizing activity. As an illustration, workers for Kaiser-Permanente of California recently struck for job concessions.

Conceivably, workers in this sector may be better candidates for organizing than public sector workers. In fact, this possibility contains an irony: if employees of corporations are easier to organize, in part because they have the freedom and willingness to strike—a right denied public-sector workers—then privatization may, in the long run, enhance the prospects for unionizing human service workers.

With the exception of this last suggestion, these recommendations are closer to the idea of organizing than they are to unionizing in the conventional sense. If so, I suspect that is a concession necessitated by relevance. Professional social workers have not been attracted to traditional union appeals, and unions have lost influence for that reason. By now, it should be clear that other tactics are necessary. Unions must break into the professions if they are to remain influential social institutions. Social work—along with other semiprofessions—represents an opportunity for unions to broaden their membership base, but to attract social workers, unions will have to think creatively about the private sector of social welfare. If unions are willing to do that, privatization may symbolize not the demise of the union movement, but its transition into the postindustrial era.

NOTES

1. The Heritage Foundation has a reputation for advocating the sale of public commodities and facilities.

2. David Donnison, "The Progressive Potential of Privatisation," in Julian LeGrand and Ray Robinson, (eds.) *Privatisation and the Welfare State* (London: Allen and Unwin, 1984), pp. 45–57.

3. Mary Richmond, *Social Diagnosis* (New York: Russell Sage Foundation, 1917).

4. Howard Jacob Karger, *The Sentinels of Order: Social Control and the Minneapolis Settlement House, 1900–1950* (Latham, Maryland: University Press of America, 1987).

5. Allen F. Davis, *American Heroine: The Life and Legend of Jane Addams* (New York: Oxford University Press, 1973).

6. National Association of Social Workers, *Social Casework: Generic and Specific* (Washington, D.C.: 1974).

7. Harold Wilensky and Charles Lebeaux, *Industrial Society and Social Welfare* (New York: Macmillan, 1965).

8. Robert Barker, *Social Work in Private Practice* (Washington, D.C.: National Association of Social Workers, 1984).

9. F. D. Chu and S. Trotter, *The Madness Establishment* (New York: Grossman, 1974).

10. Michael Lipsky, *Street-Level Bureaucracy* (New York: Russell Sage Foundation, 1980).

11. Fred Wiseman, *Welfare* (Zipporah Films, 1974).

12. George Konrad, *The Caseworker* (New York: Harcourt, Brace, and Jovanovich, 1974).

13. David Stoesz, "Corporate Welfare," *Social Work*, 31 (July-August 1986).

14. Sheila Akabas, Paul A. Kurzman, and Nancy S. Koblen (eds.) *Labor and Industrial Settings: Sites for Social Work Practice* (New York: Council on Social Work Education, 1979); Martha Ozawa, "Development of Social Services in Industry," *Social Work* (November 1980); and Dale Masi, *Human Services in Industry* (Lexington, Mass.: D. C. Heath, 1982).

15. James T. Decker, Richard Starrett, and John Redhorse "Evaluating the Cost-Effectiveness of Employee Assistance Programs," *Social Work* 31 (September-October 1986).

16. David Stoesz, "The Family Life Center," *Social Work* 26 (September 1981).

9

Computer Technology and the Human Services

HOWARD JACOB KARGER
AND LARRY W. KREUGER

Neither professional associations nor public sector unions have systematically addressed the effects of technology on the social service workplace. Although some unions have confronted many of the ramifications of increased workplace computerization, little actual attention has been focused on the psychological and sociological affects of the current technological retooling in both public and private social services. This chapter will examine some of the psychological, sociological, and power relationships that characterize the new technology of the social service workplace.

An examination of the effects of computers in the social service workplace must be grounded in the present technology, and in the experiences of human service workers who encounter that technology. However, before looking at the consequences of technology in human services, several points should be noted.

For one, little research exists on the effects of computer technology on human perceptions, self-fulfillment, and human happiness. Furthermore, a dearth of research exists to show that technology deforms the human spirit. Most of what is known about the effects of technology is based on survey research of debatable generalizability, and on impressionistic observation.

Secondly, computer technology in the human service agency is not experienced in the same way by all subjects, and it is used differentially by various sectors of the social welfare network. The use of technology in social services run the gamut from the traditional nonautomated office where few, if any, machines are present, to the fully automated agency.

The traditional office relies on paperwork, verbal encounters, and informal relationships to establish communication. The semiautomated office is characterized by the use of one or two micro- or minicomputers which perform key work tasks. Although computers are used, the semiautomated office still relies on face-to-face office encounters for accomplishing work. On the other hand, the fully automated office is one where most communication occurs within an electronic network of micro-minis and mainframe computers, and where meaningful work is impossible to accomplish without the use of automated equipment.

Many, if not most, of the smaller private social welfare organizations are characterized by traditional or semiautomated office structures. Computers are used in these agencies for bookkeeping, scheduling, and word processing. For most of the professional human service staff the confrontation with computers is minimal and probably benign. However, for public-welfare social workers, especially income-maintenance workers, computer encounters often constitute a major part of their daily task environment.

Lastly, the relationship of staff to computers is mediated by the power and control the individual worker is able to exert on various applications of the technology. For example, social welfare administrators (who voluntarily use computers) may view that relationship with a greater sense of control because they have the power to turn the machine on and off at will. Their relationship to the computer is often one of dominance and subordination. In that sense, voluntary users of technology are likely to have the power to squelch the whirring of the motor on their own terms, and hence they perceive technology as a handmaiden and useful tool. Even if only an illusion, the willful user of computers exerts psychological control over the tool and its domain.

On the other hand, the involuntary user perceives the technology not as a subordinate entity to be used at will, but as an omnipresent force that monitors and controls work. To the involuntary user, the computer may be seen as a symbol of the encroachment of technology into the texture and fabric of work. For the income-maintenance worker in public welfare, who often has a caseload of 300, microcomputers can be a chain that binds them to a desk, demands their full attention, and unabatingly requires precision. Multiple methods for executing a task are discouraged—if not outrightly prohibited—by the unrelenting binary logic of software. Creativity is subordinated to precision and standardization, and the operator is transformed into an extension of the machine's logic. In the end, work is routinized, operations are formally codified and may become inflexible to the individual worker's preferences, and the creativity of the worker may be demeaned by the standardization in the form and content of work.

Forced to compete in the technological marketplace, the involuntary user faces an almost Sisyphean task. Even before the social worker masters the present technology, it may become virtually obsolete. Living in dread of a newer and more complex technology, the involuntary user is engrossed in a catch-up game. For many workers it is akin to a ring pull on a merry-go-round: just when they begin grasping the ring it is pulled farther away. Hence, the nontechnologically adroit worker often does not experience the same elation at confronting a new and more potent technology as the voluntary user. In fact, when forced to adopt a new technology the involuntary user often experiences vulnerability, dependence, and powerlessness.

To examine technology without locating it in a framework that bespeaks its political and organizational roots is to obfuscate rather than illuminate its hazards and potentialities. In short, the impact of technology is dependent upon the organizational and hierarchical context in which it is located. Although realizing that the major impact of technology is felt most acutely by the involuntary user, the remainder of the chapter will address the ramifications of computers for professional human-service workers who, for the most part, are involuntary users.

High technology manufacturers promote their products as saviours that will ultimately eliminate the drudgery of labor, rationalize organizational and administrative processes, and increase productivity. Most of the available materials emphasize the design and implementation of computer technology rather than its impact on workers and the overall environment of the workplace. Discussions revolve around bytes, drives, and modems, rather than on the psychological effects of technology and the potential displacement of the less technologically competent worker.

Moreover, an *a priori* assumption exists that technology is good, and people who question that supposition often face the opprobrium of their colleagues. The technological apostate is perceived as an unenlightened vestige of a time barely remembered, or, at best, an annoyance. The power of the technological elite (computer specialists, systems managers, and so on) lies in their ability to control the debate and cast it in their own terms: that is, efficiency and rationality.

PLAUSIBLE EFFECTS OF COMPUTER TECHNOLOGY ON HUMAN SERVICES

The computeristic distortion of time in the social service workplace leads to several unintended consequences. The temporal plasticity characteristic of human service interviews begins to appear as a badly managed slice of time. Wasted moments and the often desultory nature of interviews beg to be rationalized, and unstructured moments are perceived as needing to be filled with product.

Process in technology is a standardized series of routine assignments intended to accomplish a given task, with the process itself having only instrumental integrity. Hence, the belief in process becomes denigrated at the altar of production—process is a tangential activity in the world of computers and technology. In short, the world of computers is often a hostile and barren one for the process-oriented human service worker.

This emphasis on "product" can take the shape of behavioristic forms of treatment. In that sense, the process inherent in microcomputer technology determines, albeit indirectly, the shape of practice. The subtle power of the computer to shape perceptions and control the process of time clearly has unintended yet profound consequences for the human service profession.

The reliance on technology may also cause what Craig Brod calls "technostress." Brod's thesis is that users adapt to computers with either a fearful or ambivalent anxiety, or with a symbiotic relationship in which the user loses his or her capacity to relate to others. Brod's category of the "techno-centered" individual is one in which the user experiences an increase in factual thinking, has poor access to feelings, insists on efficiency and speed, lacks empathy, has a low tolerance for ambiguity and, in severe cases, exhibits aberrant and antisocial behavior coupled with an inability to think intuitively.[1]

Perhaps the most problematic issue is the tendency of computers to routinize tasks and thus center the intelligent aspects of a job inside the machine rather than the employee. Jobs may be broken down so that they require little training and, in the end, the denigration of mental labor results in de-skilling rather than increasing the currency of the social worker.

COMPUTERS AND THE IDEOLOGY OF SOCIAL SERVICES

Nurtured by technology, this idiographic perspective encourages the development of a technocratic ideology geared to processing raw materials more efficiently. Rooted in Max Weber's notion of *Zweckrationalitet*, this value-free administration often results in narrow technological considerations which override a richer assessment of crucial goals and the most appropriate means for achieving them.[2]

Technocratic ideology encourages the creation of a subcommunity of technologically oriented "insiders." Guided by instrumental reasoning, this group of technocrats control the information flow within the organization, establish *de facto* norms for performance, manipulate symbols and data, and help mold the organizational culture of the workplace. Highly placed technocrats increasingly function as the power behind the throne in many organizations.

Instrumental reasoning leads to instrumental relationships. When a worker is viewed as a cog in the wheel of rationality, and the goal of the workplace is to replicate the efficiency of machines, employees become expendable objects to be manipulated. The instrumentality of workplace interaction symbolizes the subordination of human relations to the needs of productivity: concern, respect, dignity, warmth, and appreciation become qualities to be manipulated in the quest for efficiency. Instrumental relationships also contribute to alienation, and to what Jurgen Habermas, in another context, calls the "structure of silence": an environment characterized by little active dialogue with the social structure, passive participation, and the loss of any preexistent democracy.[3]

Although it appears that computers exercise considerable influence on the nature of work, interorganizational relationships, the capacity of the agency to achieve goals and to manage available resources, and the composition of organizational power; what is unknown, however, is the intrinsic cost associated with its widespread use. Furthermore, benefits of computerization are clearer in terms of efficiency than effectiveness.

Labor unions have warned of the potential drawbacks of automation in terms of worker displacement and the resulting economic and social dislocation. Questions abound regarding the worker who lacks the technological skills to compete in the contemporary marketplace. Will technology be creating clients out of colleagues? In short, too little is known about the consequences of the current romance with computers.

HUMAN SERVICE WORKERS AND HUMAN CHOICES

The major problem for social workers may not result from the technology *per se*, but from the way it is manipulated to redesign work. Nevertheless, the reaction of human service workers to the technological imperative can take a multitude of forms. The subsequent choices, although stratified, present some perspectives that workers may adopt.

Rebellion

At the core of any internal organizational transaction (the distribution of sanctions, access to scarce resources, structural opportunities, and so forth) lies the concept of power and dependency. To the extent that office workers lack control over environmental pressures, their tasks are dependent upon those who manage the environment. According to Blau, power and dependency are on opposite sides of any transaction.[4] Those who suffer at the hands of technology are dependent upon those who control it. Lurking in the background, however, is the implicit threat of major structural alterations should the less powerful decide to revolt.

Rebellion can take many forms. On the covert side, rebellion may be expressed by an increase in the number of sick days, "blue Mondays," and subtle forms of passive-aggressive behavior. On the overt side, dissatisfaction may be expressed through efforts to collectively organize labor unions or worker organizations.

Accommodation

Lacking the means or opportunity to rebel, office personnel may give up hope of winning the technology battle. Worker concessions can take the form of outright resignation, with accompanying efforts to emotionally adjust by rationalizing the new technology. Accommodation to the inevitability of social change, and to the technological baggage that accompanies it, is by no means a recent phenomenon. Labor history is replete with attempts to manage the technical obsolescence of manual and cognitive skills. Subtle and not so subtle changes in office schedules, work loads, "down time," and numerous other adjustments fall under the category of accommodations.

Nihilism

Nihilism in human service organizations may be expressed as a conscious or unconscious belief that conditions in the organization are so reprehensible as to warrant destruction for its own sake. The destruction of the work environment can include technical sabotage of software or hardware (planting program bugs), oversights in the set-up or alignment of equipment, failure to follow rules of data storage, and so forth.

Demands for Constructive Change

Demands for constructive change may include employee demands for greater self-management, collective negotiation (such as collective bargaining) regarding the scope and intensity of office automation, and ongoing technical training. Demands for constructive change may be expressed through the formation of white collar unions.

Learning Survival Skills

Learning survival skills differs from accommodation by degree rather than category. The worker who learns survival skills has not resigned from the technical demands of the workplace but, as a conscious actor, has developed new modes for survival. Developing survival skills encompasses learning new technological skills to correctly anticipate trends, and developing the ability to assess and respond to technostress.

Survival skills include adjustments to new technology and to new forms of office conduct. For example, office humor is one form of adjustment that can soften the hard edge of the computer-dominated workplace.

Learning specialized "techno-skills" is an important ingredient in automation survival. Such skills include typing, knowledge of techno-terms (bytes, ROM/RAM, and so forth), accommodating automation schedules (such as when to print out a report), and learning to survive computer disasters by placing the blame on something (software bug, program glitch, or power surge) or someone else (poor training, poor upkeep, and so forth).

Another survival skill is the ability to correctly anticipate the direction of office automation. This includes moving early to acquire appropriate technical skills, thereby securing a position in the work-flow process which guarantees some control over new technology. Another techno-skill is learning to monitor, evaluate, and respond to various automation adjustments (technostress) in oneself and others. If Brod and others are correct, and computer interaction leads to a loss of relational skills, then human services are obliged to develop mechanisms for dealing with such stress.

STRATEGIES FOR DEALING WITH TECHNOLOGY

Some strategies for dealing with the effects of technology include:

1. Development (or discovery) of agency pockets of informal "*Gemeinschaft*-like" opportunities relatively free from bureaucratic intervention. During coffee breaks, at lunch, in the restroom, and during lulls in routine office work, individuals may find opportunities to interact on a more personal, "brute being" level. The development of such "technology-free" space should be encouraged.

2. Erving Goffman suggested that individuals function within a framework of "fronts" or interactive membranes that protect them from direct confrontation with others.[5] A front is that part of the self that the individual allows to come through. The individual may choose to hide behind a protective front or operate within the parameters of an "official self," while keeping intact much of what is really felt or believed. In effect, the individual controls his or her "presentation of self" to others and thus preserves a sense of personal autonomy. Such protective shields should be recognized as an important mechanism for the separation of self from technology.

3. Individuals likewise carry around an unseen yet real sense of "*Umwelt*," or a psychosocial space where personal security and feelings of well-being can develop.[6] The individual defines his or her "territory" which then functions as a moving bubble of security (desk space, bathroom stall, "safe distance," and so forth). The *Umwelt* should be viewed as a sacred boundary which ought not be invaded by technological gadgetry.

4. Technical specialists should be forced to speak in English-language sentences.

Moreover, technocrats should be charged with translating the nonordinary language of symbolic logic and technological argot into everyday office vernacular. The responsibility for presenting "technological subuniverses of meaning" to the rest of the world should appropriately be lodged with those who advocate for its utility.

5. The "Pareto optimum" should be enforced; namely, no policy, program, or office activity should be undertaken unless it can be demonstrated in advance to help at least one person and harm no one. If such an optimum condition cannot be guaranteed, then the proposed technological change should be delayed. A trial period for implementation of computer technology is one way to assure that the technology is appropriate and manageable.

6. All office workers affected by a decision to automate should be allowed to participate in the decision-making process. Advance notice should be given by management, and consultation with unions around computer issues should be required. To implement technological changes by administrative fiat is to further the development of monolithic office structures that concentrate power in the hands of a few technical specialists. It should be remembered that the common office citizenry wage the automation war, not the technological generals.

7. Office workers who participate in various hands-on automated activities should be provided additional medical insurance coverage for eye strain and related physical maladies associated with computer usage. Ergonomical office furniture, having proven benefits for posture, should be provided for all office workers, especially those bound to the sedentary office position associated with computer use.

8. Employees possessing insufficient technical skills should be given the choice to receive fully compensated technical training during working hours, or the opportunity to migrate to a nonautomated position providing equal pay or other remuneration.

CONCLUSION

Some "antitechnology" critics have characterized computers as having the power to determine their own future development. At best, that is magical thinking. Current technology is still in the service of human masters. The course of technology is therefore not determined by some internal machine logic or an axiom of science, but by the needs of the political, social, and economic system.

What is true for computer technology is also generally true for social service organizations. For example, through efficiently managing information, social services can help clients gain easier access to vital resources. Computer technology can also help the human service worker experience relief from the endless hours of case recording, filing, case retrieval, and so forth. Humane and client-centered evaluation programs can help caseworkers develop more refined skills and provide empirical evidence of the efficacy of given treatment modalities. Conversely, computerized information systems may allow client files to be accessed by agencies whose motives are dubious, and rigid evaluation programs may force caseworkers into fixed treatment modes.

Apart from mild questions regarding the impact of computer technology on the psychological and perceptual abilities of workers, professional social-work associations have remained mute on the issue. Although attempting to address some of the more egregious aspects of computer technology, union inquiries have exhibited a similar shallowness. For example, *Facing the Future: AFSCME's Approach to Technology* states that unions have demanded a variety of protection for employees who must operate computers, including frequent rest breaks, alternating computer work with other work, prohibition of work measurement, regular eye exams for VDT operators, training programs, and pay differentials and upgrading.[7]

Although valid, these union demands beg the larger issues surrounding the organization of work. Specifically, what are the perceptual and psychological consequences of constant interaction with machines rather than human beings? What is the effect of computers on the relations of power in the workplace? These and other questions must be asked if social workers and labor unions are to understand the ramifications of computers in the social service workplace.

Computer technology is only a small part of the growing trend toward the industrialization of human services. The following chapter will locate social work and technology in the larger framework of the industrial model of production.

NOTES

1. See Craig Brod, *Technostress: The Human Cost of the Computer Revolution* (Reading, Mass.: Addison-Wesley, 1984).

2. See for example, Stephen Alter, *Decision Support Systems: Current Practices and Continuing Challenges* (Lexington, Mass.: D. C.Heath, 1980); Gary Brewer, *Politicians, Bureaucrats and Consultants* (New York: Free Press, 1974); Thomas Collins, "Social Science Research and the Microcomputer," *Sociological Methods and Research*, 9 (May 1981), pp. 438–460; and Peter Keen and Michael S. Morton, *Decision Support Systems: An Organizational Perspectivel* (Reading, Mass.: Addison-Wesley, 1978).

3. See Jurgen Habermas, *Legitimation Crisis* (Boston: Beacon Press, 1975).

4. Peter Blau, *Exchange and Power in Social Life* (N.Y.: Wiley, 1964), p. 119.

5. Erving Goffman, *The Presentation of Self in Everyday Life* (Garden City, N.J.: Doubleday, 1959).

6. Erving Goffman, *Behavior in Public Places: Notes on the Social Organization of Gatherings* (N.Y.: Doubleday, 1963).

7. American Federation of State, County and Municipal Employees, *Facing the Future: AFSCME's Approach to Technology*, Washington, D.C.: AFSCME, 1984.

10

De-Skilling Social Workers: The Industrial Model of Production and the Delivery of Social Services

HOWARD JACOB KARGER

Professional social work associations and public sector unions have failed to adequately examine the effects of technology on the social service field. Social work organizations have often viewed technological schemes as heralding in a more professionalized form of social services, while traditional unionism has frequently viewed administrative technologies as being within the managerial purview of the employer. This situation has resulted in the unchecked development of technology with few external controls exerted on either methodology or overall goals.

The intent of this chapter is to examine the effects of the industrial model of production on the delivery of social services. Although the chapter will examine technology and systems rationalization, it will do so with the understanding that they are merely tools used in the service of the industrial model of production. In addition, the chapter will also explore the consequences of the industrial model of production on the work life of social workers. Lastly, the author will suggest some criteria to be used in the development of alternative measures of worker and agency productivity.

Stated simply, the thesis of this chapter is that when the industrial model of production is utilized in the social services, it produces an effect upon the client, worker, and agency which is damaging to the well-being of each. Moreover, overemphasis on the quantitative aspects of production forces social services to adopt an industrial model of production in which the accepted measure of success is not the quality of services provided, but the number of people processed.

SOCIAL SERVICES, FUNDERS, AND TECHNOLOGY

Technological management of the social service workplace is rooted in the industrial age of rationality and efficiency. Attempts at rationalizing social services are not a recent phenomenon. Movements toward efficiency were visible as early as the Charity Organization Society (COS), which was created to rationalize the nascent social welfare complex. The COS emphasis on rationality was further refined when principles of Taylorism were adapted to the social welfare establishment. A strong division of labor, specialization of task and function, and bureaucratic and hierarchical systems of management were well entrenched in the social services by the middle 1920s.[1] In short, social service technology did not arise out of a vacuum, but out of a set of historical circumstances both indigenous to the profession and embedded within the overall structure of modernity.

Nonetheless, demands for greater system rationality have increased over the last fifteen years. This pressure has been fueled by a combination of inflation and recession, a dwindling of fiscal resources earmarked for social welfare, the intense competition for capital between the social welfare state and the military-industrial complex, a growing feud with the corporate sector over taxation, and federal deficit spending that has reached catastrophic proportions.

Concomitant with fiscal austerity is an apparent increase in job dissatisfaction among private- and public-agency social workers, many of whom are reporting severe problems in relation to "burnout" and low agency morale.[2]

Perhaps not surprisingly, this job dissatisfaction comes on the heels of the adoption of highly sophisticated management technologies including scientific management (such as management by objectives or goal attainment scaling), attempts at greater quantification of client/worker contact hours, a plethora of designs used to evaluate and measure how worker time is spent, and so forth. Given the recent fiscal constraints in both public and private social welfare agencies, it can be expected that greater economic rationalization through increased technological monitoring, downward reclassifying of social work positions, and the general diminution of social work jobs constitute a likely future scenario.[3]

The response of many social welfare managers to diminished funding has focused on the development of more sophisticated technologies. Before continuing, however, a definition of technology is useful. Charles Perrow defines technology as

the actions that an individual performs upon an object, with or without the aid of tools or mechanical devices, in order to make some change in that object. The object, or "raw material," may be a living being, human or otherwise, a symbol, or an inanimate object. People are raw materials in people changing or people processing organizations; symbols are materials in banks, advertising agencies, and some research organizations; the interactions of people are raw materials to be manipulated by administrators in organizations; boards of directors, committees, and councils are usually involved with the changing or processing of symbols and human interactions, and so on.[4]

For our purposes, technology will be defined as "how the work is done"; that is, the machinery (computers), software, styles and philosophies of management, and the general design, organization, and execution of agency work.

The engine that drives technology is the desire to cut costs, specifically the costs of labor. The savings for the agency, organization, or industry is established through increasing both the scale and intensity of production. Utilizing technology optimally results in higher productivity—an increase in the qualities produced. (In human service organizations the "quantity" produced is the number of clients processed.) The overall goal of human service technology is to process more (or the same amount) of clients at the lowest cost.

Standardizing the mode of production requires that raw materials be perceived in a normative fashion. Clients and workers must therefore have attributes that are dependable (whether or not that is the case in reality), there must be a prescribed notion of the role of each, and exceptions to the production process must be overlooked or rejected. In short, the production process must be normative for the system to achieve any kind of rationalization. Perrow makes a similar argument:

Techniques are performed upon raw materials. The state of the art of analyzing the characteristics of the raw materials is likely to determine what kind of technology will be used. (Tools are also necessary, of course, but by and large, the construction of tools is a simpler problem than the analysis of the nature of the material and generally follows the analysis.) To understand the nature of the material means to be able to control it better and achieve predictability and efficiency in transformation. We are not referring here to the "essence" of the material, only the way the organization perceives it to be.... The other relevant characteristic of the raw material, besides the understandability of its nature, is its stability and variability; that is, whether the material can be treated in a standardized fashion or whether continual adjustment to it is necessary. Organizations uniformly seek to standardize their raw material in order to minimize exceptional situations. This is the point of de-individualizing processes found in military academies, monasteries and prisons, and the superiority of the synthetic shoe material Corfam over leather.[5]

THE DE-SKILLING OF SOCIAL WORKERS

The values, philosophy and culture of social work are at odds with the values of technological rationalization. Specifically, social work places a high premium on human interaction and process, is labor-intensive, and has a nonlinear view of the world.

When complex technology pays little attention to the "terrain" (the actual work duties) of social services, social work skills become devalued, and the professional currency of social workers is diminished.

Technocrats attempt to conform the production process to fit the strengths and needs of a particular technology. Therefore, social welfare technologies will try to conform social work practice into a system that can be rationalized, measured and evaluated. For example, if a particular quantitative methodology is effective, social work must become quantitative in its orientation. Because evaluative criteria are inherent in the technology, if social work fails in its quantitative goals (for example, numbers of people receiving service), it is evaluated as ineffective. In that sense, the technology determines the practice and the tail wags the dog. The confusion about means and ends rigidifies social work practice, and in the end, the engine that drives social work becomes evaluative technology rather than the other way around.

In order to fully utilize the quantitative strength of human service technologies, human interactions must be reduced as much as possible into quantifiable terms. (The strength of technology lies in measuring the product and not the terrain of social service.) The net result of human service technologies is that the criteria for determining success are removed from the control of the social worker, and, subsequently, placed within the domain of the technology. Through its emphasis on efficiency—a view of efficiency tied to quantity rather than quality—technology attempts to replace labor power for less costly machine power. Moreover, it is easier to measure the productivity of machines than humans because machine production is usually more constant.[6]

Social service technology fits under the aegis of industrial production in several other important ways. Both industrial and social agency production demand standardization of the raw materials of production (client and workers).[7] Utilizing the industrial model of production forces a nonroutinized type of work (social work in this case) into a routinized and standardized framework. For example, the objective of operations research, at least as used in social work, is to develop an unobstructed and continuous assembly-line process devoid of organizational and production obstacles. Contrary to Hage and Aiken, the development of an assembly-like process is clearly applicable to social service organizations.[8] In short, the principle inherent in routinized work tasks suggests that if clients are stable and uniform, and if much is known about the process of treatment, a routine work flow will follow.[9,10]

Routinization exacerbates the division of labor and locates the agency's decision-making functions within an insulated context. If a job is made routine, the worker can only made decisions related to a small task. (In order for tasks to be routine, they must be particular, specific, and measurable.) Moreover, the more routine the task the less the worker knows about the overall functioning of the agency, and, thus, is not well enough informed to have significant input into agency decisions. The enforced ignorance of the workers allows them to remain in a passive and compliant state. Even within the context of their routinized task, workers may not be allowed to control the decision-making aspects of their job. Thus, routinized tasks allow for a division of labor that centralizes decision making within an administrative cadre and attempts, albeit often unconsciously, to relegate the worker to a world of organizational impotence.

Unique problems arise when routinized tasks are introduced into the social service field. According to Eliot Friedson, professionalism is the quality of being free, self-directed and autonomous.[11] A professional regulates his or her work. Conversely, an occupation that cannot direct or control the production and application of knowledge and skill to the work it performs is not a profession.[12] The routinization of social service delivery is problematic for the social worker who, as a result of educational dogma, believes professionalism to be a central mandate of social work. Friedson sums up the dilemma:

It has been felt by many writers that the worker, as well as the client, suffers from the bureaucratization of production by a monocratic administration. Lacking identification with the prime goals of the organization, lacking an important voice in setting the formal level and direction of work, and performing work which has been so rationalized as to become mechanical and meaningless, the worker functions as a minute segment of an intricate mosaic of specialized activities which he is in no position to perceive or understand, and is said to be alienated.[13]

As a consequence of the technological mandate to increase efficiency, productivity, and profits, the tasks of workers must be reduced to simple routines approximating the logic of machine production. Workers become transformed from competent individuals into machine-like components which possess only the most basic knowledge of their work environment. These workers become defined as mere "factors of production." This expropriation of knowledge removes workers from the essence of dignity and worth and completes their transformation into marketable and replaceable commodities.[14] Social work practice—through the exigencies of technology—must therefore become specialized, its tasks mechanized, and its final mission made more fully automatic.[15]

"Decomplexifying" social work skills allows less qualified people to operate social services. Hence, with the downward reclassification of social work positions, the trivialization of social work becomes more widespread. Technology demands component parts that it can measure, and in the glow of technology's preeminence, what was formerly a skill (insight, empathy, and so forth) becomes an anachronism of pretechnology. The caseworker whose skill is ill-defined in the terms used by technocrats is subordinated to the skilled technician who can measure behavioral change. Because technology must measure and what is not quantifiable cannot be measured, behavioral change must become the sole barometer of effective casework.[16] Insight that cannot be measured is extraneous to the technology, and, hence, cannot be included in most rigorous evaluative strategies.

When a sophisticated technology does not pay attention to the organization of social work, and when that technology is mastered by only a few, severe dislocation and stratification occur in the workplace. In particular, social service technocrats oversee social workers who cannot compete in the technological arena. Thus, the preexisting relations of power become transformed into a stratified system of power relationships in which the new technocrats lord over what has become the lower echelons of the profession. In effect, less technologically adept social workers operate under orders from their technocratic managers. The value of social workers, and their ability to decide on the fundamental questions that affect their practice, are diminished in light of the new power relationships resulting from the new technology.

The adoption of complex managerial techniques leads to the importation of technologically trained non-social work managers (MPAs or MBAs). This importation often results in the colonialization of social work by other professions. These managers, who try to produce cost-efficient, productive, and rational services, often have little understanding of the terrain of social work practice.

A profession which no longer values its practitioners becomes de-developed. With its valued talent imported, and little place to export its professionals, social work reduces itself to an economic colony of other disciplines. In effect, social work imports its masters and trains their subordinates. Furthermore, many social workers fit neither the old way that is disappearing nor the new way for which they are not trained. With only their labor to exchange, professional social workers are threatened with economic obsolescence. Unless social workers can work more cheaply or gain new high-technology skills, they will become subordinated to inferior work roles. Unfortunately, social work curricula are already bursting and have little room for more high-technology skills without compromising the "knowledge of the terrain."

The technological cycle effects the superfluousness of social workers who possess interpersonal skills. In effect, these social workers form an underclass in the high-technology social-welfare field. Finally, the de-

valuation of the skilled line worker leads to lower wages and the proletarianization of social workers.

Because technology builds on itself, and increasingly more technology
is needed to be competitive, the cycle of de-development grows more
widespread. Each new technological advancement means that greater
numbers of social workers are disenfranchised, and, for many, they are
made obsolete. In short, every new development requiring complex technological skills drives a nail deeper into the coffin of the traditional
relations of power in the social work profession.

The de-skilling cycle nears completion when the worker doubts and
finally devalues his or her own skills. With that devaluation comes a
subsequent decline in self-concept and a diminution in the purpose of
work. Work becomes labor and labor, alienated work.[17] The worker who
was active now becomes passive, and he or she who was once a subject
is now an object. In other words, technology dissolves the labor process
as one conducted by workers and reconstitutes it as a process conducted
by management.[18]

The cycle of de-skilling is completed when the trivialization of social
work becomes a reality. At the core of this trivialization is the devaluation
of the social worker's capital and the reduction of social work skills into
mechanical operations.

The technological mandate is enforced by the agency and, often, by
the profession itself. Resistance to the technological imperative is pun-
ished either through repudiation or agency sanction. In any case, the
refusal to capitulate engenders substantial risks. The transformation of
social workers into mere factors of production is antagonistic to work;
it violates the human conditions necessary for work and produces alienation through the mindlessness of routine tasks.

RECOMMENDATIONS

The rationalization of social work is evident in social work practice
and administration. Moreover, rationalization is a fact of life and will,
in all likelihood, become a permanent fixture of social work. Rationalization has both benefits and penalties; however, while the benefits have
long been extolled, the penalties remain underexamined. Although not
exhaustive, the following recommendations suggest a direction for the
rationalization of social services:

1. The notion of productivity must be reassessed. Productivity for its own sake
   must be discarded; in its place should be a reconstituted form of production
   located within in a human context. Productivity must be redefined to reflect
   the best interests of clients and workers, and alternative means of measurement and evaluation must be created.

Technology appropriate for the social welfare field must be developed and utilized. Utilization of appropriate technology presupposes the need to redefine efficiency in human rather than technological terms. This redefinition of efficiency hinges on reevaluating the goals of social service, because efficiency is nothing more than a measurement of predetermined goals.

Social service planning should be based on the needs of workers and clients and flow from a humanistic framework rather than a machine-like notion of productivity. This assumes a thorough assessment of the needs of workers and the creation of an alternative ideology around the role of work in modern life.

In order to create appropriate technological assessments, a "regional" approach must be devleoped to evaluate the various sectors (for example, child welfare or mental health) of the profession. Each "region" must then develop its own specific forms of technology that evaluate its locality (practice area of social work, such as casework, group work, and so on). The idea that one evaluative technology can be used across the board is not only misleading, but, in the end, will compromise the profession. Attempts to homogenize the terrain by superimposing a nonindigenous technology will only make it appear ineffective.

2. Social service organizations need less mechanistic practice models and more humane and democratic organizational forms. Hierarchical organizations which pit worker against supervisor and center decision making on a select few must be replaced by more collegial work formats that allow for greater initiative and worker control.

3. Social service technology should be easily understood by those who will be expected to implement it. This does not mean using only rudimentary and crude forms of technology, but, instead, using forms of technology that can be mastered by practitioners with social work training. Undoubtedly, even middle-range technology may necessitate the moderate retraining of some social service personnel. Technologies must also be flexible and open to input by social work personnel. Lastly, new technologies must by dynamic and easily altered to the conditions of social work practice.

CONCLUSION

This chapter has attempted to show the consequences of the use of inappropriate technology in the social welfare field. Primary among those consequences is the de-skilling of social workers and the devaluation of the social work profession. Choices regarding the use and development of technology are unavoidable, and demands for the accountability of social services are omnipresent. While technological choices must be made, the criteria for those decisions must be carefully scrutinized. As part of those deliberations, new criteria must be developed which are based on notions of effectiveness grounded in the human dimension of work rather than in a machine-like view of efficiency.

Professional social-work associations have not systematically addressed the issue of workplace technology. When the issues are discussed, it is often in the context of applauding the increased efficiency associated with technological gains. Furthermore, because at least some of the members of professional associations are technologically oriented administrators, a debate becomes problematic. What could therefore be a promising ground for a dialogue between unions and social work associations is all but nonexistent. Moreover, if pushed, the position of social work associations might well be antithetical to that of unions.

In an optimistic scenario, professional social-work associations and public sector unions could help develop humane and democratic social-service technologies that could become a potent force in changing the face of social welfare services in the United States.

NOTES

1. Roy Lubove, *The Professional Altruist* (N.Y.: Atheneum, 1975).

2. See, for example, Srinika Jayaratne and Wayne E. Chess, "Job Satisfaction, Burnout, and Turnover: A National Study," *Social Work*, 29 (September/October 1984), pp. 442–452; Herbert Freudenberger, "Staff Burnout," *Journal of Social Issues*, 30 (Winter 1974), pp. 459–465.

3. On the relationship of declassification to the future of social service, see Peter J. Peccora and Michael J. Austin, "Declassification of Social Service Jobs: Issues and Strategies," *Social Work*, 28 (November/December 1983), pp. 421–426; and H. Jacob Karger, "Reclassification: Is There a Future in Public Welfare for Trained Social Worker?" *Social Work*, 28 (November/December 1983), pp. 427–434.

4. Charles Perrow, "A Framework for the Comparative Analysis of Organizations," *American Sociological Review* 32 (April 1967), p. 195.

5. Ibid., p. 196.

6. For a fuller description of the proclivity of machines to replace labor, see Lewis Mumford's "The Mechanical Routine" in Eric and Mary Josephson's *Man Alone* (New York: Dell Publishers, 1962), pp. 114–122.

7. Perrow, "A Framework for the Comparative Analysis of Organizations," p. 196.

8. See Jerald Hage and Michael Aiken, "Routine Technology, Social Structure, and Organizational Goals," in Yeheskel Hasenfeld and Richard A. English, (eds.), *Human Service Organizations* (Ann Arbor: University of Michigan Press, 1974), p. 298.

9. Routinized tasks are similar to what Eugene Litvak refers to as uniformity of tasks. See "Models of Bureaucracy Which Permit Conflict," in Hasenfeld and English, (eds.), *Human Service Organizations*, passim.

10. Ibid., p. 419.

11. Eliot Freidson, "Dominant Professions, Bureaucracy, and Client Services," in William R. Rosengren and Mary Leyton, (eds.), *Organizations and Clients: Essays in the Sociology of Service* (Columbus, Ohio: Charles E. Merrill Publishing Company, 1970), p. 74.

12. Ibid., p. 75.

13. Ibid., p. 81.

14. Although not directly related to social work practitioners, David Gil provides an interesting assessment of the violence inherent in the workplace. See David G. Gil, "Reversing Dynamics of Violence by Transforming Work," *Journal of International and Comparative Social Welfare*, 1 (Fall 1984), p. 7.

15. While not directly related to social work, Mumford gives an interesting analysis of the criteria for machine technologies. Mumford, in *Man Alone*, p. 118.

16. A good example of an exaggerated position in the technological debate can be seen in Walter Hudson's "First Axioms of Treatment," *Social Work* 23 (January 1978), p. 65. Hudson maintains that "if you cannot measure the client's problem, it does not exist." The second corollary states that "if you cannot measure the client's problem, you cannot treat it."

17. For an analysis of the symptoms and causes of alienation in public welfare, see Howard J. Karger, "Burnout as Alienation," *Social Service Review* 55 (June 1981), pp. 271–283.

18. Stanley Aronowitz, *False Promises* (N.Y.: McGraw Hill, 1973).

IV

ETHICS, STRUGGLE, ANTIUNIONISM, AND THE FUTURE

11

Social Workers and Unions: Ethical Dilemmas

FREDERIC G. REAMER

Social workers have been active in the world of work since the earliest days of the profession. Precedents set by the welfare secretaries of the early twentieth century have led over the years to the full-fledged emergence of industrial social work as a specialty within the profession. Today, social workers occupy a variety of visible positions in the world of work, as union officials and in union- or management-sponsored employee assistance programs (EAPs), personnel and corporate social responsibility departments, training and affirmative action offices, and human resource units. They may function primarily as clinicians, administrators, trainers, advocates, organizers, planners, or researchers.

Certainly social workers' involvement in the world of work has changed dramatically during the profession's years. During some periods—notably during the 1930s and 1940s—there have been especially close ties between social workers and organized labor. Over time, however, the relationship has changed. As a group, social workers are less directly involved in union affairs and the labor movement. The focus has shifted toward the delivery of social services and to personnel matters. Along with other areas of the profession, in recent years, social work in industrial settings has moved from a preoccupation with issues of rights and social justice toward clinical and direct practice issues.

The diverse functions performed by contemporary social workers in the world of work represent more than an impressive display of technical talent related to counseling, case management, administration, labor relations, organizing, and so on. They also represent a wide range of occasionally conflicting assumptions about the fundamental aims and mission of the profession. To some, social workers employed by multi-national corporations to counsel troubled employees serve as handmaidens to and apologists for harsh, profit-driven capitalist entities, thus contravening the central values of social work. From this perspective, social workers should seek instead to liberate workers from the intoxicating control of mercenary corporations, not to mend them to better serve their masters' purposes. Social work should be aligned with labor and the proletariat, both practically and ideologically.

For others, social workers are obligated to acknowledge realistically the nature of the world in which we live: people need work, business and industry offer it, and it is therefore important for social workers to help the parties involved in this joint enterprise to function smoothly. Social workers may contribute by counseling, training, promoting affirmative action, and the like. From this vantage point, the aims of business and social work are compatible.

Clearly, an examination of the status of social work in business and industrial settings cannot overlook such critical value issues. Ultimately, they provide the foundation for the professional goals we embrace, but such value preferences also have important practical significance. Conflicting aims eventually convert into conflicting duties.

The value conflicts encountered by social workers in the world of work are largely a function of the duties they perform. For instance, a social worker who provides services to union members in an employee assistance program may face hard choices concerning the confidentiality of information about a seriously impaired worker. A social worker active in union affairs may have to make difficult choices concerning strikes and picket lines that may jeopardize clients' welfare. A social worker employed in a corporation's personnel division may be involved in difficult ethical choices concerning layoffs, plant closings, or affirmative action.

Below I will examine these value and ethical choices and discuss their implications for social workers. I will focus especially on social workers' "divided loyalties" to clients, employers, and the general public (that is, confidentiality and "whistle blowing" in the work setting), and on social workers' involvement in strikes and related social action. I will conclude with a discussion of the relevance of ethical theory to the variety of value choices social workers face in the world of work.

DIVIDED LOYALTIES

Every practitioner with formal social-work training has been imbued with the time-honored belief that one's principal duty is to clients. The prescription is the centerpiece of the profession, and the mandate seems clear: protect and advance the client's interests, above all else.

However, as every seasoned professional knows, the mandate is blurred around the edges. On occasion, the practitioner must wrestle with competing interests presented by one's employers, other clients, and members of the public at large.

Some settings are more complicated than others. For example, social workers in military, correctional, and industrial settings share a common dilemma: Who is the client, and to whom is one primarily loyal? Clinical social workers in these settings generally use the same professional skills as their counterparts in family service agencies, mental health centers, and private practice, yet along with their paychecks comes at least a tacit assumption that the ends of the organization are to be served as well. These social workers are employed to assist those whose lives are somehow troubled, but they are also expected to recognize that their service is intended to advance their employers' interests, interests that may clash with those of their individual clients.[1]

The social worker in industrial settings confronts divided loyalties in a variety of ways. As employee assistance counselors in management-sponsored programs, they sometimes find themselves caught between their commitment to assist clients confidentially, and subtle or explicit expectations by management that social workers will share critical information germane to a worker's performance. As Dale A. Masi observes, "Confidentiality is more of an issue in the workplace than in a community mental health clinic or social agency because of the uniqueness of the host setting. Competition for jobs, as well as an environment that does not necessarily understand employees' personal problems, mandate a clearly defined and enforced confidentiality policy."[2] Fortunately, managers now generally accept the reality that social workers must be able to ensure workers of confidentiality; violations of confidentiality are rare indeed.[3]

Special problems related to worker confidentiality and privacy arise when there is the possibility of harm to third parties. Social workers are well aware of the stringent requirement that client rights to privacy are paramount, and that according to the National Association of Social Workers (NASW) Code of Ethics, confidential information should be shared with others, without the client's consent, "only for compelling professional reasons."[4]

Although there is no precise definition of "compelling professional reasons," it is widely accepted that in extreme circumstances—such as when a client poses a serious threat of violence to a third party—confidentiality may be breached. The precedent-setting case of *Tarasoff vs. Regents of the University of California* established the professional's obligation to take steps to protect third parties in such instances.[5]

The employee assistance counselor needs to be aware of the limitations *Tarasoff* and other legal regulations (such as mandatory reporting laws concerning child abuse and neglect) place on confidential information shared by workers (for example, when a worker reveals plans to injure a third party, such as a spouse, child, or fellow worker). This circumstance can be faced by any social worker, regardless of setting.

Social workers in industrial settings occasionally face another, unique predicament. In these instances an employee brings to a social worker's attention wrongdoing within the organization that constitutes a threat to public safety. A social worker may be privy to confidential information about fraud, abuse, misrepresentation, or safety.

Typically the worker faces a painful choice between virtuous disclosure or malfeasance and silence. Many employees know that whistle-blowers sometimes suffer mightily because of their moral instincts. They run the risk of being fired, transferred, harassed, and ostracized. Their motives may be questioned and their reputations sullied. The applause and appreciation received from colleagues who admire courage, decency, and candor may pale in comparison to the scars incurred by the honorable disclosure. Vincent Barry presents the dilemma succinctly:

Truthfulness, non-injury, and fairness are the ordinary categories of obligations that employees have to third parties, but we can still ask: How are workers to reconcile obligations to employers or organizations and others? Should the employee ensure the welfare of the organization by reporting the fellow worker using drugs, or should she be loyal to the fellow worker and say nothing? Should the secretary carry out her boss's instructions, or should she tell his wife the truth? Should the accountant say nothing about the building code violations, or should she inform authorities? In each case the employee experiences divided loyalties. Resolving such conflict calls for a careful weighing of the obligations to the employer or firm, on the one hand, and of those to the third party, on the other. This process is never easy.[6]

There is an added complication for the employee-assistance social worker in whom such a confidence has been placed, especially if the social worker's client has decided not to blow the whistle. In addition to the choice between loyalty to the firm and protection of third parties, the social worker must also factor in the obligation as to what to treat as confidential information.

Employee-assistance social workers caught in such a bind at times conclude that their only choice revolves around either silence or full-scale whistle blowing. Such is rarely the case, however. By now there is considerable consensus that such troublesome decisions need to be approached deliberately, incrementally, and cautiously. Careful consideration must be given to the whistle-blower's motives, the use of internal mechanisms to resolve the matter, the quality of available evidence, and the likelihood that whistle blowing will be effective.[7] In most instances there are intermediate options, although ultimately bold whistle blowing may be necessary.

The employee-assistance social worker's approach to ethical choices related to privacy, confidentiality, and whistle blowing is likely to be affected by his or her own employment status. A social worker employed by a corporation to supply in-house services to its employees may feel some pressure, subtle or otherwise, to have fairly loose standards regarding the confidentiality of information shared by workers. After all, the argument goes, management runs the show. As such, management hires the social worker, and it has a right to know when an employee's private troubles (such as substance abuse or poor mental health) may detrimentally affect the corporation. In this respect, the employee-assistance social worker's bind is not significantly different from that of the military or prison social worker. In addition to careful editing of verbal communications, in-house employee-assistance social workers also need to ensure the confidentiality of records. Measures need to be taken to restrict access to file cabinets, computer-based records, reports, and so on. Strict guidelines ought to govern the extent to which management (especially personnel departments) have access to information about employees.

The problem of management pressure tends to be less severe when corporations contract with independent agencies to provide employee-assistance services. Even here, however, there are no guarantees. Staffs of independent social service agencies have an understandable incentive to please corporate management. Future contracts may depend on it. Nonetheless, employee assistance workers must be diligent in their efforts to uphold their principal obligation to their clients. This problem of social worker as "double agent" is least severe when employee-assistance services are sponsored directly by unions.[8]

Although it is tempting to conclude that union-sponsored services minimize these hazards, we must also acknowledge the dilemma they introduce. Unions also face the prospect of offering mixed messages to members when they assume some responsibility for their personal problems. As Leroy Johnson observes in his discussion of union-sponsored alcoholism services: "A unilateral program puts the union in a conflict of interest position. On the one hand the traditional role is defending the member from job action discipline, but at the same time the leadership is engaged in establishing the program of performance monitoring and exercising of discipline."[9]

SOCIAL WORKERS AND JOB ACTION

Strike votes rarely take place without considerable angst. There is the inevitable push-and-pull of job security, benefits, personal disruption, company loyalty, and principle. The clash of interests arises whether one screws bolts into new automobiles, answers a telephone, drives a delivery truck, or catches footballs for a living.

For social workers, along with other professionals who provide human services, there is a special burden. Social workers are in the business of serving others, and there is a widespread assumption in the profession that one's professional obligations to clients ordinarily should take precedence over personal interests. The NASW Code of Ethics is clear and concise: "The social worker's primary responsibility is to clients."[10]

As a result, a chronic tension exists in the profession. As union members, social workers periodically face difficult choices at the point of a strike vote. As colleagues of members of other unions, social workers must periodically decide whether to support job actions by refusing to cross picket lines.

The dilemma is particularly troublesome for public-sector social workers and social workers in settings that provide critical services, such as health care. The debate is old, yet it persists because of its intractability. Moreover, while the arguments are familiar, they are hardly hackneyed. From one vantage point, social workers are public servants and thus occupy positions of trust and obligation. It would be unconscionable for social workers to betray the poor, mentally ill, infirm, abused, and neglected in order to advance their own interests. Granted, their claims may be legitimate, but, like police officers and fire fighters, the job comes with certain strings attached—strikes are not acceptable.

Critics, on the other hand, argue that social workers are particularly vulnerable to abuse. The presumption of altruism invites managers to take advantage of social workers' benevolent instincts. To counter such temptation, social workers must retain the right to strike, even if they are not always taken seriously. According to Victor Gotbaum—then Executive Director, District Council 37 of the American Federation of State, Council, and Municipal Employees, AFL-CIO, the largest union of municipal employees in the nation—the right to strike may actually enhance labor relations.

We need the possibility of a strike. Take what I call the Red China experience. When the Red Chinese did not have the atom bomb, they were the most militant and irresponsible of sovereign states. They wanted Russia to invade the United States; they were flexing their nonexistent muscles. But as soon as they got the bomb, the Chinese became much more responsible, because they could also create havoc. The same thing happens with workers.[11]

Social workers have always struggled to reconcile their principal concern about clients' welfare and their right (or need, perhaps) to strike. Bertha Reynolds acknowledged the conflict decades ago, when she con-

cluded that "in the history of unionization in social work it is impossible
to separate the two notions of protecting one's own condition as a worker
and safeguarding the right to treat clients ethically."[12]

Clearly, social workers are ambivalent about striking. Ronald H. Bohr,
Herbert I. Brenner, and Howard M. Kaplan report on social workers'
reactions to a work stoppage by psychiatric aides in a large metropolitan
state hospital in Pennsylvania.[13] Social work staff were evenly divided as
to whether they should have joined the walkout. Helen Rehr found a
similar split in social workers' reactions to a strike of nonprofessional
workers at Mount Sinai Hospital in New York City;[14] half the staff remained on the job while the other half refused to cross the picket line.[15]
Similar disagreement prevailed during a second strike at Mount Sinai
Hospital twenty-five years later.[16] Ernie S. Lightman also reports considerable variation in social workers' opinions about the legitimacy of a
strike. In his survey of a sample drawn from the Metropolitan Toronto
branch of the Ontario Association of Professional Social Workers, Lightman found that over half (53 percent) of the respondents disagreed with
the statement, "Social workers provide an essential service [that] should
not be interrupted by a strike."[17] Twenty-nine percent agreed with the
statement, and 18 percent were uncertain. As Lightman notes, "Such a
conflictual and power-based approach toward decision making sits un-
comfortably with many social workers who prefer to believe that good
faith and reasoned interchange can resolve any work-related problem.
At the same time, conflict and power do not fit easily with many traditional social work values."[18]

Although social workers tend to feel uncomfortable with the prospect
of a strike, many are able to justify it is a last resort, especially if the
principal aim is to enhance the quality of care made available to clients.
For example, Lightman found that while only 50 percent of his sample
of Toronto-area social workers would consider striking to enhance fringe
benefits, 86 percent would consider striking to enhance quality of service
for clients.[19] Even NASW, through its Ad Hoc Committee on Advocacy,
has acknowledged the possibility that extreme measures, which may
harm clients in the short run, may be necessary to ensure quality care
in the long run: "To what extent does one risk injury to his clients'
interests in the short run on behalf of institutional changes in the long
run? . . . One cannot arbitrarily write off any action that may temporarily
cause his clients hardship if he believes the ultimate benefits of his action
will outweigh any initial harm."[20] In its Personnel Standards, NASW
explicitly opposes "laws or policies that prohibit strikes by employees."[21]

SOCIAL WORK AND SOCIAL ACTION

Social workers in industrial settings face several additional ethical issues related to the social action aims of the profession. The first concerns

the persistent and troubling debate concerning affirmative action principles. Social workers are bound by their Code of Ethics to prevent and eliminate discrimination. Belief in the need to promote and protect the rights of minority and oppressed individuals is one of the central tenets of the profession.

However, social workers, along with the general citizenry, seem quite divided about the merits of affirmative action. Arguments on both sides of the issue seem compelling, and thus divide the profession.

The arguments in favor of affirmative action in hiring reduce to the following: affirmative action is necessary in order to right past wrongs, compensate those who have been affected (or their descendants), and ensure that discriminatory practices do not continue. In contrast, critics argue that affirmative action constitutes reverse discrimination against contemporary majorities, requires that they compensate wronged individuals who may not be alive, encourages the hiring and retention of less qualified or unqualified individuals, encourages conflict among employees, and in the end, is demeaning, insulting, and paternalistic.[22]

The debate is complex, controversial, and evolving. It certainly will not be settled in these pages. Social workers active in union affairs and personnel departments must continually examine the merits of prevailing views on affirmative action and their consistency with traditional social work values. The answers will not come easily.

The challenge is somewhat less daunting with respect to the issue of comparable worth. Social workers generally embrace the need for significant changes in pay scales for men and women who are paid unequal wages for comparable tasks. Important principles of equity and justice are at stake. Only the most ardent supporters of free enterprise seem willing to argue against comparable worth. They tend to claim that women have freely chosen lower-paying jobs—perhaps in exchange for more flexible schedules or less taxing work—and thus are not entitled to any special consideration. For example, Phyllis Schlafly, well-known critic of the Equal Rights Amendment, claims that comparable worth is "basically a conspiracy theory of jobs.... It asserts that, first, a massive societal male conspiracy has segregated or ghetto-ized women into particular occupations by excluding them from others; and then, second, devalued the women's job by paying them lower wages than other occupations held primarily by men.... Not a shred of evidence has been produced to prove these assumptions."[23]

THE RELEVANCE OF ETHICAL THEORY

Of course, social workers active in industrial settings are not the only members of the profession who meet up with hard ethical choices. Social workers in all settings face comparable dilemmas, whether they address the needs of the poor, disabled, neglected, abused, elderly, mentally ill, or addicted. In each arena, ethical choices arise related to direct practice, program design and administration, and relationships among colleagues.

The form of the ethical issues varies with the settings and populations. Social workers in health care settings are likely to encounter choices related to death and dying, informed consent, and the patient's right to know. Social workers in psychiatric settings are likely to encounter choices related to behavior control, privacy, and confidentiality. Social workers in emergency shelters are likely to encounter choices related to the allocation of limited resources.

Although philosophers have wrestled with moral and ethical choices for centuries, professionals have examined ethical issues systematically only in recent years, beginning especially in the late 1960s. This is not to say that prior to this period the topics of ethics and values were absent in professional literature and discourse. Rather, there is ample evidence to suggest that in the late 1960s there began an unusually intense, concentrated effort to identify and address ethical issues in professions such as medicine, law, journalism, social work, nursing, law enforcement, business, public administration, engineering, and the military.[24]

In the early years of the various professions' history, much of the discussion of ethics focussed on matters of professional etiquette. Since the late 1960s, however, the focus has been on conflicts of professional duty and the nature of hard choices. For example, the legal literature addresses attorneys' obligations when clients perjure themselves. The engineering literature discusses the professional's obligation when he or she uncovers defective products. The business literature raises questions about conflicts of interest and corporate social responsibility. The journalism literature broaches ethical problems related to the protection of sources and First Amendment rights.

There is a central theme in contemporary discussions of professional ethics. Experienced practitioners know that most ethical issues are not complex. In most instances, social workers are clear about their obligation to keep information confidential, tell the truth, obey the law, and respect clients' right to self-determination. These are not the hard issues.

On occasion, however, these *prima facie* duties clash in such a way that in order to fulfill one ethical obligation, the practitioner must violate another. If a social worker suspects child abuse, she cannot simultaneously keep information confidential and obey the mandatory reporting law. A social worker who is counseling a self-destructive client may not be able simultaneously to respect his right to self-determination and ensure his safety.

Such is the nature of hard ethical choices, including those faced by social workers in industrial and business settings. How should a social worker decide whether it is appropriate to share confidential information with an impaired client's employer? Is it permissible for a public-sector social worker to strike? Should an employee-assistance social worker participate in the administration of a mandatory drug screening program?

The NASW Code of Ethics contains some suggestive guidelines. For instance, several principles seem relevant to the issue of strikes:

II.F.10. The social worker should withdraw services precipitously only under unusual circumstances, giving careful consideration to all factors in the situation and taking care to minimize possible adverse effects.

IV.L. The social worker should adhere to commitments made to the employing organization.

VI.P.5. The social worker should provide appropriate professional services in public emergencies.

The first principle (II.F.10) suggests that participation in a strike may be justifiable under extreme circumstances, as long as steps are taken to minimize harmful consequences. However, the second principle (IV.L) suggests that social workers must fulfill commitments to their employers, commitments that may be inconsistent with a strike. Similarly, principle VI.P.5 suggests that strikes may not be justifiable if they coincide with a public emergency.

Unfortunately, the Code of Ethics by itself does not provide a clear guide for social workers who face the prospect of a strike. This is not a defect in the code, for no code of ethics is able to provide precise, situation-specific advice for the wide range of ethical judgments called for in practice. As the preamble to the NASW code states: "In itself, this code does not represent a set of rules that will prescribe all the behaviors of social workers in all the complexities of professional life. Rather it offers general principles to guide conduct, and the judicious appraisal of conduct, in situations that have ethical implications. . . . Specific applications of ethical principles must be judged within the context in which they are being considered." As Rehr observes in her assessment of the divisive strike at Mount Sinai Hospital: "No single individual social worker can create the model for the social work profession. He can only reflect the ideal as set forth by his professional organization's commitment to specific ethics. In the situation of a strike, personal and professional conflicts arise. The fact that social workers can interpret and act upon a code of ethics in diametrically opposed ways suggests the confusion engendered by their own emotions."[25]

For some time, philosophers have recognized the need to look beyond statements of general ethical principles. The philosophical literature is filled with speculation about ways of making ethical judgments and the criteria that ought to guide such decisions.

The arguments generally fall within two major schools of thought. On the one hand are those arguments that claim that certain actions are inherently right or wrong as a matter of principle—or good or bad in the moral sense. This is known as the deontological perspective, a term derived from the Greek word meaning duty or obligation. From this point of view, it would be ethically unacceptable for a social worker to break a promise of confidentiality made to a company employee, or to break a commitment to an employer. Such principles as promise keeping, truth telling, contracts, and obedience to the law are inviolable, regardless of extenuating circumstances.[26]

In contrast, a utilitarian perspective holds that the morality of action depends on the goodness of the consequences. Thus, promises ought to be kept and contracts ought to be respected as long as they lead to good consequences, but if a broken promise or a violated contract would result in a greater good, so be it. In common parlance, this case-by-case approach (generally known as act-utilitarianism) holds that the ends can justify the means. Thus, affirmative action—which may violate the rights of some in the short run—may be justifiable because of the long-term benefits. Disclosing confidential information may be justifiable if doing so ultimately enhances a life or protects others. A short-term strike—which may harm clients for some limited time period—may be justifiable if it leads eventually to improved care and quality of service.[27]

Clearly, each position has its merits and limitations. The deontological view supports values consistent with the central mission of social work—honesty, fidelity, justice, and the like, but from the critic's perspective, it is naive to uphold such virtues without exception, as a form of "rule worship."[28] In some instances, the greatest good for the greatest number requires the temporary or occasional violation of these ideals. Of course, motive matters. We would not want to see the spirit of utilitarianism distorted to justify trampling on the rights of a minority, merely to produce a greater benefit for a privileged majority. There must be limits. We would not want to justify the coercion of employees in order to maximize corporate profits. We would not want to deprive oppressed groups of employment opportunities to enhance the careers of an affluent majority. Compromises may be necessary at times, but they must be principled.

The persistent, centuries-long debates about theories of ethics suggest the deceptiveness of simple solutions. We are skilled at identifying ethical conflicts in the professions, and we are able to construct sophisticated arguments to support each side of a complex debate. If we try hard enough, compelling reasons can be found to support nearly every position, with the exception of the most egregious points of view.

Such is the nature of ethical dilemmas. Important matters often are not simple matters. The complexity of the debate should not, however, discourage us from participating in it. Professionals probably will always disagree about the ethics of strikes, affirmative action, whistle blowing, and so on, but diplomatic, spirited debate pushes us to think through what we value and to defend the conclusion. The result may not satisfy everyone, but it is likely to be principled.

Social workers active in the world of work must be skilled at counseling, administering, organizing, and advocating. Technical proficiency is essential. In the end, however, we must acknowledge the central place of values and professional ethics. It is upon such fundamental beliefs that our professional actions depend.

NOTES

1. Sheila H. Akabas, and Paul A. Kurzman, "The Industrial Social Welfare Specialist: What's So Special?" in Sheila H. Akabas and Paul A. Kurzman, (eds.), *Work, Workers, and Work Organizations: A View from Social Work* (Englewood Cliffs, N.J.: Prentice-Hall, 1982), p. 221.

2. Dale A. Masi, *Designing Employee Assistance Programs* (New York: American Management Associations, 1984), p. 119.

3. Paul A. Kurzman, "Industrial Social Work (Occupational Social Work)," in National Association of Social Workers, *Encyclopedia of Social work*, 18th ed. (Silver Spring, Md.: National Association of Social Workers, 1987), p. 906.

4. National Association of Social Workers, *Code of Ethics* (Silver Spring, Md.: National Association of Social Workers, 1979), Principle II.H.1.

5. *Tarasoff vs. Regents of the University of California*, [(1976) 17 Cal. 3D 425]. Quoted in Donald Brieland, and Samuel Z. Goldfarb, "Legal Issues and Legal Services," in National Association of Social Workers, *Encyclopedia of Social Work*, 18th ed., Vol 2. (Silver Spring, Md.: National Association of Social Workers, 1987), pp. 28–34.

6. Vincent Barry, *Moral Issues in Business*, 3rd ed. (Belmont, Calif.: Wadsworth, 1986), p. 239.

7. Ibid., pp. 238–267. See also Norman Bowie, *Business Ethics*, (Englewood Cliffs, N.J.: Prentice Hall, 1982), p. 143; and Gene G. James, "In Defense of Whistle Blowing," in Vincent Barry, (ed.), *Moral Issues in Business*, pp. 259–67. Also see Richard T. DeGeorge, "Ethical Responsibilities of Engineers in Large Organizations," *Business and Professional Ethics Journal*, (1), 1 (1981), pp. 1–14.

8. Akabas and Kurzman, *Work, Workers, and Work Organizations*, p. 222.

9. Leroy Johnson, "Union Response to Alcoholism," *Journal of Drug Issues*, (11), 3 (1981), p. 267.

10. National Association of Social Workers "Code of Ethics," Principle II.F. (Silver Spring, Md.: NASW, 1979).

11. Victor Gotbaum, "Public Service Strikes: Where Prevention is Worse than the Cure," in Richard T. DeGeorge and Joseph A. Pichler, (eds.), *Ethics, Free Enterprise, and Public Policy* (New York: Oxford University Press, 1978), p. 158.

12. Bertha Reynolds, *Unchartered Journey* (New York: Citadel, 1956), p. 237.

13. Ronald H. Bohr, Herbert I. Brenner, and Howard M. Kaplan, "Value Conflicts in a Hospital Walkout," *Social Work*, (16), 4 (1971), pp. 33–42.

14. Helen Rehr, "Problems for a Profession in a Strike Situation," *Social Work*, (5), 2 (1960), pp. 22–28.

15. It is interesting to note that physicians and nurses were instructed by their respective professional organizations to continue providing patient care. However, the New York City chapter of the National Association of Social Workers stated that "each employee has a right to determine for himself whether or not to report to work." See Rehr, "Problems for a Profession."

16. Dena Fisher, "Problems for Social Work in a Strike Situation: Professional, Ethical, and Value Considerations," *Social Work*, (32), 3 (1987), pp. 252–254.

17. Ernie S. Lightman, "Social Workers, Strikes, and Service to Clients," *Social Work*, (28), 2 (1983), pp. 142–148.

18. Ibid., p. 143.

19. Ibid., p. 145.

20. National Association of Social Workers, Ad Hoc Committee on Advocacy, "The Social Worker as Advocate: Champion of Social Victims," *Social Work*, (14), 2 (1969), p. 19.

21. National Association of Social Workers, *NASW Standards for Social Work Personnel Practices* (Silver Spring, Md.: National Association of Social Workers, 1975).

22. In Tom L. Beauchamp, and Norman E. Bowie, (eds.), *Ethical Theory and Business* (Englewood Cliffs, N.J.: Prentice-Hall, 1979). See also Keith Davis and Robert Blomstrom, "Business, Minorities, and Less-Advantaged Persons," pp. 595–603; Jules Cohn, "Affirmative Action Programs: Their Impact in the Corporate World," pp. 603–608; Sidney Hook, "Discrimination, Color Blindness, and the Quota System," pp. 608–611; Judith Jarvis Thomson, "Preferential Hiring," pp. 616–621; Robert Simon, "Preferential Hiring: A Response to Judith Jarvis Thomson," pp. 622–624; and Tom L. Beauchamp, "The Justification of Reverse Discrimination in Hiring," pp. 625–635. See also Barry, *Moral Issues in Business*; and William J. Kilberg, "Ethical Considerations in Civil Remedies: The Equal Employment Context," in Richard T. DeGeorge and Joseph A. Pichler, (eds.), *Ethics, Free Enterprise, and Public Policy* (New York: Oxford University Press, 1978), pp. 116–124.

23. Quoted in Barry, *Moral Issues in Business*, p. 376.

24. For discussion of the nature of and reasons for this growth of interest in professional ethics, see Daniel Callahan and Sissela Bok, (eds.), *Ethics Teaching in Higher Education* (New York: Plenum, 1980); and Frederic G. Reamer and Marcia Abramson, *The Teaching of Social Work Ethics* (Hastings-on-Hudson, N.Y.: The Hastings Center, 1982).

25. Rehr, "Problems for a Profession," p. 27.

26. See William K. Frankena, *Ethics*, 2nd ed. (Englewood Cliffs, N.J.: Prentice-Hall, 1973); Beauchamp and Bowie, *Ethical Theory and Business*.

27. This is a simplified overview of major schools of ethical theory. For a more detailed discussion, see Frankena, *Ethics*; Roger N. Hancock, *Twentieth-Century Ethics* (New York: Columbia University Press, 1974); and Frederic G. Reamer, *Ethical Dilemmas in Social Service* (New York: Columbia University Press, 1982).

28. J. J. C. Smart and Bernard Williams, *Utilitarianism: For and Against* (Cambridge: Cambridge University Press, 1973).

12

Social Workers and Public-Sector Labor Relations: A Case Study of the Missouri Department of Social Services and the Communications Workers of America

HOWARD JACOB KARGER

This chapter examines general labor relations principles that impact on the unionization of public-sector social workers. Although the chapter differentiates social workers from other public workers, it is not the intent of the author to suggest that social work unionization is so exceptional as to make it a special case. Nevertheless, there are some differences in the expectations and work conditions of social workers that warrant closer scrutiny.

The relationship between the Missouri Department of Social Services (DoSS) and the newly emergent Communications Workers of America (CWA), Public Employees Division, will be used as a case study to illustrate the tensions and conflict that often permeate labor relations in the public sector. In addition, this examination will also illustrate some key principles inherent in the matrix of public-sector labor-management relations.

The Missouri Department of Social Services was not chosen as a case study because it represents an egregious example of a mismanaged state agency, but because it exemplifies an ambivalent attitude held by many welfare administrators toward public employee unions.

CWA COMES TO MISSOURI

By 1984 DoSS was ripe for unionism. A private research organization commissioned in 1984 by the Missouri legislature reported that:

Current salaries for merit system positions in the State of Missouri lag substantially behind those paid within the State by private industry and local governments for the same and comparable services. The salary gap for merit positions is calculated at -18.8 percent if one takes an average of the statewide, private industry, and local salary gaps for benchmark classes.[1]

According to CWA, the average 1984 pay of state workers in Missouri was $1,220 per month. Missouri ranked forty-eighth in the nation in terms of public employee salaries, ahead of only West Virginia and Mississippi. CWA further maintained that salaries for many clerical, caseworkers, and beginning-level youth workers were so low that "some qualify for food stamps, energy assistance, reduced or free lunches for their children, and subsidized housing (Section 8)."[2]

Previous salary increases for DoSS employees were meager. In 1981 raises amounted to 2 percent; in 1982 they were $600 per year plus 1 percent of the employee's current salary; and in 1983 the wage increase was only $240. When CWA compared the Missouri salary increases to contiguous states its case became even more powerful:

State	% Increase F.Y. '82-'84
Oklahoma	27%
Kansas	16%
Iowa	16%
Nebraska	11.5%
Missouri	2% to 4% depending on annual salary[3]

The State of Missouri's fringe benefit system was as vulnerable to criticism as its salary scale. CWA literature noted that "only 8 states pay less than Missouri toward the cost of family coverage; in only 1 of those states do employees contribute more than Missouri workers."[4] When the cost of coverage rose in 1983, Missouri increased its contribution by fifty cents and benefits were reduced. The 1983 retirement benefits under the Missouri State Employees System were exactly the same as they were in 1972.

Armed with issues such as pay inequity, meager fringe benefits, inordinate job pressures, and comparable worth, CWA began a two-year campaign to organize DoSS. Using adroit organizing and shouldering costs that exceeded $250,000, CWA finally signed a resolution with the State of Missouri on May 14, 1985. As a testament to its success, CWA could boast that by March of 1985 (two months before the resolution was signed), it had signed up over 2,000 members out of a potential bargaining unit of 5,500.

POLITICS AND PUBLIC-SECTOR UNIONISM

Conflict came early to the uneasy relationship between CWA and the State of Missouri. On March 23, 1985, CWA sent a letter to potential union members claiming that "the improvement in last year's COL [cost of living] and this year's proposed COL and repositioning is *solely due to CWA efforts.*"[5] Angered by CWA's claim, Missouri Senator Edwin Dirck and Representatives Al Nilges and Marvin Proffer wrote to Joseph O'Hara, then Director of DoSS:

It has come to our attention that...[CWA] is distributing literature to... [DoSS] employees which seems to indicate that they were primarily responsible for the passage of the eight percent cost of living increase, and the repositioning package....

It is incredible that an independent organization is attempting to take credit for this plan.... From our perspective, CWA had nothing to do with the passage of this plan.... [W]e are requesting that you have a copy of this letter posted in each office of the Department of Social Services.[6]

Labor-management relations in the public sector is often a political activity played out on the legislative stage. In the absence of collective bargaining—as in the case of Missouri—this political drama occasionally takes on the proportions of a melodrama.

Richard Freeman maintains that "public sector employers have not fought union organization of their workers to the extent that private sector employers have. Public officials cannot break the spirit or letter of the law as management has done in the private sector."[7] Whether the state of Missouri has broken the spirit, if not the letter of the law, is an issue beyond the limited scope of this chapter. However, Division of Family Service (DFS) employees perceive a threat associated with their membership in CWA. Even as early as 1982—the beginning stages of CWA organizing—one potential member wrote to Vic Crawley (a CWA organizer) stating, "I received a letter about your organization last week and I circulated it around the department.... Eighteen people signed the letter out of approximately thirty-five people. I am hoping that the information I have given you will be kept strictly confidential."[8]

The situation worsened, when in the summer of 1985, the state of Missouri hired Ivan Schraeder, an attorney, as its labor consultant. Although supposedly neutral, Schraeder began to circulate a series of memorandums which CWA viewed as a *casus belli*. For example, one memo issued in February, 1986, informed supervisors that they may:

express [the] opinion that [the] union is not wanted or needed.

indicate that unionization may interfere with [the] employee's ability to discuss and resolve problems without outside interference.

identify [the] disadvantages of unions (dues, fees, assessments, job insecurity, loss of money during strikes, loss of job flexibility, etc.).

explain how authorization cards may be used rather than as explained by [the] union.

In that same memo, Schraeder went on to suggest that supervisors should:

show interest in employees beyond work effort to develop loyalty.

deny union access to premises under certain conditions;

campaign against need for unionization;

    (1) communicate

    (2) communicate

    (3) communicate[9]

Ironically, many of Schraeder's memos were distributed to DFS supervisors, several of whom were union members. Schraeder's written correspondence followed on the heels of his statement that "a happy employee is a non-union employee."[10]

The effect of Schraeder's comments and memos was exacerbated by a letter written by Joseph O'Hara, then Director of the Department of Social Services, in which he informed Vic Crawley that:

A recent review of . . . DoSS payroll records has identified [15] DoSS employees who are having . . . CWA dues deducted . . . but who, by virtue of occupying a supervisory or managerial position or one designated as "confidential," are excluded from the CWA bargaining unit. . . .

[in reference to a DoSS employee] . . . he is excluded from the CWA bargaining unit and . . . he must immediately resign from his position as CWA steward or face dismissal from his aforementioned position with DFS.[11]

Two out of the fifteen members cited were actively involved with the union, and the employee referred to in O'Hara's memo was the treasurer of a CWA local.

While parts of Schraeder's counsel may not have been inflammatory, the general ambience of labor-management relations in Missouri was so embittered that reasonable dialogue was next to impossible. In response to Schraeder's memos, Crawley wrote that:

Over and above these anti-Union documents, he [Schraeder] was quoted as saying that: "there will be no first line Supervisors in the Union by the end of the year." . . . Because of a new Supreme Court ruling in the State [allowing for the bargaining unit exemption of employees categorized as "confidential"], he has requested that Supervisors write job descriptions for clerical employees using action type of words such as: they . . . file confidential memos, type confidential memos or have access to confidential memos. These activities could lessen the number of employees eligible for union representation by 500.[12]

In a state without collective bargaining or arbitration for public employees, state legislators act as arbiters of the first and last resort. Functioning like parents of estranged siblings, legislators are forced to mediate in all squabbles regardless of their significance. The absence of collective bargaining for state employees forces costly legislative time to be consumed by the frequent and often petty conflicts that occur between public sector unions and state managers.

The lack of public-sector collective bargaining inhibits the development of a mature form of labor-management relations. Since unions are continually forced to solicit the support of legislators, little incentive is provided for the kind of dialogue and compromise that should ideally characterize labor-management relations. Moreover, when legislative lobbying is substituted for "across-the-table" negotiations and bargaining strategies, an infantile process of labor-management relations is encouraged, whereby neither unions nor state managers develop the sophistication and skills required in a mature bargaining process.

Labor-management relations in the public sector is both political and ideological. In many states public welfare directors are political appointments, and thereby accountable to the reigning ideology of the administration. If welfare directors—at least in the current political climate—have aspirations of achieving higher political office, they may be required to exhibit their ideological purity by cutting welfare budgets and by showing a visible disdain for public employee unions. In that sense, politics and ideology have a major impact on the relationship of state managers to public sector unions.

The ideological predisposition of politically appointed state managers stands in contrast to merit-system state bureaucrats concerned with both agency growth and an increase in their power base. Protected by civil service or merit systems, these middle- or upper-level bureaucrats are often in conflict with political appointees who view their agencies as a stepping stone to higher political office.

The antagonism between political appointees and merit-system bureaucrats is based almost entirely on political considerations. Specifically, the conflict centers around the configuration of power within state agencies, and in particular, on the scurrying about for power and position. In order to ease these inherent tensions, the two parties often create an uneasy truce which, by implication, acknowledges the power of the other.

Public employee unions represent a third force in the power dynamic of state agencies. Subservient to neither state agencies nor career bureaucrats, unions are perceived as a force that demands a piece of the already divided pie of power. Faced with the union's demand for influence in state agencies, career bureaucrats and political appointees often engineer a rapprochement—at least around the problem of public sector unions—designed to curtail the potential power of the new contender.

Given the control exercised by both merit system bureaucrats and political appointees, the two-pronged attack on CWA is predictable. It is therefore not surprising that Missouri's higher-placed public servants are reluctant to accept the legitimacy of CWA and its constituents.

Unlike private-sector employers who have experienced unionism since the middle 1930s, public administrators are relative novices in unionized labor-management relations, and many are convulsing from its effects. It is hoped that in time a new wisdom, equilibrium, and a rearrangement of state agency power will emerge.

WORK AND CAPTIVITY IN THE PUBLIC SECTOR

In the last two decades lawmakers have tried to bring the industrial model of labor relations to the public sector. The consequences of this attempt have been both good and bad for public workers. For example, certain blue-, white-, and pink-collar public workers thrive well under the industrial model. On the other hand, professional employees such as social workers in protective services, group homes, and crisis-related work, find themselves in a conundrum.

Often forced to work on weekends and nights, and unable to control the crisis-related nature of their work, these social workers find themselves at a disadvantage working under an industrial model of labor relations. For many social workers, the responsibility to clients takes precedence over agency concerns about compensatory time and the curtailment of costs. Moreover, if these social workers adhered to strict schedules, the reprobation from both the agency and the community would be deafening. It may be this perceived responsibility to clients that accounts for the reluctance of social workers to adopt more militant trade-union tactics.[13]

Social workers are forced to operate under two different sets of rules: professionalism requires flexibility but the industrial model of labor relations demands uniformity of purpose, task, and function.[14] The attempt to integrate these oppositional forces often results in a "no-win situation."

Albert Hirschman points out that individuals and societies have two basic strategies they can use to combat social or economic problems: exit-and-entry and voice.[15] Exit-and-entry is the classic economic mechanism whereby one exercises freedom of choice or occupational mobility. In this scenario the dissatisfied worker leaves his or her job for a better one. A high quit-rate penalizes the bad employer and rewards the good one. According to Hirschman, this mechanism ultimately leads to greater efficiency in the economic system.

The "voice" mechanism refers to using communication, registering dissent, participating in the democratic process, bargaining, and collective action. A single worker using his or her "voice" in the workplace runs the risk of being fired. On the other hand, a collective workplace voice is protected by laws such as the National Labor Relations Act.

It is likely that under ideal marketplace conditions exit-and-entry mechanisms are legitimate. However, labor market conditions are rarely ideal, and in the public sector, mobility is often curtailed by the idiosyncratic nature of certain jobs. For example, the tasks of an income-maintenance worker are so idiosyncratic that twelve years of casework only prepares a worker for another twelve years. Income-maintenance workers have no corollary job in the private sector and longtime workers perceive little occupational mobility.

The problem of mobility is not as severe for social-service or child-protection workers, but it is nevertheless present. While some social workers can make the shift to private social-welfare agencies, many lack the required educational credentials. Rino J. Patti and Charles Maynard found that 70 percent of the positions in social service and 76 percent of the positions in mental health required a master's degree.[16] It is estimated that 50 percent of all social workers have no formal social work education.[17] In some regions, many income-maintenance and social workers possess only a high school degree. A letter written by DFS workers in one Missouri county illustrates the problem:

In regard to SB 533 (Wiggins), the licensing of social workers bill: We would be agreeable to the bill ONLY if current DoSS social workers were exempt. As of April, 1985, we had only 9 out of 70 workers and supervisors with a degree in social work.... The rest of us would likely be forced to resign should this bill pass without this amendment.[18]

In spite of curtailed job mobility, the DFS turnover rate in 1984 for St. Louis City was 10.7 percent; for St. Louis County, 15.5 percent; for Greene County (Springfield), 19.2 percent; and for Jackson County (Kansas City), the overall state-wide turnover rate for DFS was 13.9 percent (excluding metropolitan areas).[19] These figures compare unfavorably with the private sector where the separation rates in 1985 ranged from 0.8 percent in the smaller firms to 1.6 percent among financial institutions.[20]

Traditional economic theories of labor-force participation have limited utility in explaining many of the problems encountered by public-sector social workers. Faced with the prospects of restricted job mobility, embittered labor-management relations, conflicts between client needs and agency policies, and the variegated problems inherent in public sector employment, it is not surprising that DoSS workers opted to speak with a collective voice. A letter written by DFS employees to Missouri legislators eloquently summarizes the dilemma:

We would like to make our legislators aware of the current attempt to do away with overtime for Social Service Worker II's. Our work concerns families in crises, and few crises are limited to 8:00 to 5:00. If we are to continue to help our clients, we must be allowed to be there when they need us most. We must also be paid for working these difficult hours. We appeal to you for support in this area. Our administration *appears* [original emphasis] to be no longer supportive of either the clients or workers.

We want you to know that income maintenance caseworkers are being required to do on the average of one and one-half caseloads (per worker) without error, and with severe penalty should errors occur. Four errors in one year may result in punitive ratings and threats of dismissal. We are exhausted and feel that further "punishment" cannot result in positive change, although reasonable expectations and incentives might.... Our administration *appears* [original emphasis] to be no longer supportive of either the clients or their own workers.[21]

ARE PUBLIC SECTOR UNIONS GOOD?

Stated succinctly, the fundamental question of this chapter remains: Is public sector unionism in Missouri (and by implication, elsewhere) good for social workers, clients, the state, and the community? In large part, the answer to that question depends on the perspective of public agency administrators. Freeman and Medoff maintain that unionism can be understood as having two faces: the "monopoly face" and the "collective voice/institutional response face."[22] These two views of unionism lead to fundamentally different conclusions regarding the worth and utility of public sector unions.

Adherence to the "monopoly face" perspective leads managers to maintain that unions create a monopolistic demand for higher wages, dilute management authority by substituting a system of industrial jurisprudence (seniority, grievances, and so on) for managerial discretion, decrease productivity as a result of union work rules, and lead to the autarkic control of unions by corrupt and nondemocratic elements.

Proponents of the "collective voice/institutional response face" believe that unions improve morale, lower quit-rates, increase productivity, reduce wage inequality, encourage industrial democracy by demanding more professional management techniques in lieu of paternalistic and authoritarian administrative fiats, and provide an important voice for society's downtrodden.

The collective voice face suggests important ways that DoSS—and by implication other state welfare agencies—can use unions to its advantage.

For one, maintaining a voice at the workplace should reduce quit-rates.[23] Lower quit-rates mean lower training and hiring costs, less disruption in the functioning of work groups, and less interruption in client service. Lower quit-races alone should result in higher productivity of DoSS employees, particularly given the 1984 separation of 20.9 percent in urban counties.

Union emphasis on seniority may also prove beneficial to the social service workplace. The ideological perspective of unionism requires that promotions, pay, and other rewards be dependent upon length of service. Merit pay is discouraged and hence rivalry among workers should be less pronounced, resulting in an increase in the amount of informal help, training, and assistance workers are willing to provide one another. On the other hand, seniority may hinder productivity by providing fewer rewards for competence and initiative. The preferred tradeoff is an empirical question that is yet unanswered.

Unionism can improve agency efficiency by pressuring management to tighten job performance standards, increase accountability, and to discard arbitrary, paternalistic, and authoritarian management practices in favor of explicit rules governing workplace behavior. In a case study of over 100 unionized firms, Sumner H. Slichter, James H. Healy, and Robert E. Livernash concluded that "the challenge that unions presented to management has . . . created superior and better balanced management, even though some exceptions must be recognized."[24]

Lastly, public employee unions may be instrumental in opening up important avenues of communication between management and workers. Grievances (despite their innate antagonism) may be a useful mechanism to inform management of the existence of deleterious workplace conditions or policies. Moreover, unions can help to more wisely balance the dollar spent on wages and compensation packages by apprising management of the worker's desires.

Whether unions are good or bad for workers, society, clients, and agencies depends on the "face" one chooses to observe. If management focuses on the monopoly face, antagonism in labor-management relations is the probable outcome. If on the other hand, state agency administrators choose to focus on the "voice" aspect of unionism, more convivial arrangements are possible. Regardless of the "face," public employee unions are not an ephemeral phenomenon, but a fact of life that is likely to be a durable and long-term part of the public sector.

CONCLUSION

This chapter has attempted to explore the relationship between public-sector social workers and labor unions by analyzing CWA and the Missouri Department of Social Services. As part of that examination, the chapter analyzed the conditions leading to the unionization of DoSS workers and attempted to investigate the relationship between politics and public sector unionism. It is hoped that this inquiry will illustrate some fundamental principles that must be operationalized if peace in the public workplace is to be realized.

Labor-management relations in the public sector is frequently characterized by bitterness and conflict instead of joint strategies based on creative solutions to welfare-state problems. If labor relations in the public sector is to become more convivial, a new labor-management paradigm of mutual trust and cooperation must emerge. Perhaps this new paradigm could even be a model for labor relations in the private sector.

NOTES

1. Public Administrative Service, "Executive Summary," McLean, Virginia, December 13, 1984, pp. 1–3.

2. CWA, "State Wage Increase," CWA Legislative Fact Sheet, CWA Conference–1984, CWA District 6, St. Louis, Mo., 1984, n.p.

3. Ibid.

4. Ibid.

5. Untitled letter sent to Missouri state workers, CWA Local 6382, St. Louis, Mo., March 23, 1985.

6. Letter from Al Nilges, Chairman, State of Missouri House Appropriations Committee for Social Services and Corrections; Marvin Proffer, Chairman, State of Missouri House Budget Committee; and Edwin Dirck, Chairman, State of Missouri Senate Appropriations Committee to Joseph J. O'Hara, Director, Division of Social Services (DoSS), June 25, 1985.

7. Richard B. Freeman, "Unionism Comes to the Public Sector," *Journal of Economic Literature*, 24 (March 1986), p. 49.

8. Letter to Vic Crawley, CWA, District No. 6, St. Louis, Mo., July 19, 1982.

9. Ivan L. Schraeder, Labor Relations Specialist, "What Supervisors May SAY and DO, "Exhibit C," Office of Administration, Jefferson City, Mo., February 20, 1986, n.p.

10. Schraeder acknowledged that comment to the House Labor Committee of the Missouri Legislature, "Minutes, House Labor Committee," Missouri Legislature, Jefferson City, Mo., April 15, 1986, n.p.

11. Letter from Joseph J. O'Hara, Director, Missouri Department of Social Services to Vic Crawley, Administrative Assistant to the Vice President, CWA, District 6, St. Louis, Mo., March 10, 1986.

12. Memorandum from Vic Crawley to Lynn Amen, CWA Representative, "Missouri Department of Social Services Anti-Union Activities," CWA, District 6, St. Louis, Mo., February 25, 1986.

13. See Leslie Alexander, Philip Lichtenberg, and Dennis Brunn, "Social Workers in Unions," *Social Work*, 25 (May 1980), p. 222. Alexander notes that most social workers interviewed in her study were opposed to strikes, slowdowns, sickouts, and so forth, and instead preferred arbitration.

14. For a fuller argument of this point see Howard Jacob Karger, "The Industrial Model of Production and the Delivery of Social Services," *Journal of Sociology and Social Welfare*, 16 (Fall 1986), pp. 17–22.

15. Albert O. Hirschman, *Exit, Voice, and Loyalty* (Cambridge, Mass.: Harvard University Press, 1971).

16. Rino J. Patti and Charles Maynard, "Qualifying for Managerial Jobs in Public Welfare," *Social Work*, 23 (July 1978), p. 292.

17. Howard J. Karger, "Reclassification: Is There a Future in Public Welfare for the Trained Social Worker?" *Social Work* 28 (November/December 1983), p. 429.

18. Letter from DFS employees to Senators and State Representatives, CWA, District 6, St. Louis, Mo., March 25, 1985.

19. Missouri Division of Family Services, "Social Service Worker Turnover, Calendar Year–1984," Division of Family Services, Jefferson City, Mo., 1984, n.p.

20. Bureau of National Affairs, "Report 4th Quarter, 1985," (Washington, D.C.: The Bureau of National Affairs, March 6, 1986), n.p.

21. Division of Social Service (DoSS) employee letter to State Senators and Representatives, CWA, District No. 6, St. Louis, Mo., ca. 1984.

22. See Richard B. Freeman and James L. Medoff, "The Two Faces of Unionism," *The Public Interest*, 57 (Fall 1979), p. 75.

23. The relationship of unions to lower quit rates was found to be positively correlated in a large study done by Richard B. Freeman and James L. Medoff titled *What Do Unions Do?* (New York: Basic Books, Inc., 1984), pp. 94–110.

24. Sumner H. Slichter, James H. Healy, and Robert E. Livernash, *The Impact of Collective Bargaining on Management* (Washington, D.C.: Brookings Institution, 1960), p. 951.

13

Professionalization and Unionization: Compatible After All?

LESLIE B. ALEXANDER

According to some observers, many social workers share a general feeling that the increasing unionization of social workers at both the MSW and BSW levels is a serious challenge to social work's professionalism.[1] The perception of unionization as "unprofessional" is a commonly held though untested assertion. The related view that unionization and professionalization are inherently antagonistic and mutually exclusive is problematic: it fails to account for the slow yet steady rate since the 1930s of unionization of professional workers of all types, including social workers, psychologists, lawyers, engineers, occupational therapists, and college professors.

Although membership is currently declining in blue-collar unions, many white-collar unions, including those that organize professionals, are showing dramatic gains in membership. As of 1978 it was estimated that about 30 percent of all professional and technical employees (excluding managers and the self-employed) were represented in collective bargaining efforts.[2] Union activity is strongest among professionals in education, government service, and the entertainment and communication industries, and less prevalent among doctors, lawyers, scientists, and engineers. Since the early 1970s, unionization has also made great strides in the health care field. Although there is evidence of accelerating participation in unions by social workers, there are no firm statistics on the number of professional social workers belonging to the three major unions organizing social workers nationally: the American Federation of State, County, and Municipal Employees; Service Employees International Union; and the National Union of Hospital and Health Care Employees.[3]

One way around the seeming paradox between the negative view of unionization for professionals and its growth is to examine unions and professions theoretically, as ideal types. Such a contrast is useful for two reasons. First, this comparison seems to underlie the widespread sentiment in social work that unions are unprofessional. More important, such a comparison of ideal types results in the inevitable conclusion that unionism and professionalism as principles, unionization and professionalization as processes, and unions and professional associations as modes of organization are, in fact, contradictory and incompatible. It is only when the realities are examined, both of the less-established professions such as social work and of the unions organizing them, that the compatibility and mutual reinforcement emerge. The paradox disappears and a more substantive debate about the pros and cons of unionization for professionals is possible.

The occurrence of unionization and professionalization as complementary processes, then, appears least likely when both are examined as ideal types exemplifying the most mature and successful of each. For example, the ideal model of unionization could be the automobile or steel worker's unions. The model of the industrial union, which includes all workers in a given industry regardless of skill or occupational specialty, is chosen deliberately, since it appears to underlie most discussions that contrast professions and unions. In addition, the major unions organizing social workers and many other professional workers have been industrial in form. The contrast between craft unions—organizations of workers engaged in a single trade and using similar skills—and professions is much less pronounced. The ideal model of professionalization might be law or medicine, especially as exemplified by self-employed, independent practitioners.

At this level of analysis, unionization and professionalization seem to have little in common, other than both being processes that represent collective, protective efforts in behalf of their membership and aimed at upward social mobility.[4] Useful dimensions on which to compare as ideal types the two organizational forms—the union and the professional association—are patterns of membership, overall philosophy, and tactics.

MEMBERSHIP

Regarding membership, unions have typically been associated with wage workers involved in manual labor for low pay. The professional association on the other hand, is generally associated with middle-class people involved in nonmanual, more esoteric, prestigious, and lucrative work. Class and status differences have been stressed continually in the literature, beginning with A. M. Carr-Saunders and James Wilson's classic work on professions in 1933. In their view, those aspiring to professional status should avoid unions at all costs: "Indeed, association with that movement [labor] is generally regarded, even among the more economically dependent of professions, as calculated to depress rather than elevate their social status and is therefore avoided even in cases where one might expect it to be sought after."[5]

The resistance to unionization on the grounds of prestige has endured, forming part of what C. Wright Mills defined in the 1950s as the "principled" rejection of unions by many white-collar employees.[6] The following is another example of this principled rejection:

The "after all, we are all workers" approach has served to alienate many professional persons from the labor movement who might otherwise be sympathetic. Unionism's endeavors to organize professional personnel by appeals to worker solidarity, when professionals regard themselves as a group set above the common herd, has been a tactic as self-defeating as it is persistent.[7]

The cleavage created by differences in status and image seems almost insurmountable.

Another important dimension of membership patterns relates to the exclusionary practices of both unions and professional associations. Both exclude potential members, but on the basis of more or less opposite criteria. Unions typically reject those above a certain level in the organizational hierarchy—for example, those defined as management—whereas professional associations tend to exclude members on the basis of insufficient education or experience.

For professionals who are union members, these exclusionary practices typically mean that eligibility for membership in their professional association is for their lifetime, whereas eligibility for union membership is short-term, lasting only until the individual is promoted into management. Unions' eligibility criteria also result in a fair amount of turnover, with a large percentage of the membership being younger, professionally less experienced individuals who remain eligible for union membership only for a few years until they are promoted into management. Although promotion into management is detrimental from the unions' perspective, it is synonymous with advancement from the professional point of view.

PHILOSOPHY

There is also considerable variation in the overall philosophy and goals of the two modes of organization. In the union's ethos, a very real and inherent conflict of interest exists between union members and man-

agement. No such inherent adversary relationship exists in the professional ethos. In addition, although both modes have protective functions,
union activity is more narrowly confined to this domain, focused primarily on improving wages, hours, and conditions of work. Whereas
higher standards are an expected though often denied consequence of
unionization, success on the instrumental dimension—the realization of
economic and job benefits—is most critical to a union's success. Although
the "expressive" or ideological purpose of unions is apparent and important, the primary function is to accrue economic and job-related
benefits rather than to provide something in which to believe. The expressive dimension is clearly secondary in the minority of cases. Much
more so than professions, unions are basically institutions of the job
market whose development and traditions are greatly influenced by economic developments. The established professions lack this extreme dependence on outside economic influences.

The professional spirit, on the other hand, extends beyond narrow
economic and protectionist issues.[8] Concern for the enhancement of
standards, proficiency within the profession, reputation in the community, service to clients, and, above all, autonomy, are all within its
expansive interest, Whereas the union's claims to financial gain are primary, the professional association lays claim first and foremost to autonomy and independence on the job. The union generally can influence
only the conditions of work, leaving the determination of who does the
work and the nature of its content up to management; professional
autonomy, however, includes defining and controlling the nature of the
work, not just the surrounding conditions. Autonomy, then, is a requisite
for the full flowering of the service ideal, another important hallmark
of the professions.

At an ideal level, professionals stress the primacy of the public good,
whereas unions stress the primacy of private benefit. However, by definition, professionals are not as immune to financial lure as their rhetoric
of service might imply. In fact, financial success and high prestige are
inevitable and necessary requisites of full-fledged professional status.
Though generally masked in professional rhetoric, substantial financial
gain is indispensable to assure professional status.

Nevertheless, although the professional association does seek collective
advancement, the professional ethos both allows, and in fact emphasizes,
individual mobility. Striving for upward mobility is the rule rather than
the exception. Among the professions, individual advancement is based
on merit; however, unions stress seniority. Although union members
are not without hopes for individual gains in status, this is not part of
the official union value system. Above all, union philosophy stresses
egalitarianism and the good of the collectivity. As Marie Haug and Marvin Sussman have stated, "the slogan of 'all for one and one for all'

suggests disapproval for individual climbers."[9] In fact, the epitome of the professional is the autonomous individual practitioner, whereas the epitome of the unionist is the staunch group member.

According to an idealized perspective, in the unlikely event that professionals would unionize, their individualistic, elitist emphasis would favor a craft rather than an industrial union. Given a typical social agency, one would expect to find the professional social workers in one bargaining unit and the clerical and maintenance workers in another. Nonprofessionals would definitely be ineligible for membership in the professional bargaining unit, and the professionals would fight to keep it that way.

TACTICS

A final point of comparison involves the difference in tactics and rhetoric of the two modes of organization. The classic tactics of unions, which emerge from their basic and open power struggles with management, involve a range of applications of power—from slowdowns to pickets to strikes. Union rhetoric, which often involves a public admission of bitterness and hostility, commonly includes such terms as "arsenal of weapons," "open warfare," "enemies," "class solidarity," "demands," "grievances," "militancy," and "rights." The adversarial tone is readily apparent; so also is the prevailing collectivist spirit.

Professional associations, on the other hand, are not as blatantly involved in power struggles but rather emphasize more cerebral tactics, such as developing codes of ethics, raising standards of practice, promoting good community relations, and expanding the knowledge base. Although some professional associations, notably the American Nurses Association, the American Association of University Professors, and the National Education Association, have engaged in collective bargaining, the more usual route for professional associations to take in solving economic problems is through formation of vocational bureaus, publication of minimal salary scales, and development of personnel committees and programs. Theirs is the rhetoric of "service," "individual merit," "standards," and "consensus." The overall tone is dignified, cerebral, and conciliatory.

In the same connection, the purpose and tactics of the professional association result in much less intimate involvement in the daily lives of members than the union has. The professional association deals at the level of broad public relations. Unions, on the other hand, through their structure of locals and shop stewards and their emphasis on collective bargaining and redress of grievances, are much more involved on a day-to-day, intimate level with their members. Their protection is more immediate, more specific, and probably more effective.

INCOMPATIBLE VIEW

If unions and professions are judged by ideal standards, then the conclusions reached by noted authorities such as Northrup and Carr-Saunders and Wilson seem inevitable: the two are inherently incompatible. Their basic membership patterns, philosophies, and tactics are so irreconcilable that they could not coexist without each continually violating the sacred prerogatives of the other. For convenience this will be termed the "incompatible" view of professional unionism.

According to this view, which assumes ideal standards of unionism and professionalism, any type of unionization among professionals, social workers included, is an anomaly. Given that today less than a third of all professional employees are covered by collective bargaining agreements, many of which are negotiated by professional societies that eschew the label of "union," the argument could be made that this view conforms most closely to reality.[10] It certainly corresponds to the often quoted rejoinder of many professionals to the idea of unionizing: "It just isn't professional." However, this line of argument evokes ideal constructs and treats all professional union members as though their unionism and professionalism were each fully mature when this not, in fact, the case.

Nevertheless, some explanation is still needed for the group of exceptions: those persons claiming professional status who have also been unionized for the last forty years. At least two other rough models of professional unionism shed light on this seeming paradox. Neither is pure nor comprehensive, and they share some common features. Both orientations view unionism and professionalism as compatible under certain conditions. The first pattern might be called the transitional model and the second the hybrid model. Both orientations involve a certain reluctance and defensiveness in relation to unionization.

TRANSITIONAL MODEL

According to the transitional model, unionization and professionalization are compatible only when both processes are at early stages of development. However, professional development is always of greater interest. Although the aspiring professional is recognized as relatively weak on established indexes of professionalism, this insecure status is regarded as temporary. Full professional status is the ultimate outcome. In fact, unionism is not expected to become a permanent fixture at all, but rather will be shed as professional status becomes more secure. Unionization is regarded as a necessary and effective evil for wresting higher wages and better working conditions from management in the present.

This crude model makes certain assumptions. The union is expected to serve a purely instrumental function—the acquisition of economic and job security, both of which are requisites for secure professional status. The union is regarded strictly as a means rather than an end. This orientation assumes that as both unionization and professionalization mature, union and professional prerogatives will inevitably clash. This does not matter, however, since unionization is only a transitional stage in the pursuit of full professional status.

This model perhaps best represents the widespread although unwritten assumption of some reluctant professional union members. It also corresponds to the reality that for many professionals, union membership will indeed be only transitory. When professionals are promoted to supervisory positions, they are generally classified as management and are no longer eligible for union membership. This transitional model is deficient, however, in several important respects. Although it contains elements of truth, it cannot account for the following circumstances, most of which were evident by the late 1940s. First, it ignores the reality that several aspiring professions, including social workers, teachers, nurses, and librarians, have not rejected unionization, even though their professional status is more secure now than in the 1930s and 1940s when they first began to unionize. Unionization is not a transitional phenomenon for these groups.

Second, the model is too optimistic about the prospects of many occupations for obtaining professional recognition, particularly in regard to the high status, high income, and autonomy associated with the established professions.[11] In a thorough and provocative review of the empirical evidence regarding patterns of professionalism, Irwin Epstein and Kayla Conrad point out the limited descriptive and predictive validity of measures of social work professionalism as either an independent or intervening variable. They conclude:

[A more empirically based, deprofessionalized model] would view claims to social work professionalization as in fact expressions of social work professionalism— an *ideology* associated with *aspiration* to professional status rather than as an expression of the central norms of social work as a "professional community."[12]

Third, this orientation fails to take into account the environmental constraints, especially the highly bureaucratized context, in which most professionals work. Fourth, it fails to account for an inevitable interactional process: when unions and professionals interact over time, unions become more professional and professionals become more proletarian. As a result, new hybrid forms of organization develop, drawing from both unions and professions, yet different from either in their classic sense. In other words, a process of diffusion takes place.

HYBRID MODEL

The hybrid model of organization, sketched briefly by Harold L. Wilensky, seems to account better for the development of most unions of professional workers.[13] This approach assumes that many occupations aspiring to professional status will not achieve it in the traditional sense of the word, that is, in terms of the prestige, power, and financial success of the established professions such as medicine or law. The hybrid approach also judges these new professions on different terms—not merely as weak imitations of the established models but as different forms that should be judged on their own merits. The model assumes that when unions and professionals interact over time, each begins to assume some of the characteristics of the other; new forms emerge that borrow from, but do not entirely conform to, either the traditional union or the traditional professional model. The result might be one new form that combines the functions of a union and a professional association, or it might be two parallel forms. In the latter instance, union and professional forms remain separate but borrow from and influence each other. In both instances, the need for union protection, particularly in the areas of salary and working conditions, is seen as a permanent requirement.[14]

Much consideration has been given to the differences between the emerging professions, which are represented by the hybrid model, and the established professions. Whether referred to as the "new," "less established," "emerging," or "semi" profession, social work conforms to the general pattern that emerges from this discussion. Obviously, the newer professions command less prestige, have shorter training periods, and are less lucrative than the more established professions of law and medicine. However, Wilensky's parsimonious discussion, which captures the basic arguments made by others, identifies two other critical points of comparison:

1. Newer professions are salaried and housed in bureaucracies, both of which can threaten autonomy and the service itself.
2. Also, because their knowledge base is either too broad and vague or too narrow and restricted, the claims of these professions to exclusive jurisdiction and autonomy are threatened.

For example, Wilensky cites social work's broad yet vague knowledge base as being one of the major obstacles to full professional status.

Although the issue of social work's weak knowledge base is critical, it is much less controversial than the issue of the professional in the bureaucracy, which Charles Perrow has described as "certainly the hottest single topic in the field of organizational analysis during the early 1960s."[15]

The topic of the professional in the bureaucracy is obviously a complex one, but for understanding the hybrid model of professional unionism, several points are important. First, as Wilensky, Eliot Freidson, and Perrow, among others, have cogently pointed out, it is incorrect to think of bureaucratization and professionalization as inverse processes. While recognizing certain real constraints of bureaucratic life, Freidson points out that, at least in the case of health services, many of the dysfunctional consequences attributed to bureaucratic oranizations might be more accurately attributed to the professional organization of medicine.[16] In other words, many of the rigid, mechanical, and authoritarian attitudes and much of the inadequate coordination that alienate and depersonalize clients are due more to the dominance of the medical profession in health care administration than to the bureaucratic characteristics of health care.

Perhaps too much has been made, then, of the disparity between the two modes. Perhaps a bureaucratic setting is not as limiting to professional practice as has been traditionally emphasized. To quote Wilensky:

There is another way to view what is happening to professionalism: it is not that organizational revolution destroys professionalism, or that newer forms of knowledge (vague human-relations skills at one extreme, programmed instruction at the other) provide a poor base for professionalism, but simply that all these developments lead to something new. The culture of bureaucracy invades the professions; the culture of professionalism invades organizations.[17]

If bureaucracies are threats to professionals, so too are professionals threats to bureaucracies. They lack appreciation for rules and regulations, they focus on the unique rather than the routine aspects of the client's situation, and they demand authority in matters relating to the client and the organization. Besides, the obvious reality today is that most professionals, physicians and lawyers included, practice within bureaucratic settings. The individual practitioner is becoming an anomaly.

The issue of bureaucracy has also been emphasized in the literature on professionals in unions. Almost all the authors in this field view the bureaucratic setting as predisposing professional workers to unionize, particularly when the bureaucracy becomes extremely large and impersonal. One of the classic works in the field, Archie Kleingartner's *Professionalism and the Salaried Worker Organization*, seems to make the bureaucratic context the critical variable by defining such occupational groups as teachers, nurses, and social workers as salaried professionals in contrast to self-employed, autonomous professionals such as physicians and lawyers.[18] Granted, newer professionals do not have the status or income of the established professions. Instead, in Kleingartner's terms, they maintain the rhetoric but lack the essence of professional status. However, in light of the reevaluation of bureaucratic influence, this point seems to have been overemphasized.

Given the hybrid model of organization, what characteristics distinguish unions of professionals from unions of blue-collar workers? Just as fundamental differences have been observed between established and emerging professions, so too have distinctive differences in structure and style been observed between unions of professional and blue-collar workers. For example, bargaining units in professional unions often tend to be smaller and more scattered; they also have a tendency—with teachers a primary exception— to reject the use of strikes and other more extreme pressure tactics in favor of arbitration and mediation.[19] The potential use of the strike, in particular, creates a serious dilemma for many professional union members. However, as Kleingartner has queried:

If the union does not establish a strong collective bargaining mechanism, what can it do that the traditional professional association cannot do? And can the union be strong in collective bargaining unless it is willing to use the strike weapon?[20]

Use of strikes has always been a major issue in the debate within social work over unionization. Some recent data on the use of strikes by a select group of social workers suggest that for most of them, the threat of a strike is more a matter of form than substance, since no-strike (and no-lockout) clauses are commonly included in labor contracts covering social workers. Also, evidence suggests that many social-work union members strongly favor arbitration over strike action.[21]

More recently, reflecting the ethics of professionalism, many unions of professionals have also demanded that the scope of collective bargaining be expanded to include such things as size of classes and case-loads, course content, and office space—prerogatives previously regarded as belonging to management.[22] In some cases, union members have also demanded that they be able to meet to discuss professional issues on work time.

Notwithstanding such structural differences, which distinguish unions of professionals from those of blue-collar workers, perhaps most attention has been devoted to differences in style and tone, which reflect the middle-class, professional bias.[23] For example, among unions of professionals, the class struggle or inherent conflict between the union and management has usually been underplayed, with workers often expressing dual loyalty to both management and the union; euphemisms have been used (such as calling a grievance committee an "office relations" committee); middle-class organizers have been used; and merit, rather than seniority, has been stressed for promotions. Finally, unionization is presented as a way to promote, rather than impede, professional standards.

This appeal to potential members to view unions as a means of securing professional status reflects a certain defensiveness against the idea of union membership on the part of these professionals. However, it represents a much less standoffish and extreme reaction than that displayed by certain engineering and nursing associations in the 1940s and that persists today. In those two instances, the professional associations adopted strong and open campaigns to deter their members from joining unions and began to engage in collective bargaining themselves. Union affiliation was to be avoided at all costs.[24]

Such dramatic, defensive maneuvers reflect a principled rejection of unions that is not so much in evidence today. In fact, there is still evidence that professionals join unions for much the same reasons as blue-collar workers. Just as Mills predicted in 1951, Kleingartner concludes almost thirty years later:

White-collar workers may join unions as a purely defensive act. However, increases in white-collar unionization depend also on the relative merits of the case rather than on an emotional experience.... They tend to see the union as an organization that can get things done. They may not like the unions, but neither is there much evidence of the traditional principled opposition.[25]

Although unions of professionals do have some distinctive structural and stylistic features, just like blue-collar unions they are basically evaluated and valued on instrumental dimensions. The potential for professional unions to serve functions of association and social change is present just as it is for blue-collar unions; however, their primary purpose and emphasis is also the same as that of blue-collar unions: obtaining higher wages, better hours, and better working conditions.

CONCLUSION

The analysis of unions and professions as ideal types reveals the conditions under which the two modes are compatible: when both unionism and professionalism are at mature levels of development. When the structure and style of existing professional unions are examined, it becomes clear that unions of professionals are comparable to neither traditional professional associations nor traditional unions. Rather, a process of diffusion takes place. A new hybrid form of organization develops, drawing from, yet different from, both unions and professional associations in the classic sense. Recognizing this diffusion process resolves the seeming paradox in the unionization of professionals.

Since the mid–1940s, the professional associations of social workers have officially endorsed the right of individuals to bargain collectively and to be represented by a union of their choice.[26] Nevertheless, a prin-

cipled or ideological rejection of unionization still persists among many
social workers. Despite the growth of union membership among professionals of all kinds including social workers, few writers have challenged
this erroneous position in the professional social work literature; nor
has it received much attention at professional meetings. Given the growing dissatisfaction among some service workers about the content and
context of their work life, the potential for unionization seems ever
greater.

A number of reasons exist for professionals of all kinds to reject unionization, such as the potential for rigidity in the addition of more bureaucratic apparatus in the form of the union; doubts about its ability
to obtain significantly better wages and working conditions, particularly
in the public sector; and general problems of worker-union alienation,
such as the failure of some union leaders to reflect the views of their
members or charges of financial improprieties on the part of some union
leaders. However, equally convincing reasons exist for professionals to
unionize. For example, the union can provide more immediate protection for workers than professional associations. Unions can also effect
improvements in basic working conditions for professionals, thereby
improving service delivery to clients. In addition, by broadening the
scope of collective bargaining explicitly to include certain issues regarding the profession and social change, unions can also enhance service
delivery. Furthermore, although they have generated significant con-
troversy and had mixed success, definite historical precedents exist in
social work for such an expansive view of unionism. Social work unions
in the 1930s and 1940s espoused not only traditional bread-and-butter
union issues, but also issues of domestic social reform, war and peace,
and professional development as well.[27]

The primary point is that all these pros and cons are legitimate issues
in professional unionization, and they should be raised to the level of
open debate within the profession. To reject unionization because it is
allegedly "unprofessional" is supported by neither the theoretical base,
the historical record, nor the current reality.

POSTSCRIPT

Almost ten years have passed since this article was completed. At that
time, when the existing literature and interest about social work unionization was so limited, the use of an ideal-type analysis to contrast unionism and professionalism as principles, unionization and professionalization as processes, and unions and professional associations as
modes of organization seemed a useful way to prod more open debate
about unionization within the profession. In my view, the so-called "principled" rejection of unions by many white-collar employees, so eloquently

articulated by C. Wright Mills in 1951, aptly characterized the attitude of many social work professionals in the 1970s, and, I might add, seems to persist today as the mainstream view.[28] I tried further to demonstrate in the article that this pervasive principled rejection of unionization was not well supported by the historical record in social work, by theoretical discussions in the labor management and occupations and professions literature, or by the empirical reality that social workers and members of other occupational groupings, laying claim to professional status, were continuing to join labor unions at a slow but steady rate. I concluded that a hybrid model of organization, sketched briefly by Wilensky over thirty years ago, seemed to better account for the development of unionization among professionals. This model assumes that as unions and professions interact over time, a diffusion process takes place, whereby each assumes some of the characteristics of the other. These new forms borrow from, but do not necessarily conform exactly either to traditional union or traditional professional forms.

This article did not result in a rash of either favorable or hostile reactions in the literature. The only real challenge was offered by Ernie S. Lightman in 1982.[29] Two aspects of this article merit comment. First, using a sample of Canadian social workers, he found that the majority of his respondents saw no incompatibility between unionization and professionalism, but rather viewed union membership as instrumental in attaining service goals. Although an obvious challenge to my untested assumption that unionization and professionalism were viewed as antithetical by many professional social workers, it should be noted that there are firm contrasts between unionization among social workers in Canada and the United States, which might account for Lightman's results. As recently described by Joan Pennell, while definite similarities about the union scene for social workers in both countries exist, there are also distinct differences, especially in terms of more favorable national ideology toward unionization and more favorable labor relations legislation in Canada.[30] Both of these factors are influential in explaining why few Canadian social workers and most American social workers remain unorganized.

Returning to the Lightman article, the second aspect meriting comment is his persuasive argument that my discussion of the union side of the union-professional incompatibility debate was less convincing than my discussion of the professional side of this debate. In developing his argument, Lightman went on to establish the important point that:

the union is nothing more and nothing less than the embodiment of the collective will of its members. It is structurally neutral toward the attainment of the service ideal and any other goals, and it has no independent corporate existence, outcomes, priorities, or processes. As a democratic entity, the conceptual union will pursue professional goals and service ideals if this is the wish of the membership; it will assume a bureaucratic anti-professional stance if this is desired.[31]

Although Lightman does not interpret it this way, this conceptual portrayal seems entirely compatible with a hybrid interpretation of the organizational form that emerges when professionals join unions. If unions don't make some adaptations to professionals, and vice versa, the diffusion process I have discussed obviously won't take place.

So where do we stand on the union-profession compatibility debate in 1987? Among others, S. K. Khinduka from a social work perspective and Robert Dingwall and Philip Lewis's edited volume from the sociology of occupations and professions literature, have ably documented the recent ferment and reassessment of professions in the professions and occupations literature.[32, 33] At the very least, the term "profession" can no longer be treated as if it were a generic concept, but rather as one rooted in particular socioeconomic and political contexts. The historical and emergent character of the concept deserves much more emphasis as does the fact that there are competing conceptualizations of professional activity and of professionalization. The reification of professionalism has come under attack and the fact that social work—as well as the more established professions—is currently in a state of flux is better understood. Additionally, as pointed out by Ronald Davis in this volume, this historical perspective also offers a firm challenge to those studying professionals in bureaucracies. Bureaucracies, like professions, are no longer viewed as immanent structures, but as "everchanging and emergent social forms."[34] The kind of guiding theoretical perspectives seem compatible, therefore, with the hybrid conceptualization offered by Wilensky over thirty years ago.

From the union perspective, while unfavorable union stereotypes still persist in the wider society[35] and in spite of the fact that the proportion of all unionized employees in the United States has continued to fall in the past decade,[36] there is also empirical evidence that recently it has been professional and technical employees who have continued to outpace other white-collar groups in winning union elections.[37] Although the professionals most amenable to unionization have been those working in large bureaucracies, whose economic conditions are least secure, whose pay is the lowest, and who have the least control over workplace conditions, Robert L. Aronson has provided recent evidence that unionism has also been growing more rapidly among private-sector professionals in the United States than had generally been assumed.[38, 39] Even though Aronson argues that the number of professionals yet to be organized in the private sector remains small, more recent data on social workers indicate, at least for social workers belonging to NASW, an increasing move toward private sector employment.[40] Given the fact that comparatively low pay and economic insecurity characterize social work jobs, whether in the private or public sector, a continuing impetus for social worker unionization should remain.

Aronson also notes some trends that bear on the union-professional compatibility debate. Drawing upon several national sources dealing both with professional occupational and labor union data, Aronson concludes the following: First, contrary to widely held expectations, professional workers voted not for independent unions and professional associations devoted to collective bargaining, but for representation by mainstream international and national unions, much like other workers. The four main unions organizing social workers, AFSCME, the Service Employees International Union, the Communications Workers of America and the National Union of Hospital and Health Care Employees, are all main-stream, industrial unions. Aronson goes further to state that the resist-ance of professional workers to unionism and collective bargaining, which has long been assumed in the industrial relations literature, seems to be weakening, perhaps rapidly, over a wide spectrum of occupations and industries. He explains, "Union win rates during 1973–79 were not only higher in professional units than in other units but also maintained their level in professional units while declining in other units."[41] While Aronson interprets this to suggest that unionism might be a reflection of de-professionalization rather than the source of the latter, a view of professional unionization as a diffusion process could also be a reason-able interpretation.

There are several other trends that bear on the union-professional compatibility debate. From the wider union perspective, the AFL-CIO, through its Department for Professional Employees and through indi-vidual unions affiliated with that department, has been increasingly con-cerned in the last fifteen years about making union and professional prerogatives more compatible. In addition, although perhaps they are not as forceful as they once were, national unions can and do provide a progressive voice on important social issues of the day, including, for example, the need for additional expenditures for day care, health care, and public welfare. The Coalition of Labor Union Women, as well as individual unions organizing social workers, has lobbied extensively on feminist issues such as wage discrimination, the need for improved day care, and sexual harassment on the job.[42] All of these are areas that coincide with social work's progressive agenda and with the increasing feminization within the profession.

Looking at social work more specifically, G. L. Shaffer and K. Ahearn's examination of over 100 collective bargaining contracts between 1981 and 1984 reveal some success on the part of unions organizing social workers to negotiate contract provisions relating to professional con-cerns. Even though formal contract provisions were directed mostly to issues around caseload determination, informal mechanisms such as the establishment of labor-management councils or committees that address professional standards, policies, and ethical concerns that impact clients were also operative.[43] A more recent push by some unions organizing social workers to develop stress management programs for workers is another example of a union-sponsored activity for workers that ultimately impacts the quality of service delivered to clients. In addition, just as the unions mentioned above have lobbied for issues important to social work on the national level, there has also been extensive lobbying activity by unions on the local level in support of the homeless, day care, and health care, and against funding cuts in social services of all kinds.

Although I have been critical about the lack of responsiveness of either NASW or many prominent social work leaders to social worker unionization, and have noted the minimal empirical attention paid to the subject in the professional literature and in the curricula of most social work programs, I am at the same time quite encouraged by the recent founding of the Bertha Capen Reynolds Society.[44] Bertha Capen Reynolds was herself a longstanding union member and a firm supporter of union activity for social workers throughout her professional career.[45] This society, which consists of progressive social workers and includes both practitioners and academics, has the potential to provide a home base for progressive expression and activism within the profession. It is also a group that supports professional social-service delivery of a high quality and sees social worker unionization as one important vehicle for assuring the delivery of such services. Social work union members are an important and vocal component of its membership. Although the society is only two years old and struggling, it has the opportunity to provide highly visible support for union activity in the profession.[46] The lack of such a formal organizational voice within the profession, since the demise in the late 1940s of Social Service Employee Union Locals of the United Office and Professional Workers of America, has kept social worker unionization activity somewhat hidden from the awareness of the mainstream of the profession and has left the erroneous impression that the unionization of social workers is a recent innovation and a departure from social work traditions.[47]

At present, both in terms of academic consideration and empirical reality, unions and professionals remain compatible after all and are working to become ever more so.

NOTES

1. See, for example, Howard Hush, "Collective Bargaining in Voluntary Agencies," *Social Casework*, 50 (April 1969), pp. 210–213; Charles S. Levy, "Social Workers and Unions," in Levy, (ed.), *Social Work Ethics* (New York: Human Sciences Press, 1974), pp. 195–208; and Lawrence C. Schulman, "Unionization

and the Professional Employee: The Social Service Director's View," in Simon Slavin, (ed.), *Social Administration: The Management of the Social Services* (New York: Haworth Press, 1978), pp. 460–468. Three recent pro-union works also mention this attitude. See Gary L. Shaffer, "Labor Relations and the Unionization of Professional Social Workers: A Neglected Area in Social Work Education," *Journal of Education for Social Work*, 15 (Winter 1979), pp. 80–86; Milton Tambor, "The Social Worker as Worker: A Union Perspective," *Administration in Social Work*, 3 (Fall 1979), pp. 289–300; and Jeffry Galper, *Social Work Practice: A Radical Perspective* (Englewood Cliffs, N.J.: Prentice-Hall, 1980), pp. 159–161. However, the perception of incompatibility between unions and professions does appear widespread among MSW union members. See Leslie B. Alexander, Philip Lichtenberg, and Dennis Brunn, "Social Workers in Unions: A Survey," *Social Work*, 25 (May 1980), pp. 216–223.

2. Bureau of Labor Statistics, U.S. Department of Labor, *Directory of National Unions and Employee Associations*, 1979, Bulletin No. 2079 (Washington, D.C.: U.S. Government Printing Office, forthcoming), Table 14. Because technical and professional workers are lumped together, the number of professionals represented by collective bargaining is obviously less than 30 percent. See also Eileen B. Hoffman, *Unionization of Professional Societies*, Report No. 690 (New York: Conference Board, 1976), pp. 41–42.

3. Jerry Wurf, "Labor Movement, Social Work Fighting Similar Battles," *NASW News*, 25 (February 1980), p. 7.

4. See Marie Haug and Marvin Sussman, "Professionalization and Unionism: A Jurisdictional Dispute?" in Eliot Friedson, (ed.), *The Professions and Their Prospects* (Beverly Hills, Calif.: Sage Publications, 1973), pp. 89–104.

5. A. M. Carr-Saunders and P. A. Wilson, *The Professions* (Oxford, England: Clarendon Press, 1933), p. 329.

6. C. Wright Mills, *White Collar* (New York: Oxford University Press, 1951). For a more recent statement, see Magali S. Larson, *The Rise of Professionalism* (Berkeley: University of California Press, 1977), p. 236.

7. Herbert R. Northrup, "Collective Bargaining by Professional Societies," in Richard A. Lester and Joseph Shister, (eds.), *Insights into Labor Issues* (New York: Macmillan Co., 1948), p. 157.

8. The ideas about professions in this section come primarily from Eliot Freidson, *Professional Dominance: The Social Structure of Medical Care* (Chicago: Aldine Publishing Co., 1970); William A. Goode, "The Theoretical Limits of Professionalization," in Amitai Etzioni, (ed.), *The Semi-Professions and Their Organization* (New York: Free Press, 1969), pp. 266–313; and Everett C. Hughes, "Work and Self," in Hughes, (ed.), *Sociological Eye* (Chicago: Aldine-Atherton Co., 1971), pp. 283–427.

9. Haug and Sussman, "Professionalization and Unionism," p. 102.

10. Hoffman, "Unionization of Professional Societies," p. 1.

11. See Goode, "The Theoretical Limits of Professionalization," p. 267; Harold L. Wilensky, "The Professionalization of Everyone," *American Journal of Sociology*, 70 (September 1964), pp. 137–158; and Nathan Glazer, "The Schools of the Minor Professions," *Minerva* 12 (July 1974), pp. 346–364.

12. Irwin Epstein and Kayla Conrad, "The Empirical Limits of Social Work

Professionalization," in Rosemary Saari and Yeheskel Hazenfeld, (eds.), *The Management of Human Sciences* (New York: Columbia University Press, 1978), p. 178.

13. See Wilensky, "The Professionalization of Everyone."

14. See Archie Kleingartner, "Collective Bargaining Between Salaried Professionals and Public Sector Management," *Public Administration Review*, 33 (March-April 1973), pp. 165–172.

15. Charles Perrow, *Complex Organizations* (Glenview Ill.: Scott Foresman & Co., 1972), p. 55. The social work literature has followed the same pattern as the more general works: an overemphasis on the more dysfunctional aspects of bureaucracy in the early 1960s, with more balance since then. See, for example, Peter M. Blau and W. Richard Scott, *Formal Organizations* (San Francisco: Chandler Publishing Co., 1962); and Nina Toren, "SemiProfessionalism and Social Work: A Theoretical Perspective," in Amitai Etzioni, (ed.), *The Semi-Professions and Their Organization* (New York: Free Press, 1969). See also Epstein and Conrad, "The Empirical Limits of Social Work Professionalization," pp. 176–177.

16. Eliot Freidson, "Dominant Professions, Bureaucracy, and Client Services," in Yeheskel Hasenfeld and Richard A. English, (eds.), *Human Service Organizations* (Ann Arbor: University of Michigan Press, 1974), pp. 428–448.

17. Wilensky, "The Professionalization of Everyone," p. 150.

18. Archie Kleingartner, *Professionalism and the Salaried Worker Organization* (Madison: University of Wisconsin, Industrial Relations Research Institute, 1967), p. 50. However, Kleingartner does not emphasize the salaried relationship as much in his later article, "Collective Bargaining Between Salaried Professionals and Public Sector Management."

19. See Everett M. Kassalow, "The Prospects for White-Collar Union Growth," *Industrial Relations*, 5 (October 1965), p. 40; George Strauss, "Professionalism and Occupational Association," *Industrial Relations*, 2 (May 1963), p. 15; and Bernard Goldstein, "The Perspective of Unionized Professionals," *Social Forces*, 37 (May 1959), p. 323.

20. Kleingartner, *Professionalism and the Salaried Worker Organization*, p. 55.

21. Alexander, Lichtenberg, and Brunn, "Social Workers in Unions," p. 219. For a historical perspective, see Leslie B. Alexander, "Organizing the Professional Social Worker: Union Development in Voluntary Social Work, 1930–50," unpublished Ph.D. dissertation, Bryn Mawr College, 1977. For a more general discussion see Levy, "Social Workers and Unions"; Shaffer, "Labor Relations and the Unionization of Social Workers"; and Al Nash, "Local 1707, CSAE: Facets of a Union in the Nonprofit Field," *Labor History*, 20 (Spring 1979), pp. 256–277.

22. See Kleingartner, "Collective Bargaining Between Salaried Professionals and Public Sector Management"; and Dennis Chamot, "Professional Employees Turn to Unions," *Harvard Business Review*, 54 (May–June 1976), pp. 119–127.

23. See, for example, the quarterly issues of *Interface*, published by the Department for Professional Employees of the American Federation of Labor-Congress of Industrial Organizations. This theme is also recurrent in the newsletters and bulletins of all the major unions that organize professionals. For a fascinating account of the accommodations made by a union local to social work professionalism, see Nash, "Local 1707, CSAE."

24. Northrup, "Collective Bargaining by Professional Societies," pp. 134–143; and Hoffman, "Unionization of Professional Societies," pp. 40ff, 52–55.

25. Archie Kleingartner, "The Organization of White-Collar Workers," *British Journal of Industrial Relations*, 6 (March 1968), pp. 82–83. See also *Mills, White Collar*, p. 309.

26. See *Personnel Practices in Social Work* (New York: American Association of Social Workers, September 1946), p. 4. This prounion position was revised and reaffirmed in 1968, 1971, and 1975. See *NASW Standards for Social Work Personnel Practices* (New York: National Association of Social Workers, 1968, rev. 1971 and 1976).

27. See Alexander, "Organizing the Professional Social Worker"; Leslie B. Alexander and Milton Speizman, "The Union Movement in Voluntary Social Work: 1930–1950," *Social Welfare Forum, 1979* (New York: Columbia University Press, 1980), pp. 179–187; John Earl Haynes, "The Rank and File Movement in Private Social Work," *Labor History*, 16 (Winter 1975), pp. 78–98; and Jacob Fisher, *The Response of Social Work to the Depression* (Cambridge, Mass.: Schenkman Publishing Co., 1980).

28. Antiunion views are rarely openly stated in professional journals. A recent exception to this is Dena Fisher, "Problems for Social Work in a Strike Situation: Professional, Ethical, and Value Considerations," *Social Work*, 32 (May–June 1987), pp. 252–254.

29. Ernie S. Lightman, "Professionalization, Bureaucratization, and Unionization in Social Work," *Social Service Review*, (1), 56, pp. 130–143.

30. Joan Pennell, "Union Participation of Canadian and American Social Workers: Contrasts and Forecasts," *Social Service Review*, 61 (March 1987), pp. 117–131.

31. Ibid, p. 133.

32. S. K. Khinduka, "Social Work and the Human Services," in *Encyclopedia of Social Work*, 18th Ed., Vol. 2 (Silver Spring, Md.: National Association of Social Workers), pp. 681–695.

33. Robert Dingwall and Philip Lewis, (eds.), *The Sociology of the Professions: Lawyers, Doctors and Others* (New York: St. Martins Press, 1983). See especially the article by Eliot Freidson.

34. Celia Davies, "Professionals in Bureaucracies: The Conflict Thesis Revisited," in Dingwall and Lewis, *The Sociology of the Professions*, pp. 177–194.

35. R. B. Freeman and J. L. Medoff, *What Do Unions Do?* (New York: Basic Books, 1984).

36. L. T. Adams, "Changing Employment Patterns of Organized Workers," *Monthly Labor Review*, (2), 108, pp. 25–31.

37. M. Goldfield, "The Decline of Organized Labor: NLRB Union Certification Election Results," *Politics and Society*, (2), 11, pp. 167–210.

38. S. G. Brint and M. H. Dodd, *Professional Workers and Unionization; A Data Handbook* (Washington, D.C.: AFL-CIO, Department of Professional Employees, 1984).

39. Robert L. Aronson, "Unionism Among Professional Employees in the Private Sector," *Industrial and Labor Relations Review* 38 (April 1985), pp. 352–364.

40. "Membership Survey Shows Practice Shifts," *NASW News*, 28 (1983), pp. 6–7.

41. Ibid., p. 361.

42. G. T. Martin, Jr., "Union Social Service and Womens Work," *Social Service Review*, 59 (January 1985), pp. 62–73. Note also Pennell's (see Pennell, n. 30 above) conclusion that feminist and union goals seem increasingly compatible.

43. G. L. Shaffer and K. Ahearn, "Unionization of Professional Social Workers: Current Contract Developments," Paper No. 2, Unionized Workers Project, University of Illinois, 1982; and Shaffer, personal conversation, February 28, 1985.

44. Leslie B. Alexander, "Unions in Social Work," in *Encyclopedia of Social Work*, 18th Ed., Vol. 2 (Silver Spring, Md.: National Association of Social Workers), pp. 793–800.

45. Bertha Capen Reynolds, *An Unchartered Journey: Fifty Years of Growth in Social Work* (New York: Citadel Press, 1963).

46. See, for example, *The Bertha Capen Reynolds Society Newsletter*, Vol. 1 (Nos. 1 and 2), 1986.

47. Alexander, "Unions in Social Work," pp. 794–795.

Postscript

The landscape of public sector unionism is littered with ineluctable problems as well as extraordinary opportunities. Marked by a complex blend of ambitions, successes and failures, a statement by Jerry Wurf, former director of AFSCME, captures the hope of public sector unionists:

Public employee unionists have a singularly modest goal, but some observers have called it revolutionary. Their goal is to reach a day when it will be possible for representatives of public employees everywhere to sit down with public officials as equals, and negotiate a fair contract covering wages, hours, and working conditions. When that day arrives, public employees will be freed from arbitrary management authority, and the delivery of public services will be freed from political manipulation. We have made progress, but we have a long way to go.[1]

Despite Wurf's aspirations, a number of obstacles portend significant changes for public sector unions. Primary among them is the proliferation of privatized, for-profit social welfare services. The rapid growth of privatized social services is a phenomenon rooted in the frenzied expansion that has marked the welfare state since the middle 1960s, and in the ongoing need for entrepreneurs to discover fertile areas for investment. If anything is surprising about the privatization movement, it is not its existence, but why it took so long to take hold.

Privatized social service is promoted as the public sector answer to escalating costs and low productivity. For example, private-sector corporations who desire to increase profits by lowering overhead and labor costs relocate to developing nations. For public-sector managers, that option is obviously impossible. An alternative to third world relocation is to transfer social services to private contractors, thereby relieving the public sector of the burden of labor relations, the responsibility for maintaining quality social services, and the onus for providing a reasonable wage for employees.

In many ways, the low pay characteristic of certain nonunionized sectors of the private social service workforce (such as orderlies, nursing assistants, and maintenance staff) mirrors the same proletarianization of the work force that occurs in developing countries. In effect, privatized social services may help to exploit the underclass, many of whom work for wages that qualify them as social service recipients. In the worst scenario, the contracting out of services results in the substitution of a relatively better-paid public-employee labor force for a more impoverished one. This strategy parallels the classic tactics employed by runaway corporations which close plants in the industrial North only to open them up again in developing countries or the nonunionized South.

Regardless of its value, because of formidable capital backing, the political support it receives from the highest levels of government, and its untoward promises, privatized, for-profit social services have become a permanent fixture in the American economic landscape as well as a reality that public service unions must live with.

Privatization will ultimately require public sector unions to pursue a more aggressive policy of recruiting private-sector social workers, many of whom are employed in smaller agencies. While necessary, this kind of small-scale organizing will undoubtedly put a great strain on the fiscal resources of unions.

On the other hand, the rise in corporate social welfare may also result in increased numbers of social workers clamoring for unionization. Seduced by promises of more pay, less restrictive work environments, professional autonomy, and greater prestige, many social workers will obviously be attracted to the lure of the corporate welfare sector.

Eager to leave the public sector—a motive partly fueled by the assumption that private is always better than public—some of the most qualified social workers will opt for the promises held out by corporatized social services. However, as social workers find that their initially higher salaries evaporate as the market produces more trained professionals; as they realize that the profit motive has more salience in the private sector than service goals; when they discover that as organizations grow larger the bureaucratic structure of corporate social services replicates public agencies; and, finally, when they realize that they have less job security than in the public sector; a disillusioned cadre of social workers ripe for unionization may emerge.

A second obstacle facing unionized social workers is the realization that a public- or private-sector strike is not a fearsome weapon. Most social work strikes have been unsuccessful, and, perhaps more importantly, managers, bureaucrats, and legislators appear to not fear them. Arnold Weber maintains that:

Public management will have little incentive to succumb to sanctions unless the service is "essential" in the sense that its curtailment will mobilize the consumer and impose political "losses" on the executive...[in referring to a 1969 Chicago strike of social workers] there were no competitors vying for the opportunity to provide funds and services to indigent persons. The strike did not diminish revenue to the agency...the department was able to distribute the monthly welfare payments without interruption.... The inability of social worker unions to impair a politically sensitive service helps to explain the consistent defeats of strikes by social workers all over the country.[2]

In the end, public-sector social workers service mainly poor clients, their services are not generally seen as essential, and from the perspective of the general public, a social work strike does not seriously endanger their welfare. To attenuate this handicap, unionized social workers must build an independent power base among vulnerable client groups, consumer action groups, interested professional organizations, and private sector unions (many of which are not ardent supporters of public service unions).

A third obstacle involves the ideological problems inherent in business unionism. Traditional notions of trade unionism often fail to address many of the concerns of professional social workers. For example, some years ago I had the opportunity to meet a large group of social workers, all of whom were committed union members. Although concerned about salaries, this group seemed more disturbed by their inability to provide the highest quality of service possible to clients. The problems discussed by this group centered around unmanageable caseloads, administrative insensitivity to clients, incompetent colleagues, and inadequate resources. When I brought these concerns to the union staff, they responded by pointing out that they had engineered significant raises, better grievance procedures, and so forth. Two themes emerged from this encounter: conventional trade union leaders seemed uncomfortable in usurping the traditional prerogatives of management, and an insensitivity existed to the concerns of professional union members. This problem of union insensitivity is additionally heightened by the influx of various unions into the public sector. In many cases, the only experience many of these unions have had has been with private sector.

A fourth impediment to unionization involves the diverse and often chaotic nature of public sector labor laws. The nonuniformity of these labor laws, rules, and regulations, coupled with an often politically opportunistic interpretation, leads many states to have a turbulent system of labor relations. Moreover, even in the most liberal states, no public worker possesses the same legal rights as his or her private-sector counterpart. Grandiloquent arguments about states' rights and the differences between public- and private-sector employment are at best anachronistic.

Abridgment of employee rights occurs in the public as well as the private sector. Consequently, employee protection and the right to collective bargaining must be guaranteed for all workers if workplace democracy is to be universally applied. Until a uniform code of labor relations is enacted, and the antilabor legislation in many states is struck down, the full potential of public sector unionism cannot be realized.

Unions must recognize that although bread-and-butter issues are important to social workers, this group is also concerned with professional issues that bear directly on their ability to serve clients. Leslie Alexander is correct. Unions must struggle to fuse traditional unionism with the professional concerns of social workers and, therefore, they must find new ways to advocate for enhanced service goals.

Unions can strengthen links with social workers by more fully utilizing their talents. For instance, unions can use social workers to provide essential social services to unions members. Moreover, social workers can be used as a valuable resource in the competition with corporations over the provision of Employee Assistance Programs (EAPs).

Another barrier to unionization involves EAPs. The increased monopolization of the economy has led to a form of feudalism in which large numbers of people desire to live under the umbrella of security they believe is found in large corporations. Like feudal serfs, many American workers expect corporations to provide the protection and services they desire, often including the provision of social services. Although initially reluctant, some corporations are beginning to realize the emotional and psychological rewards that can be reaped from this kind of employee dependence.[3]

Employer-initiated EAPs run counter to the interests of unions for two reasons: they produce worker loyalty to the corporation rather than the union, and increased dependency on the corporation discourages workers from joining unions (many workers may feel that embracing unionism represents the betrayal of corporate benevolence). In order to increase worker loyalty and to combat the invasion of the corporation into the emotional life of its employees, unions must begin to provide their own EAP programs. These EAPs can be either administered directly by the union or through joint cooperation with management.

Unions must revitalize their commitment to providing social services. Programs such as the AFL-CIO's Department of Community Services ("the first, largest, and only national delivery system of social services in the U.S. labor movement"), the United Labor Agency, and the Community Services Department of the United Auto Workers must be strengthened.[4] In addition, a "human contract" that takes an interest in the health, welfare, and living conditions of the worker must be expanded and promoted as part of the collective bargaining process.[5]

Another obstacle to unionizing social workers involves professional organizations. For example, professional social work associations must understand that collective bargaining bespeaks dignity rather than charity, and that it represents a means for turning begging into negotiations. Moreover, collective bargaining fits well within the context of self-determination, one of the most cherished social work values. In its pure form, collective bargaining is a mainstay of democracy; it represents a meeting of minds as opposed to a decision rooted in arbitrary rules and regulations. The underlying philosophy of collective bargaining is clearly congruent with self-determination and social work's emphasis on democracy.

If professional associations are to encourage unionism, they must begin by educating their constituency around the biases and misconceptions held about public unions. For example, Dale A. Masi maintains that, "Trade unions continue to view the professional practice of social work as isolated from both the world of work and the workers as a target population."[6] Although a popular belief, little evidence exists to support Masi's claim.

Social work curricula are for the most part devoid of content on collective bargaining and unionization, even for administrative-track students at the master's level. According to Gary L. Shaffer, "Most social workers have not been prepared by education or experience to deal effectively with union issues."[7] Masi maintains that, "knowledge of . . . union problems, the subtleties and nuances of labor/management relationships, and the grievance procedure of the collective-bargaining agreement is essential in order for a social worker to function in the workplace."[8] At minimum, social work curricula should contain content on collective bargaining, public-sector labor laws, negotiations and impasse procedures, the scope of bargaining, unit determination, and the process of union certification.

Despite occasional setbacks, public sector unions appear to be durable. Jerry Wurf, former president of AFSCME, observed that:

We've come a long way, and it hasn't been easy. In state after state, governors aspiring to strengthen or reinstate political patronage have attempted to crush public employee unionism. In several southern communities, workers who had the audacity to seek union recognition were confronted with the full fury of the conservative local establishment.

One of the more difficult tests of the will of public employees occurred in Memphis in 1968. . . . He [Mayor Loeb of Memphis] provoked a strike in which workers who had very little were required to make great sacrifices for themselves and their union. Dr. Martin Luther King gave his life in support of that strike.

In Memphis and elsewhere, we've taken the worst public management has thrown at us—and we're still there.[9]

Regardless of any ambivalence felt by some quarters of the profession, the union movement in social work is entrenched. As such, professional social workers will continue to be unionized in significant numbers— some will become ardent trade unionists, others will be relatively uninvolved in union matters, and still others may assume important positions within the union hierarchy.

Furthermore, despite divisive issues such as reclassification and social work licensure, there appears to be an overall complementarity of purpose and goals between public sector unionism and professional social workers. It is likely that unions and professional social work associations are generous enough in spirit to accommodate each other.

NOTES

1. Jerry Wurf, "Union Leaders and Public Unions," in Institute for Contemporary Studies, *Public Employee Unions: A Study of the Crisis in Public Sector Labor Relations* (San Francisco, California: Institute for Contemporary Studies, 1976), p. 174.

2. Arnold R. Weber, "Paradise Lost; Or Whatever Happened to the Chicago Social Workers," *Industrial and Labor Relations Review*, 22 (1969), p. 337.

3. This form of feudalism is cheaper for the capitalists, because unlike their predecessors, they don't have to feed and lodge their economic serfs.

4. Dale A. Masi, *Human Services in Industry* (Lexington, Massachusetts: Lexington Books, 1982), p. 38.

5. For greater elaboration on the human contract, see Ibid., pp. 39–40.

6. Ibid., p. 33.

7. Gary L. Shaffer, "Labor Relations and the Unionization of Professional Social Workers: A Neglected Area in Social Work Education," *Journal of Education in Social Work*, (15), 1 (Winter 1979), p. 84.

8. Masi, *Human Services in Industry*, p. 45.

9. Jerry Wurf, "Union Leaders and Public Sector Unions," in Center for Contemporary Studies, *Public Employee Unions: A Study of the Crisis in Public Sector Labor Relations* (San Francisco, California: Institute for Contemporary Studies, 1976), pp. 176–177.

Selected Bibliography

Akabas, Sheila, Paul A. Kurzman, and Nancy S. Koblan, (Eds.). *Labor and Industrial Settings: Sites for Social Work Practice*. New York: Council on Social Work Education, 1979.

Akabas, Sheila, and Paul A. Kurzman, (Eds.). *Work, Workers, and Work Organizations: A View from Social Work*. Englewood Cliffs, N.J.: Prentice-Hall, 1982.

Alexander, Leslie B. "Organizing the Professional Social Worker: Union Development in Voluntary Social Work, 1930–1950." (Doctoral Dissertation, Bryn Mawr College, 1976.)

———. "Professionalization and Unionization: Compatible After All?" *Social Work*, Vol. 25, No. 6 (November 1980), pp. 476–482.

———. "Unions in Social Work." In National Association of Social Workers, *Encyclopedia of Social Work*, 18th Ed., Vol. 2. Silver Spring, Md.: NASW, 1987, pp. 793–800.

Alexander, Leslie B., Philip Lichtenberg, and Dennis Brunn. "Social Workers in Unions: A Survey." *Social Work*, Vol. 25, No. 3 (May 1980), pp. 216–223.

Alexander, Leslie B., and Speizman, Milton. "The Union Movement in Voluntary Social Work." In the National Conference on Social Welfare, *Social Welfare Forum, 1979*. New York: Columbia University Press, 1980, pp. 179–187.

Anderson, Mary. *Woman at Work*. Westport, Connecticut: Greenwood Press, 1973.

Aronson, Robert L. "Unionism Among Professional Employees in the Private Sector." *Industrial and Labor Relations Review*, Vol. 38 (April 1985), pp. 352–364.

Bohr, Ronald H., Herbert I. Brenner, and Howard H. Kaplan. "Value Conflicts in a Hospital Walkout." *Social Work*, Vol. 16, No. 4 (1971), pp. 33–42.

Bremner, Robert. *From the Depths*. New York: New York University Press, 1964.

Brint, Steven G. and Martin H. Dodd. *Professional Workers and Unionization: A Data Handbook*. Washington, D.C.: Department of Professional Employees, AFL-CIO, 1984.

Burke, Donald R. "The Impact of Unions on Social Welfare Agency Management." (Doctoral Dissertation, University of Pennsylvania, 1970).

Chamot, Dennis. "Professional Employees Turn to Unions." *Harvard Business Review*, Vol. 54 (May–June 1976), pp. 119–127.

Chitnis, Nancy and Gae Tigelaar. "Impact of a Strike on Graduate Students." *Social Work*, Vol. 16, No. 2 (April 1971), pp. 65–68.

Cole, Elma Phillipson. "Unions in Social Work." National Association of Social Workers, *Encyclopedia of Social Work*. New York: NASW, 1977, pp. 1550–1555.

Coleman, Jill. "The Struggle Within: Fighting Red-Baiting and Sexism in the Union." *Catalyst*, Vol. 5, No. 17/18 (1985), pp. 51–56.

Davis, Allen F. *Spearheads For Reform*. New York: Oxford University Press, 1967.

DiBicarri, Eda. "Organizing in the Massachusetts Purchase of Service System." *Catalyst*, Vol. 5, No. 17/18 (1985), pp. 45–50.

Dingwall, Robert and Philip Lewis, (Eds.). *The Sociology of the Professions: Lawyers, Doctors and Others*. New York: St. Martins Press, 1983.

Epstein, Irwin and Kayla Conrad. "The Empirical Limits of Social Work Professionalization." In Rosemary Saari and Yeheskel Hasenfeld (Eds.). *The Management of Human Sciences*. New York: Columbia University Press, 1978.

Fisher, Dena. "Problems for Social Work in a Strike Situation: Professional, Ethical, and Value Considerations." *Social Work*, Vol. 32, No. 3 (May–June 1987), pp. 252–254.

Fisher, Jacob. *The History of the Rank and File, 1931–6*. New York: New York School of Philanthropy, 1936.

——. *The Response of Social Work to the Depression*. Boston: Schenkman, 1980.

Flynn, John P. "Collective Bargaining in Professional Social Work Education." *Journal of Education for Social Work*, Vol. 16, No. 3 (Fall 1980), pp. 101–109.

Foner, Philip. *Women and the American Labor Movement*. New York: The Free Press, 1979.

Freeman, Richard B. "The Two Faces of Unionism." *The Public Interest*, Vol. 57 (Fall 1979), pp. 66–83.

——. "Unionism Comes to the Public Sector." *Journal of Economic Literature*, Vol. 24 (March 1986), pp. 40–53.

Freeman, Richard B., and J. L. Medoff, *What Do Unions Do?* New York: Basic Books, 1984.

Freidson, Eliot. "Dominant Professions, Bureaucracy, and Client Services." In Yeheskel Hasenfeld and Richard A. English, (Eds.). *Human Service Organizations*. Ann Arbor: University of Michigan Press, 1974, pp. 428–448.

Galper, Jeffry. *Social Work Practice: A Radical Perspective*. Englewood Cliffs, N.J.: Prentice-Hall, 1980, pp. 156–189.

Gerhart, Paul. "The Unionization of Social Welfare Employees." (Master's Thesis, University of Pennsylvania, 1966.)

Glazer, Nathan. "The Schools of the Minor Professions." *Minerva*, Vol. 12 (July 1974), pp. 346–364.

Goldberg, Jack R. "The Professional and his Union in the Jewish Center." *Journal of Jewish Communal Service*, Vol. 36, No. 3 (Spring 1960), pp. 284–289.

Goldstein, Bernard. "The Perspective of Unionized Professionals." *Social Forces*, Vol. 37 (May 1959), pp. 83–91.

Goode, William A. "The Theoretical Limits of Professionalization." In Amitai Etzioni, (Ed.), *The Semi-Professions and Their Organization*. New York: Free Press, 1969, pp. 266–313.

Gotbaum, Victor. "Public Service Strikes: Where Prevention is Worse than the Cure." In Richard T. DeGeorge and Joseph A. Pichler, (Eds.). *Ethics, Free Enterprise, and Public Policy*. New York: Oxford University Press, 1978, pp. 110–21.

Grossinger, Ken. "Organizing in the Human Service Community." *Catalyst*, Vol. 5, No. 17/18 (1985), pp. 109–114.

Grossman, Jon. "Can a Human Service Union Affect Clinical Issues?" *Catalyst*, Vol. 5, No. 17/18 (1985), pp. 57–66.

Haug, Marie and Marvin Sussman. "Professionalization and Unionism: A Jurisdictional Dispute?" In Eliot Freidson, (Ed.), *The Professions and Their Prospects*. Beverly Hills, Calif.: Sage Publications, 1973, pp. 89–104.

Haynes, John Earl. "The Rank and File Movement in Private Social Work." *Labor History*, Vol. 16 (Winter 1975), pp. 78–98.

Hoffman, Eileen B. *Unionization of Professional Societies* (Report No. 690). New York: Conference Board, 1976.

Hush, Howard. "Collective Bargaining in Voluntary Agencies." *Social Casework*, Vol. 50, No. 4 (April 1969), pp. 210–213.

Karger, H. Jacob. "The Early Unionization Movement in Social Work, 1934–1947." *Social Development Issues*, Vol. 8, No. 3 (Winter 1984), pages 73–78.

———. "Reclassification and Social Work: Is There a Future for the Trained Social Worker?" *Social Work*, Vol. 28, No. 6 (November–December 1983), pp. 427–434.

———. "Social Workers and Labor Relations in the Public Sector: The Missouri Department of Social Services and the Communications Workers of America." *Administration in Social Work*, Vol. 12, No. 1 (Spring 1988), pp. 113–19.

Kassalow, Everett M. "The Prospects for White-Collar Union Growth." *Industrial Relations*, Vol. 5 (October 1965), pp. 35–42.

Kelley, Florence. *The Autobiography of Florence Kelley*. Edited by Kathryn Kish Sklar. Chicago: Charles H. Kerr Publishing Company, 1986.

Kendellen, Gary. "The Social Service Employees Union: A Study of Rival Unionism in the Public Sector." (Master's Thesis, Cornell University, 1969.)

Kirzner, M. L. "Public Welfare Unions and Public Assistance Policy: A Case Study of the Pennsylvania Social Services Union." (Doctoral dissertation, University of Pennsylvania, 1985.)

Kleingartner, Archie. "Collective Bargaining Between Salaried Professionals and

Public Sector Management." *Public Administration Review*, Vol. 33 (March-April 1973), pp. 165–172.

———. *Professionalism and the Salaried Worker Organization.* Madison: University of Wisconsin, Industrial Relations Research Institute, 1967.

Larson, Magali S. *The Rise of Professionalism.* Berkeley: University of California Press, 1977.

Lefkowitz, Jerome. "Unionism in the Human Services Industries." *Albany Law Review*, Vol. 36 (1972), pp. 37–46.

Levine, Gilbert. "Collective Bargaining For Social Workers in Voluntary Agencies." Toronto, Ontario: Association of Professional Social Workers, 1975.

Levy, Charles S. "Social Workers and Unions." In Charles S. Levy, (Ed.), *Social Work Ethics.* New York: Human Sciences Press, 1974, pp. 195–208.

———. "Labor Management Relations in the Jewish Community Center." *Journal of Jewish Communal Service*, Vol. 41, No. 1 (Fall 1964), pp. 114–123.

Lightman, Ernie S. "An Imbalance of Power: Social Workers in Unions." *Administration in Social Work*, Vol. 2, No. 1 (Spring 1978), pp. 75–85.

———. "Professionalization, Bureaucratization, and Unionization in Social Work." *Social Service Review*, Vol. 56, No. 1, (March 1982), pp. 130–143.

———. "Social Workers, Strikes and Service to Clients." *Social Work*, Vol. 28, No. 2 (April 1983), pp. 142–147.

McCormick, Andrew, and Beryl Minkle. "Organizing Workers in the Contractual Human Services." *Catalyst*, Vol. 4, No. 2 (1982), pp. 59–71.

Martin, G. T., Jr., "Union Social Service and Women's Work." *Social Service Review*, Vol. 59 (January 1985), pp. 62–73.

Masi, Dale. *Human Services in Industry.* Lexington, Mass.: D.C. Heath, 1982.

Mendes, Richard. "The Professional Union: A Study of the Social Service Employees Union of the New York City Department of Social Services." (Doctoral Dissertation, Columbia University, 1974.)

Nash, Al. "Local 1707, CSAE, Facets of a Union in the Non-Profit Field." *Labor History*, Vol. 20, No. 2 (Spring 1979), pp. 256–277.

National Association of Social Workers. *NASW Standards for Social Work Personnel Practices.* New York: National Association of Social Workers, 1968, rev. 1971 and 1976.

Northrup, Herbert R. "Collective Bargaining by Professional Societies." In Richard A. Lester and Joseph Shister, (Eds.), *Insights into Labor Issues.* New York: Macmillan Co., 1948.

Oppenheimer, Martin. "The Unionization of the Professional." *Social Policy*, Vol. 5, No. 5 (January–February 1975), pp. 34–40.

Pennell, Joan. "Union Participation of Canadian and American Social Workers: Contrasts and Forecasts." *Social Service Review*, Vol. 61 (March 1987), pp. 117–131.

Ratner, Linda. "Understanding and Moving Beyond Social Workers' Resistance to Unionization." *Catalyst*, Vol. 5, No. 17/18 (1985), pp. 79–86.

Rehr, Helen. "Problems for a Profession in a Strike Situation." *Social Work*, Vol. 5, No. 2 (April 1960), pp. 22–28.

Reynolds, Bertha. *An Uncharted Journey.* New York: Citadel Press, 1961.

Shaffer, Gary L. "Labor Relations and the Unionization of Professional Social

Workers: A Neglected Area in Social Work Education." *Journal of Education for Social Work*, Vol. 15, No. 1 (Winter 1979), pp. 80–86.

———. "Preparation of Social Workers for Unionization and Collective Bargaining Practice." *Arete*, Vol. 8, No. 1 (Spring 1983), pp. 53–56.

———. "Professional Social Worker Unionization: Current Contract Developments and Implications for Managers." Paper presented at the National Association of Social Workers Annual Conference, Management Conference, September 12, 1987.

———. "Unionization of Professional Social Workers: Current Contract Developments," Paper No. 2, Unionized Workers Project, University of Illinois at Urbana, Champaign, 1982.

Shaffer, Gary L., and Kathleen Ahearn. "Unionization of Professional Social Workers: Staff Development and Practice Implications." Paper presented at the 7th National Association of Social Workers, Professional Symposium, November, 1981.

Schulman, Lawrence C. "Unionization and the Professional Employee: The Social Service Director's View." In Simon Slavin, (Ed.), *Social Administration: The Management of the Social Services*. New York: Haworth Press, 1978, pp. 460–468.

Schutt, Russell K. "The Politics of Work: Union Involvement by Social Service Employees." (Doctoral Dissertation, University of Illinois at Chicago Circle, 1977.)

Sherman, Wendy and Stanley Wenocur. "Empowering Public Welfare Workers Through Mutual Support." *Social Work*, Vol. 28, No. 5 (September–October 1983), pp. 12–16.

Steininger, Fred H. "Employee Unions in Public Welfare." Paper presented at the National Conference on Public Administration, American Society of Public Administration, Boston, Massachusetts, 1968.

Stieber, Jack. *Public Employee Unionism: Structure Growth, Policy*. Washington, D.C.: Brookings Institution, 1973.

Tambor, Milton. "Declassification and Divisiveness in Human Services." *Administration in Social Work*, Vol. 7, No. 2 (1983), pp. 61–68.

———. "Independent Unionism and the Politics of Self-Defeat." *Catalyst*, Vol. 3, No. 3 (1981), pp. 23–32.

———. "The Social Worker as Worker: A Union Perspective." *Administration in Social Work*, Vol. 3, No. 3 (Fall 1979), pp. 289–300.

———. "Unions and Voluntary Agencies." *Social Work*, Vol. 18, No. 4 (July 1973), pp. 41–47.

Tambor, Milton, and Gary Shaffer. "Social Work Unionization: A Beginning Bibliography." *Catalyst*, Vol. 5, No. 17/18 (1985), pp. 131–36.

Toren, Nina. "Semi-Professionalism and Social Work: A Theoretical Perspective." In Amitai Etzioni, (Ed.), *The Semi-Professions and Their Organization*. New York: Free Press, 1969.

Transue, Judith. "Collective Bargaining on Whose Terms?" *Catalyst*, Vol. 2, No. 1 (1980), pp. 25–37.

Tudiver, Neil. "Business Ideology and Management in Social Work: The Limits of Cost Control." *Catalyst*, Vol. 4, No. 1 (1982), pp. 25–48.

van Kleeck, Mary. "Our Illusions Regarding Government." Proceedings, National Conference on Social Work, 1934; Chicago, Ill.: University of Chicago Press, 1935.

———. "Common Goals of Labor and Social Work." Proceedings, National Conference on Social Work, 1934; Chicago, Ill.: University of Chicago Press, 1935.

Wagner, David and Marcia Cohen. "Social Workers, Class, and Professionalism." *Catalyst*, Vol. 1, No. 1 (1978), pp. 25–53.

Warner, Kenneth, Rupert F. Chisholm, and Robert F. Munzenrider. "Motives for Unionization Among State Social Service Employees." *Public Personnel Management*, Vol. 7, No. 3 (May–June 1978), pp. 181–191.

Weber, Arnold R. "Paradise Lost; Or Whatever Happened to the Chicago Social Workers." *Industrial and Labor Relations Review*, Vol. 22, No. 3 (April, 1969), pp. 323–338.

Withorn, Ann. "Building Democracy and Working with the Community: An Interview with Progressive Trade Union Leaders." *Catalyst*, Vol. 5, No. 17/18 (1985), pp. 67–78.

Wurf, Jerry. "Labor Movement, Social Work Fighting Similar Battles." *NASW News*, Vol. 25 (February 1980), p. 7.

Index

About the Contributors

LESLIE B. ALEXANDER is Associate Professor, Graduate School of Social Work and Social Research, Bryn Mawr College, Bryn Mawr, Pennsylvania.

HOWARD JACOB KARGER is Associate Professor, School of Social Work, University of Missouri-Columbia, Columbia, Missouri.

LARRY W. KREUGER is Assistant Professor, School of Social Work, University of Missouri-Columbia, Columbia, Missouri.

FREDERIC G. REAMER is Associate Professor, School of Social Work, Rhode Island College, Providence, Rhode Island.

DAVID STOESZ is Assistant Professor, School of Social Work, San Diego State University, San Diego, California.

MILTON TAMBOR is Staff Representative, Michigan Council Number 25, American Federation of State and County Municipal Employees, AFL-CIO, Southfield, Michigan.

DATE DUE
